RIC FLAIR

TO BE THE MAN

POCKET BOOKS

New York   London   Toronto   Sydney

RIC FLAIR

TO BE THE MAN

RIC FLAIR
with Keith Elliot Greenberg

edited by Mark Madden

World
Wrestling
Entertainment

POCKET BOOKS, a division of Simon & Schuster, Inc.
1230 Avenue of the Americas, New York, NY 10020

ISBN: 0-7434-5691-2

First Pocket Books hardcover edition July 2004

10 9 8 7 6 5

POCKET and colophon are registered trademarks of Simon & Schuster, Inc.

Designed by Richard Oriolo

Visit us on the World Wide Web
http://www.simonsays.com
http://www.wwe.com

Manufactured in the United States of America

For information regarding special discounts for bulk purchases,
please contact Simon & Schuster Special Sales at 1-800-456-6798
or business@simonandschuster.com.

This book is dedicated to my fans.

The blood, sweat, and tears were all for you.

There's a scene in *Fast Times at Ridgemont High* where one guy is giving his friend advice on how to be cool, telling him to make wherever he is the place to be. Ric Flair did that naturally. Whether he was wrestling a sixty-minute match, dancing with a harem of women in a nightclub, or just telling stories in some shithole airport in the middle of nowhere, Flair transformed wherever he was into the *only* place to be on the planet.

Even as a kid, I could tell that there was a quality about Ric Flair that made the people around him look special. He'd get in the ring with somebody, and when the match was over, his opponent had become a star. Ric had greatness, and those who came close to him took some of it with them.

INTRODUCTION
by Paul Levesque, aka Triple H

Even though he was a bad guy—my dad hated him—I just loved Ric Flair, with his "stylin' and profilin'" and his talk. To this day, I consider him the greatest interview in the wrestling business.

When I became a wrestler myself, I didn't want to be a guy who just got in the ring and earned a paycheck. I wanted wrestling to be my life. I wanted to be great. I wanted to be the "Nature Boy."

No one ever could, of course. But I've tried to emulate things that I saw in him—his work ethic as a wrestler, dressing the part of a champion, showing up on time no matter how much he had partied the night before. In every way, he's the supreme professional.

Let me state this categorically: Ric Flair is the greatest wrestler of all time. He's spanned generations, wrestling everybody from the original "Nature Boy," Buddy Rogers, to Dusty Rhodes, Hulk Hogan, Bob Backlund, Jack Brisco, Shohei "Giant" Baba, Harley Race, Roddy Piper, Antonio Inoki, Terry Funk, Ricky "The Dragon" Steamboat, Randy "Macho Man" Savage, Bret "Hitman" Hart, Bill Goldberg, Vince McMahon, and Undertaker. His personality and talent continue to endure. In the arena, at fifty-five years old, the Nature Boy gets one of the biggest reactions on our show—not because of what he's done in the past, but because he's still so entertaining today.

I laugh when I'm driving with Ric—we'll enter some town and he'll mention, almost wistfully, "This is a great place. I used to have a lot of fun here." I can only look at him and say, "Ric, did you ever *not* have fun in a town?"

The man has so many stories to tell. If he were just talking about the part of his career that everyone saw on TV, it would be riveting. Then there are the backstage tales—the crazy things that people in our universe tend to do, Ric's role at the center of that, and all the political intrigue that goes on in the wrestling business. After that, we have his private life—the way he was allegedly stolen from his birth parents and put up for adoption; his inner torment as he saw his legacy demeaned and cheapened in World Championship Wrestling (WCW); and his struggle to reconcile his wild lifestyle with his quest to become the ultimate husband and father.

Despite his public persona, Ric has managed to keep so much of this stuff a secret from even his closest friends. Now, because of this book, it's all out in the open.

Invariably, people become disappointed when they get to know their idol. Everyone's human, and the image that you build up in your mind is often unachievable. Well, I put Ric Flair on a very high pedestal. Then I got to work side by side with him every day, hear him talking on the phone to his family, and become his friend. Today, I'm one of the few people who can say that his hero exceeded the expectations.

I hope you feel the same way.

RIC FLAIR
TO BE THE MAN

I don't remember crying much as a kid. But that was a long time ago, before I left Minnesota for Charlotte, bleached my brown hair blond, and became "Nature Boy" Ric Flair. That's before I let myself-esteem depend on people with power in the wrestling business.

For the last fifteen years or so, I've been told that I'm the greatest professional wrestler who ever lived. Better than Frank Gotch or Lou Thesz, Bruno Sammartino or Verne Gagne, Gorgeous George or Hulk Hogan. Ric Flair can call himself a sixteen-time world champion. Ric Flair went on the road and wrestled every single day—twice on Saturday, twice on Sunday, every birthday, every holiday, every anniversary—for twenty straight years. I've spent more than thirty years of my life—some days good, some bad—trying

CHAPTER 1

BLACK
MARKET
BABY

to prove to myself, to my peers, and to the fans who paid anywhere from five to five hundred dollars that I could be the best at what I chose to do for a living.

When you have no equal in professional wrestling, you have no equal in the sports world. Because—despite what outsiders may think—we are not ninjas or warriors. We are a special breed who can withstand pain, exhaustion, and injury without ever coming up for air. There is no off-season in our business, and we're the toughest athletes alive.

In the ring, I've always been at home. It's what lurks *outside* of it that scares me. For every legitimate punch I've ever taken to the head, every bone I've ever dislocated or every chair that's been bent across my spine, nothing can be as ruthless as the political sabotage inside the dressing room or promoter's office. While fans were saying that I could have a five-star match with anyone at any time, behind the scenes I'd be called an old piece of shit that didn't understand the public, couldn't read ratings, and deserved to be bankrupted along with my family.

These weren't things I heard once or twice; it went on for *years.* And after a while, it almost broke me. I felt myself losing the Ric Flair strut and, in many ways, my joy for life. When I came to World Wrestling Entertainment (WWE) in late 2001 after spending most of my career representing the competition, I didn't know if the wrestlers liked or respected me, or knew about my legacy. Hell, I began to wonder if I even had a legacy at all.

So that's why on May 19, 2003, at fifty-four years old, I was standing in the center of a ring in Greenville, South Carolina, in boots and trunks, crying like a little boy. The *Raw* TV cameras were off. This was something personal between myself, the "boys"—as the members of our fraternity like to call each other—and the fans.

"I went through a period where the Nature Boy wasn't the Nature Boy," I started, confessing to people who had watched me trade knife-edge chops with Wahoo McDaniel in 1976 after I came back from a plane crash; take Dusty Rhodes's bionic elbow in 1987 while my cohorts in the Four Horsemen circled the ring; and return in 1998 after my old company, World Championship Wrestling (WCW), tried to sue me out of my profession. Either these fans had been there personally, or their fathers had been there, or their grandfathers or great-grandfathers had told them about it. For nearly thirty-five years, it had been me and them. And when the tears came down my face, I was just letting it out to a group of people who, in some ways, knew me like a part of their families.

But the bad days were over, and here in Greenville, South Carolina, I finally saw it—by the way the boys had hugged and honored me after my opponent, Triple H, carried me to one of the most satisfying matches of my career, and by the way the fans had stood and screamed and looked into my watery eyes, letting me know that, when the Nature Boy was in the ring, they'd never stopped believing.

"To be the man, you've gotta beat the man," I'd said so many times, taunting my opponents while I shoved my title into the camera. Well, I'd beaten myself, but now—in *my* mind, at least—I won back the crown. I was still "Slick Ric," "Space Mountain," "Secretariat in Disguise," a kiss-stealing, wheeling, dealing, jet-flying, limousine-riding son-of-a-gun.

This is my story. And, as I've proclaimed during many an interview, whether you like it, or whether you *don't* like it, learn to love it. *Wooooooo!*

MY MOTHER PROBABLY thought I was stillborn.

That's what they told a lot of the girls whose kids ended up with the Tennessee Children's Home Society in Memphis—their babies were dead, and they just needed to sign a couple of papers. *Adoption* papers. Most of these girls were poor and uneducated. Some were even under sedation.

They had pulled the same scam on single mothers, promising that their kids would be kept in a nice, safe place until the girls could come and get them. A corrupt judge had been in on the whole scheme, taking away infants from people on public assistance. One woman in the Western State Hospital for the Insane had a new baby with a different inmate every year. When you handed her a pen, she'd sign anything.

Years later, *60 Minutes* would do an exposé on the case. Mary Tyler Moore would win an Emmy Award for her performance in *Stolen Babies,* a cable-TV movie about the scandal. But until the governor of Tennessee called for an investigation in 1950, five thousand children had been taken away and adopted by parents from all over the United States, including Joan Crawford (whose *Mommie Dearest* daughter supposedly came from the Tennessee Children's Home Society), June

Allyson, Dick Powell, and the people I grew to love as *my* mother and father, Dick and Kay Fliehr.

My parents were both born in 1918, and had met at the University of Minnesota. My mother, Kathleen Virginia Kinsmiller, was from a town called Brainerd, Minnesota. She was a cultured woman who wrote articles for newspapers and magazines, and in 1968, she authored a book, *In Search of Audience,* about the Guthrie Theatre in Minneapolis, a place where she introduced me to people like Jessica Tandy, Henry Fonda, and Elizabeth Taylor.

My father, Richard Reid Fliehr, was salutatorian of his high school class in Virginia, Minnesota. Like my mother, he loved the theater, but he ended up taking pre-med courses, becoming a medic in the navy during World War II, and then a successful obstetrician and gynecologist.

I thought my dad was the most intelligent guy in the world. While working as an ob-gyn, he went back to school and got his master's and doctorate both in theater and English. He went on the road, performing in plays, and became president of the American Community Theater Association. Meanwhile, his practice—Haugen, Fliehr and Meeker—was one of the biggest in the Twin Cities. My dad probably delivered thousands of babies, among them wrestling promoter Gary Juster, former National Wrestling Alliance (NWA) Heavyweight Champion Gene Kiniski's kids (including his son Kelly, who wrestled in the World Wrestling Federation in the 1980s) and Superstar Billy Graham's daughter Capella.

Sadly, my parents weren't able to start a family of their own. In the mid-1940s, my mother gave birth to a daughter who died so quickly, I'm not sure if she had a name. Afterward, my mother couldn't become pregnant again, so in 1948 she began corresponding with the Tennessee Children's Home Society.

My father's salary was a bit of an issue. He was only making $3,000 a year, but my mother explained that he was doing his residency in Detroit, and that any child they adopted would live a relatively privileged life, and most likely go to college.

On the form the agency sent them, my parents were questioned about their reasons for adopting. "Unable to have one of our own," my mother handwrote, "and our love of children."

"Will you treat the child as a member of your family?" they were asked. "Yes," my mother replied.

"If the child is returned," the questionnaire inquired, "will you pay the expense of bringing it back?" My parents agreed to the condition. But once they laid eyes on the Nature Boy, I wasn't going anywhere.

DEPENDING UPON WHICH documents you read, my birth name was Fred Phillips, Fred Demaree, or Fred Stewart, and I was born in Memphis on February 25, 1949. My biological mother's name was Olive Phillips, Demaree, or Stewart. My biological father is listed as Luther Phillips.

Given all the deceit that went on between the Tennessee Children's Home Society and the authorities they paid off, I'll never really know the circumstances surrounding my birth, or what happened to me immediately afterward. The agency reported that, on March 12, 1949, "Olive Phillips and Luther Phillips did abandon and desert said child." A court later ruled that I was "an abandoned, dependent and neglected child," to be placed "under the guardianship of the Tennessee Children's Home Society," which now had the right to find me "a suitable home for adoption."

They didn't keep me around Memphis for long. On March 18, I was delivered to my adoptive parents at 6439 Devereaux in Detroit, just as the agency had dropped off other children at hotels like the Biltmore in Los Angeles—an extra amenity, I guess, for preferred customers. My parents renamed me Richard Morgan Fliehr, and eventually took me home to Edina, Minnesota, just outside Minneapolis.

Believe it or not, I never bothered looking at my adoption papers until I started researching this book. The documents were sitting in a safe in my house, and I didn't even know my birth name. I was never curious. I'm still not. I'm an only child, and as far as I'm concerned, my parents have always been my mom and dad.

They never kept my adoption a secret from me; in fact, they described it as one of the happiest events of their lives. I'd have a birthday party and then, every March 18, my parents and I would go to an Italian restaurant (I always liked Italian food) by ourselves to celebrate my "anniversary."

In the summer, we'd take vacations that lasted three weeks and drive all over the United States, from Disneyland to the Rocky Mountains to Washington, D.C., and into Canada. My dad would take me camping up in the Great Northwest. He was a strong swimmer and could swim right across the lake. When we were thirsty, we'd drink the water out of the same lake. It was tremendous.

Every year for my birthday, my father would take me to the wrestling matches. I loved watching the old American Wrestling Association (AWA), based in Minneapolis, and remember seeing guys like Verne Gagne, Bobo Brazil, Ray Stevens, and Red Bastien. I liked the interviews better than the matches, especially when the Crusher was on. Reggie "Crusher" Lisowski called himself "the man who made Milwaukee famous," and claimed that he trained by running with a beer keg on each shoulder and dancing with fat Polish women afterward. He was a big, barrel-chested guy who called chubby girls his "dollies," and his opponents "sissies" and "turkey necks." Sometimes he and his tag-team partner, Dick the Bruiser, seemed to get so excited after winning a match—Crusher liked to use the Bolo Punch and Stomach Claw—that they'd start slugging each other.

Whenever I saw the Crusher on TV, chomping on his cigar, I'd call my father over—"Dad, Dad, come watch this interview." He'd look at it for a little while, then walk away and laugh. He knew that wrestling made me happy, but it really wasn't his thing.

This is one example of how I sometimes sensed that I didn't have a lot in common with my parents. I don't know if it had anything to do with biology, or with the things we cared about; it just seemed like we lived in different worlds. They loved the theater and education. I had no interest in anything except sports. My father was incredibly handy; he could build and wire a house. I don't think my wife has ever seen me hammer a nail. And I don't want to.

FROM THE TIME I was twelve years old, I *was* Ric Flair. The teachers at Golden Valley Elementary School and Golden Valley Junior High School might have called me "Fliehr," but I was just a younger version of the guy fans later saw stylin' and profilin' on WRAL in Raleigh, then on SuperStation TBS and TNT, and today on Spike TV. I was always a chief, never a follower. I was center stage at every party, and the girls were everywhere. And, just like in wrestling, my craziest friend in junior high school was a guy named Piper.

Dan Piper came to Edina from Nashville, Tennessee. He was at least a year older than us—I think his parents kept him back—had a southern accent and rolled-up sleeves, smoked, carried a Zippo lighter, and knew how to drive. I must have been in eighth grade when the two of us stole a car and drove some girls to the dances at the Hopkins Roller Rink. It was something like thirty below zero and I didn't know how to work the car, so when I turned on the air-conditioning instead of the heater, I completely froze the engine block.

Piper was also with me the night I took my dad's car to where some girls were having a slumber party. We sneaked out a few of them in their pajamas and were in the car when one girl hit the brake pedal and a cop came over to investigate. The police had to contact the girls' families, and one of the fathers was so irate that he wanted to press charges. It was Father's Day morning when my dad arrived at the jail.

"Happy Father's Day," I said, a little embarrassed.

"Thanks," he grumbled, and took me home.

I'm sure that if I attended school now, I'd be diagnosed with attention deficit hyperactivity disorder, ADHD. I was the epitome of the disease. I couldn't concentrate and kept getting into trouble for not listening. No one ever said that I wasn't intellectually gifted. I just couldn't slow down enough to read or study. Even today, I don't really read books; I prefer *USA Today, Time, Sports Illustrated,* and boating magazines. And back then, there was no treatment for students like me.

Sometimes kids who can't handle academics take out their frustration by getting into fights. Not me, though. I may have had a few fights, but I didn't have a chip on my shoulder. There wasn't much to be angry about. I was an only child with parents who couldn't do enough for me, and a good athlete with a huge wealth of friends.

Looking back, my parents were far more lenient than I am with my younger kids. They were constantly out of town doing plays, and supposedly leaving me under the supervision of family friends. But I could always figure my way around that.

I started having sex when I was about fourteen, and just kept going. The rotation stayed in place; I never went looking for it. My priority was going out and *being* the party. At the end of the night, when all was said and done and the last bottle drunk, I just let things happen. Pretty soon, I was working on a numbers game, and the numbers piled up fast.

Over time, my little scrapes with the law also began accumulating. I got caught riding our Honda 50 motorcycle around the lake (without a license) while my parents were out of town. Then I got busted trying to use a phony ID at a liquor store. The owner was an ex-football player in a wheelchair, and the cops made me feel terrible, telling me how I nearly caused this handicapped guy to lose his business.

It all became too much for my parents, so they decided that I'd be better off in boarding school. After the ninth grade, I left Minnesota to go to Wayland Academy in Beaver Dam, Wisconsin, an exclusive school that was founded in 1855 and, according to its promotional material, "seeks to foster the development of personality, responsibility, self-discipline and friendship" among its students.

The school has a reputation for sending its graduates to places like Wellesley, Stanford, Harvard, Princeton, Northwestern, and Duke. The kids who went there for the academics got their money's worth—we were in accelerated math programs, and had to take Latin *and* French. But the students I hung around with were mainly wild rich kids with family problems, or they'd been in trouble at school or with the police, and this was an alternative to military school. We were fifteen-year-olds, the school was coed, and all of us were players. I was there about two months when I realized that my parents had sent me to heaven.

My academics still sucked, but I lettered in three sports. I played middle linebacker and fullback on the football team, threw the shot put, and wrestled, first at 181 pounds and then as a heavyweight. Since the drinking age in Wisconsin was eighteen, it was easy to get into bars with a fake ID.

It only made sense that my friends would become a bigger part of my life than my family. During the school year, I came home only for Christmas and a couple of other days. My parents would attend one of my football games every season, but they never saw me wrestle, so I felt like I was on my own. Today, I could never imagine sending a child away like that. My youngest boy, Reid, is an accomplished high-school wrestler, and one boarding school has tried to recruit him. But I won't let him go. How could I recapture that time apart from my son?

Sometimes my best friend, the General, would invite me to his family's house for the weekend. His family was very wealthy, and just being around them accelerated my taste for the finer things in life. Don't mistake me—my father was a doctor, and we were anything but poor. But while my father may have been earning $65,000 a year—a great living in the 1960s—the General's dad was literally one of the wealthiest men in the Midwest. And my parents were frugal; they saved every dime and didn't live large—which was the complete opposite of where I wanted to go.

Every spring break, the General and I would hitchhike to Florida. I'd come home to Minnesota and tell my parents that I was going to stay with the General's family for a few days. Then, after my parents dropped me off at the train station in Minneapolis, I'd start hitching in twenty-below-zero weather until I ended up in Fort Lauderdale. When we were sixteen, we rented an apartment upstairs from a beauty salon. For the whole week, the General did the owner, while I did her daughter.

One summer, I got a job as a lifeguard at a local pool in Minnesota and had my first interaction with pro wrestlers. Maurice "Mad Dog" Vachon, a former AWA Champion with a bald head and a beard and mustache that weren't quite connected to each other, would stomp and bite his opponents, then growl into the TV camera, baring his bottom teeth. I'd see him at the pool with his brother, Paul "Butcher" Vachon, and their sister, Vivian, who also wrestled. Paul and Vivian were friendly enough—not that they had much to say to a seventeen-year-old kid—but it was impossible to strike up a conversation with Mad Dog. He was very much the character he played.

I was working on becoming a water safety instructor, giving little kids lessons, when I struck up a friendship with one of the mothers. She was thirty-five and stunning. Her husband traveled a lot. We enjoyed each other's "company." This was the most exciting thing that had ever happened to me in my teenage years. This beautiful woman introduced me to new experiences in the bedroom. I thought I'd died and gone to heaven.

When I got back to school, the dean of students called me into his office to tell me that my "aunt" had driven three hundred miles to take me off-campus for the day. She gave me some advice I've never forgotten: "Ric, you're going to learn that older women like a little appetizer before dinner." I was only too happy to oblige.

I thought our arrangement was great—beyond great—but she apparently felt guilty about cheating on her husband with a minor. One day she broke down in her doctor's office and confessed everything. The doctor excused himself, went into the next office and told his partner, my father, that it would probably be best if I stayed away from their patient. My father was irate with me for what he deemed to be inappropriate behavior.

IT TOOK ME five years to graduate from high school, but thanks to my athletic credentials, colleges were still interested in me. In both 1966 and 1967, I was state private school wrestling champion. A lot of people have asked me if that's when I knew that I was going to become a professional wrestler. Well, I didn't think that far ahead. I was having too much fun, and I couldn't imagine anything past college football.

The University of Michigan wanted to recruit me, and I decided to go to Ann Arbor with the General to check out the school. We started out with $110 between us. After two nights at the Michigan Union, we were running low on cash. I heard a knock at the door and opened it. There was a black girl who worked for the hotel; she was there to collect the money we owed for the room. Knowing we didn't have the cash, I issued her a challenge. "You see my friend over here?" I said, pointing at the General. "His balls are bigger than any black guy's you've ever seen."

"I don't think so," she replied.

The General pulled down his pants. The clerk comped our lodging.

After spending the weekend at the University of Michigan with the football coach, Bump Elliot, and players like Jim Mandich (who ended up on the Miami Dolphins and Pittsburgh Steelers) and Dan Dierdorf (one of the NFL's greatest offensive tackles before he became an announcer on *Monday Night Football*), I was ready to become a Wolverine. All I needed was a letter from Jim Fierke, the dean of students at Wayland Academy, stating his confidence in my ability to pass college-level classes. But he refused to cooperate. He told me that I would get into college and just blow it. He was right, but I had hoped he would do me a favor. After all, I gave five years to that school.

Eventually I was recruited by my parents' alma mater, the University of Minnesota, by the Golden Gophers' offensive line coach, Mike McGee. I started there in 1968, playing freshman football as an offensive guard. We'd scrimmage with the varsity squad, and the coaches evaluated us. I was definitely good enough to make the team. It was just a simple question of getting my grades right.

Of course, I had other concerns. I joined a fraternity, Phi Delta Theta, and began hanging around with a football player named Mike Goldberg. Mike was a year older than me and helped give the place its *Animal House* flavor. There was another Goldberg brother, Steve, who began playing football at the school the year after I did. And on September 21, 2003, their baby brother, Bill, defeated Triple H for the WWE World Championship.

No one was really surprised when I was told that I'd have to attend summer school in order to play my sophomore year. I had been there about two weeks when the General invited me out to his house for the weekend. I told my girlfriend, Leslie Goodman—who'd later become my first wife and the mother of my kids Megan and David—that I'd be gone for about three days. It ended up being more like two months, and when I returned, she had another boyfriend. I eventually succeeded in winning her back, and the pattern of our relationship was set.

Unfortunately, that was the least of my problems. Because I cut out on summer school, I couldn't play football. I ended up hanging around campus for a couple of months with Mike Goldberg and some of my other friends, then dropped out after the fall semester.

My parents were beyond freaking out. They'd seen this kind of thing happen with me again and again, and they worried that I'd never get my feet on the ground. I understood their fears, but didn't share their apprehension.

Somehow, I sensed that the party was only getting started.

Before joining Mid-Atlantic Championship Wrestling, I bleached my hair blond, modeling myself after guys like Superstar Billy Graham and Dusty Rhodes.

After dropping out of college, I got a job selling insurance. I kind of liked it; it was a challenge, but I applied myself and did pretty well. I had friends everywhere, so I took the general agent of the company around, and we began writing up policies on them. He even wrote my dad's pension plan. In my first year, I made about $30,000, which was big money. If I'd wanted to make a career out of this, I think I would have done okay. I was certainly off to a good start.

I also started bouncing at George's in the Park, the best dinner and dance club in Minneapolis. It was an upscale place, so we didn't have too many problems. We had one guy, Ron Kane, who we called our "hit man." He was a legitimate tough guy with a metal plate in

CHAPTER 2

BREAKING INTO THE BUSINESS!

his head, and everybody in Minneapolis knew about him. If a patron was acting unruly, Ron would ask him to leave. If there was a problem, Ron issued a verbal warning, "My record's 300–0, and it's not gonna change tonight." That was usually all it took to get the person to leave.

One night, I was standing by the cigarette machine when I saw a big guy, about 300 pounds, walk in smoking a Salem. I gestured to the other bouncer and said, "Man, that looks like Ken Patera."

The other bouncer shrugged. "Kinda."

I knew all about Ken Patera because I was a weightlifting fan. I'd just read an article about him becoming the first man to press five hundred pounds. He'd been on *ABC's Wide World of Sports*. In 1968, while he was at Brigham Young University, he'd placed third in a National College Athletic Association tournament for throwing a sixteen-pound shot put nearly sixty-six feet. As a power lifter, he bench-pressed 560 pounds, squatted 820 pounds, and deadlifted 785 pounds. In his amateur career, he'd won four gold medals at the 1971 Pan Am Games, and set eighty-four national or higher-level records.

I went over and introduced myself. Ken was from Portland, Oregon, but he was in Minneapolis training for the 1972 Olympics. Verne Gagne, the American Wrestling Association world champion—and promoter—was sponsoring him. Verne had been on the 1948 U.S. Olympic wrestling team and saw potential in Ken, believing that he could have a career in professional wrestling. The plan was for Patera to start wrestling on Verne's cards after making a strong showing at the Olympic Games.

KEN PATERA: Ric wanted to know what I was doing there. I joked, "Well, you have to be *somewhere*," then told him I'd been to Minneapolis before. My brother, Jack, was defensive line coach for the Minnesota Vikings, and later head coach of the Seattle Seahawks.

Ric looked at my cigarette: "You *smoke*?" I answered, "Yeah, and I drink, too."

A few days later, Ric's parents were having a little dinner for his twenty-first birthday, and he invited me over to the house. His family was really nice. And in his room, he had a stack of wrestling magazines about four feet high. He was a real avid fan.

We ended up moving into a house together in South Minneapolis. We didn't have any furniture, but I was selling waterbeds, so I put them all over the house. One of them was round, and kids from the neighborhood would come over to jump up and down on it like a trampoline.

I call the entire time I lived with Patera my "endless summer." Ken didn't train until the afternoon, so we kept the party going as late as we wanted. For a time, he was also bouncing part-time at George's in the Park, so we'd bring a group back to the house and meet up with Mike Goldberg, who'd been in another part of town and had some other people with him. I never went to bed.

I was delighted to have Ken Patera as a friend. It was great showing him off to people, and I couldn't believe the man's strength. After we both became wrestlers, I remember helping him train for the World's Strongest Man competition in 1977. We had a harness made, and he pulled a van up and down the street. I'd never seen anyone like him.

I'd started weightlifting in high school and now began working out with Ken. Having the chance to train at his level really inspired me. But once, while we were in the gym, I had to ask him, "How can you drink and smoke and do this?"

"That's what all the athletes do in Eastern Europe, the East Germans and the Russians," he said. "I learned more about drinking vodka in Russia than I did about sports. As far as smoking goes, you don't have to be able to breathe to lift weights."

Before the Olympics, he was trying to become as big as possible. I began eating like him. We'd drink two gallons of milk and eat two dozen eggs—yolks and all—then go to Burger King for five Whoppers. He transformed everything into muscle. In my case, 40 percent of what I ate became fat.

AFTER THE '72 Olympics, Verne Gagne was going to train Patera and a couple of other guys to become professional wrestlers. I was interested in joining them, but I didn't know if Gagne would be willing to consider me. Just before I met Patera, I'd run into Mad Dog Vachon in a bar, reminded him that I'd been the lifeguard at his pool, and inquired about getting into wrestling. Mad Dog sent me to a wrestler friend, Ricky Ferrera. We had one workout in a gym with no wrestling ring, exchanged a couple of holds, went out for some beers, and that was it.

I already knew Verne's son, Greg. He'd been at the University of Minnesota while I was there, and he was a pretty good quarterback. We had different groups of friends, but I always thought of him as a fun guy. The thing was that we'd never spoken about his father or professional wrestling, and I wasn't sure if I should approach him.

You have to understand—Verne Gagne was like a god in the Twin Cities, bigger than even Bud Grant, who had led the Minnesota Vikings into the Super Bowl. Verne became the first AWA champion in 1960 and held the title ten times. North America was divided into regional wrestling territories at the time, but the AWA had expanded from Minneapolis to Chicago, Salt Lake City, Denver, Winnipeg, and eventually Las Vegas and San Francisco. Everybody knew that Verne was the power behind the scenes. His television show was one of the highest rated in Minnesota, and he had a reputation as a successful businessman in areas not related to wrestling.

In time, Patera arranged for me to have a meeting with Verne. Here I was, standing in front of this really big star that I'd grown up watching on television, and I was intimidated. I found myself looking at the floor, afraid to even make eye contact.

Verne was about to start a pro wrestling training camp and wanted only top athletes. Patera and Greg Gagne were in the class, along with another acquaintance of mine—"Jumping" Jim Brunzell, who'd later become Greg's tag-team partner in the AWA and one of the Killer Bees (with B. Brian Blair) in the World Wrestling Federation. The other two students were Bob Bruggers, a former linebacker with the Miami Dolphins and San Diego Chargers, and Hossein Khosrow Vaziri, a great amateur wrestler from Iran who was an assistant coach on the 1972 U.S. Olympic team. Later—as the Iron Sheik—Khosrow would become the World Wrestling Federation champion.

I'd always done well at sports, so I figured that if I kept getting bigger and stronger, I could make it. But Verne told me, "You know, it's not easy being a professional wrestler. In fact, it's a task and a half."

I kept looking at the floor and nodding, like I understood. But honestly, I couldn't even *begin* to make sense of what I was about to do.

KEN PATERA: I told Ric, "You were born to be in this business. This business was made for guys like you." Verne wasn't so sure–"I have five guys training already," he said, "I don't have room for six"–but he eventually agreed to put Ric through the motions with the rest of us.

Our main trainer was Billy Robinson, an Englishman who had a reputation as a shooter, meaning that if a match got out of hand, he could "shoot"–or fight for real–and "hook" his opponent with a hold that could cripple him. Billy did most of the training, with a few assistants like Don "The Magnificent" Muraco.

We'd start off running along this frozen creek, slipping and sliding. I'm not exaggerating–you'd have to wear *three* sweatsuits. The only way to stay warm was to keep moving and not slow down–the whole day, for six or eight hours.

One day, it was ten degrees. The next, it was ten *below*. We ran around this farm, not on a track, but on a customized path that went about two miles. The only one who made me look good was Ken; his legs were so big from all the squatting that they were chafing together. We had to do 500 free squats, 200 push-ups, and 200 sit-ups. I'd never trained so hard in my life. Not once had I ever done a free squat. I hadn't done push-ups in years. I wasn't used to doing sit-ups.

KEN PATERA: We were doing neck bridges, calisthenics, jumping jacks, *everything*. Then we went to work out in the ring, which was inside one of Verne's horse barns. The horses were downstairs, and the chickens were upstairs on the right. It was below-zero temperatures, with one lightbulb in the whole barn, just dangling on a wire. The slats on the barn were about an inch apart, so there were times when we'd show up to four-foot snowdrifts in the place. The chickens would be roosting on the crossbeams of the barn, shitting in the ring, so we'd have to clean the mat.

The ring was all broken down, and the ropes were fucked up. They should be tight because you're supposed to run off them, but these were actually drooping. Here's Verne Gagne, a multimillionaire, and he had the worst possible conditions for us to train in. Eventually, when it got unbearably cold, he did rent the St. Paul Armory for us. Finally, we had hot running water and flushing toilets! But before then, I tell you, it was bizarre.

In the ring, we'd do fifty front rolls, then fifty back rolls. After that,

we'd give each other fifty turnbuckle reversals–pulling a guy off one set of turnbuckles and throwing him into the set on the opposite side of the ring. Then you'd do fifty shoulder tackles, fifty flying mares, fifty suplexes . . . fuck, it was *unbelievable*. When Joe Scarpello, an old-timer who'd been an All-American at the University of Iowa, came up one day, he said, "Verne just took ten years off your career." He said we took more bumps–falls–in our training than he had in his twenty-five years in the ring. "This is brutality," he told us. "This is uncalled for."

I must have been at camp for two days when I quit. I called up Greg and said, "I'm done." I was dead. Mentally, I couldn't take it.

Greg told his dad, so Verne came over to my house, grabbed me by the shirt and threw me out on the front lawn. "It took you five years to graduate high school," he screamed. "You quit college. Well, you're not quitting this. I didn't sign you up to be a quitter."

Verne said things to me that I'm sure my father had always been tempted to say. But my dad *never* spoke to me like that. It hit a nerve, and it made me want to prove to Verne that I was better than he thought. So I went back to camp. Life didn't get any easier after that. We'd have to wait in line to wrestle Billy Robinson, who would get behind you and try to turn you on your back, and you'd have to get away. Jim Brunzell would be standing in line behind me, and I'd try to maneuver my body so Brunzell went first. I'd spend the whole time thinking, How can I get Brunzell in front of me? It was that bad.

Out of all of us, Khosrow had accomplished the most as an amateur wrestler. While everyone else was out of breath, he whipped through the exercises. But like a lot of amateur wrestlers, he was always running his mouth, like he didn't take professional wrestling seriously. "Verne Gagne or Billy Robinson couldn't beat me on their best day," he'd brag.

Robinson got wind of this, so he lined us all up one day and told Khosrow that he wanted to wrestle him first. "I heard you said I can't turn you over," Robinson challenged.

"You can't," Khosrow shot back.

Robinson had him get down, spread-eagle, in amateur position. He got on top, but didn't have the leverage to turn Khosrow over and pin him. But Robinson was an expert on "hook" style, which was illegal in the amateur ranks, and after about ten minutes, he brought the point of his knee down into Khosrow's thigh, fucking up his hip. Khosrow was in agony as Robinson turned him over and pinned him. "See? I told you I could do it," he crowed.

KEN PATERA: Khosrow hated Robinson after that. He had no respect for him. "Billy no coach," he said. "Coach don't do that to student."

Robinson *was* a prick; that's why he had trouble in different places where he wrestled. Sailor White punched him out in Montreal, then *pissed* into his wounds. The Rock's grandfather, Peter Maivia, nearly dug out his eye in another fight. Verne and Robinson were close, but outside the AWA, nobody wanted to work with Billy. They were afraid he'd fuck them up with cheap shots. And chances were that he would.

When I saw what Robinson did to the Iron Sheik, I was shocked, mortified, and ready to kill myself, all at the same time. I thought I was next, so I ended up quitting camp one more time. I told Greg, "Don't tell your dad I'm not coming back."

Greg said, "Okay," and walked away. Of course, the *second* he saw his father, he told him.

This time Verne didn't bother going to my house. He just called me on the phone and said, "I hope I don't have to come back there to get you."

That was all I needed to hear. I returned the next day like nothing was wrong.

THE ENTIRE TIME that I was in training camp, I was waiting for the "big secret" of professional wrestling to be unbottled—were the matches real, or predetermined? I kept thinking, When are they gonna tell us? But everybody was so serious that I didn't dare ask one of the trainers; in fact, I didn't even discuss it with the other guys. Verne simply wasn't going to give something like that away until he *had* to. In my case, that meant five minutes before my first match.

I was beginning to get a feeling for how things worked by hanging out in the AWA dressing room. On Saturdays, we'd head over to WTCN Studios and watch them tape the TV show. If the guys needed a go-fer, I was happy to oblige. Sometimes a few of them would call me over to the bar, just to kind of test me and see what kind of attitude I was bringing into the business. Occasionally "Cowboy" Bill Watts, Dick "The Destroyer" Beyer, or another veteran came into the promotion, and I'd be his designated driver, sitting behind the wheel and grabbing every road story or pearl of wrestling wisdom that he was willing to throw me.

Superstar Billy Graham had a tremendous physique; he'd reveal it by pulling off his tie-dye shirt to flex and kiss his biceps. I loved to listen to him do an interview, talking about his twenty-two-inch "pythons" (yes, he used the term *before* Hulk Hogan) and rambling on in that smooth-talking voice of his: "I am the reflection of perfection! The number-one selection!"

Whenever Billy had to go out of town to wrestle for another promotion, I'd be assigned to drive him to the airport in his El Dorado. He knew that I liked weight- and power-lifting, and how much I wanted to get into the business. Sometimes he'd invite me out to dinner, just to talk. I was a young guy, but he was a star, so I appreciated the time he took with me.

I also started hanging out with Dusty Rhodes, another main-eventer who had a tremendous delivery on interviews. Dusty was playing a bad guy at the time, teaming with "Dirty" Dick Murdoch as the Outlaws, but he was so cool—putting his hands behind his head and wiggling his three-hundred-pound body, or crooking his finger forward and hitting his charging foe with a big elbow.

I was infatuated with being like Dusty. At the end of training camp, Verne told us that we could do any move that we wanted. I had another student lie down on the canvas, then hit the ropes and dropped a Dusty elbow on him. Verne, the wrestling purist, went crazy. "Oh, my God!" he yelled. "Is *that* what you've learned since you've been here?"

Just before I had my first match, I asked Verne if I could be "Rambling" Ricky Rhodes, Dusty's "brother." I was ready to curl my hair like Dusty's and everything.

"No, you can't," he insisted. "Look at the name you have—Rick Fliehr. Change a few letters around, and you're Ric *Flair*. It's a good name. You don't want to tie yourself to somebody else before you even get started."

But to think how things might have turned out if Verne had said yes.

Dusty Rhodes, one of my idols when I started in the business. His rapport with the fans was incredible.

LESLIE AND I had gotten married in 1971. She had wanted me to convert to Judaism, for the sake of her grandparents more than anything else. I'd always had Jewish friends and didn't have a problem with it, but when I went to one of those religion classes and they started speaking Hebrew, I balked. I wasn't going to sit through that stuff week after week. We ended up getting married at Plymouth Congregational Church in Minneapolis, where my dad was a deacon.

As for wrestling, my parents weren't sure that I was making a wise career choice. They knew all about Verne Gagne's achievements; they just weren't confident that *I'd* be able to make a living at doing the same thing. Leslie was more supportive. Before my first match, she made me a jacket out of blue satin fabric and put fringes on it. I must have looked at myself wearing it in the mirror a dozen times. I was so proud of it.

On December 10, 1972, in Rice Lake, Wisconsin, I made my wrestling debut against George "Scrap Iron" Gadaski. Just before I stepped through the curtain, Verne instructed me, "Just go out there and do exactly what George tells you to do. You guys are gonna go through."

I hadn't heard that term before. "What do you mean, 'go through'?"

"Nobody wins. It's gonna be a draw. Simple as that."

George was the guy who set up the ring every night. In fact, around that period, I'd often ride with him in the ring truck, helping him out. He wrestled "either way," meaning that he could be the good guy one night and a bad guy the next.

He and I had no conversation beforehand. We just got in the ring and he said, "Give me a tackle." So I did.

"Slam me," he said. I gave him a body slam.

"Take a backdrop."

I bounced off the ropes, and when Gadaski bent down, I did a flip over his shoulders and onto the canvas.

The bell rang when the ten-minute time limit expired. I'd exhausted myself during the match and needed a place to rest, but everything had gone fine. I definitely passed my first test.

GREG GAGNE WAS the promoter's son, so naturally, Verne had wanted to make him a star. I spent much of my rookie year wrestling with Greg. We had become close friends, learning our trade and having fun at the same time.

In the AWA, to break character and socialize with the wrestler who beat you up on TV last week was considered a grave insult to the wrestling business. You didn't travel together. If you were in the same bar or restaurant, you didn't sit at the same table. On the road, guys would occasionally go into each other's rooms for a drink, but no outsiders were ever allowed at those gatherings.

In 1989, the World Wrestling Federation, in a bid to deregulate athletic commission supervision of wrestling in New Jersey, obliterated that code forever when it admitted, at a public hearing, that we were "sports entertainment." Believe it or not, I know some guys who are still losing sleep over that. Part of me relates to them. I feel that I've been able to make the transition to what wrestling has become today, but once in a while, things do disturb me. I don't like seeing arena employees sit and watch while my opponent and I work out a match in the ring before the doors open. Recently, I spotted a TV reporter strolling around the building with his *kids* while the guys were rehearsing. That really aggravated me. We've worked hard to create a certain mystique about this business, and it bothers me when so much of the magic is given away.

On the surface, the AWA seemed like a traditional wrestling company. As the public face of the promotion, Verne appeared to be pretty conservative. In reality, though, he was as wide open as anybody. He just picked his spots. When you partied with Verne, you knew this: at the end of the night, you'd have to wrestle your way out of there. He and Robinson *always* wanted to wrestle somebody on the floor. I figured that out after I was thrown around a few times. I kept hanging out with Verne, but once he got that look in his eye, like he wanted to torture me in front of the girls, I was out of there.

After a wrestling match, Andre the Giant was another guy who loved to party. One night in Charlotte. I saw him drink one hundred and six beers. That's a fact. (Frank Valois, his traveling companion and translator, drank fifty-four.) Another time, at a beachfront bar in Norfolk, Blackjack Mulligan and Dick Murdoch were play-fighting with Andre when one of them sucker-punched him. Andre dragged them both into the ocean, stuck their heads under the water, and started drowning them. When he let them up, they all came back to the bar laughing, but that was the business.

Andre the Giant truly was an "eighth wonder of the world," both inside the ring and at the bars.

I used to drive Andre around when he came to wrestle in the AWA. He was billed as seven-foot-four and more than 500 pounds, and he truly was an incredible sight. Larry "The Ax" Hennig once told me that Andre had an extra set of everything—two hearts, two rows of teeth. Every time I had him in the car, I found myself peeking into his mouth, looking for that extra row of teeth.

SIX MONTHS AFTER I broke into wrestling, some of the AWA guys were booked on a tour in Japan. Someone canceled out and Verne asked me, "Do you want to go there with Dusty Rhodes and Dick Murdoch?"

I was so excited. "God, I'll go anywhere with Rhodes and Murdoch."

My mistake. From the time we landed, I carried their bags. I had traveled halfway around the world to be a bellhop. They sang at the top of their lungs on the train ride between cities. We drank all night, every night. They broke down my door at the hotel, sprayed the room with a fire extinguisher, and threw all my clothes out of a tenth-story window.

That was how you became one of the boys—you got rode hard. The veterans wanted to see if you would break. I actually had it a lot easier than most.

On June 26, 1973, I was booked in a cage match for the first time in my life, against Rusher Kimura in the Japanese city of Odate. I'd never bled in a match, so Rhodes and Murdoch gave the referee a blade and told him to get some blood out of me. He cut me from one end of my head to the other. Afterward, I went into the back and asked somebody to take a picture. Rhodes and Murdoch started laughing at me—the rookie trying to be big-time. And before I could feel too much pride, I realized that they'd left me at the building, in the middle of nowhere.

After the tour, Leslie was supposed to meet me in Hawaii, but there were a few hours before her plane arrived. Rhodes and Murdoch took me to the beach, and we got so hammered that I ended up falling asleep on the sand. When I woke up, my wife had been waiting in the airport for nearly four hours.

KEN PATERA: Ric loved Rhodes and Murdoch, and he always wanted to be with them. Like him, they were completely out of control.

Rhodes and Murdoch had a cowboy gimmick, and they really played the part. They also had this friend from Louisiana who'd come up to visit them. One night they were so drunk, they drove to Louisiana, got a mule, and brought that fucker back to Minneapolis. Then they put that mule in this beautiful luxury apartment complex they were living in; the place was so new that it wasn't even finished yet. They had a couple of bales of hay and oats and water in there.

There was this downtown bar, a country-and-western place, where the stage would come out of the floor on hydraulics. A lot of the customers were motorcycle guys, and it was pretty rowdy. Well, Murdoch rode that mule into the bar and shot a fuckin' pistol off. Of course, the cops came, and a big fight ensued. Gagne found out about it a couple of days later and threatened to fire Murdoch and Rhodes. It was a big hoopla.

I know that Leslie didn't like the effect this way of life was having on Ric. I was living next door to them when she was pregnant with their daughter, Megan. They were having all kinds of problems, and

Ric was pissed off because she wanted him to quit wrestling. I told him, "Listen here, you cocksucker. I went through all this fuckin' effort to get you into this, and you're doing good. You're not quitting now."

RHODES AND MURDOCH had two saddles, a table, a couch, a few chairs and a TV in their apartment—and about eight cases of beer. I lived in the bottom part of the house for a while. I had to; Leslie kicked me out.

We'd separate, then get back together. Sometimes I'd tell her that I was wrestling in towns where I wasn't even scheduled, and just take off with Dusty and Murdoch.

Once, Dusty called up to tell me that Kay Noble—a girl wrestler who I thought was pretty good-looking—and Donna Lemke (a female wrestler who he liked) were over at his place. "I'm gonna put Kay on you like lightning on a june bug," he said, and I drove over there at 100 miles per hour.

On another occasion, we were all supposed to wrestle in Mitchell, South Dakota. Dusty said, "Why don't you take Patera's car and come with us?"

Ken had just bought a big Oldsmobile four-door and was out of town. "Ah, fuck, I can drive his car," I convinced myself. "It can't hurt to put a couple of hundred miles on it, right?"

We got out to Mitchell—in freezing temperatures, of course—and they threw me out by a farm in the middle of the night. It was pitch-black, and I was starting to look for lights. Three minutes passed, but it seemed more like an hour. Then they came back down the road, with Murdoch shooting his nine-millimeter out the fuckin' window. I'm lucky I didn't get shot, or frostbite, or both. It made me miss carrying their bags in Japan.

By the time we returned to Minneapolis, either Murdoch or Rhodes had burned a cigar hole in the Oldsmobile's upholstery. Strawberry cake was smeared everywhere. It no longer looked like a brand-new car.

I thought Patera was going to kill me.

KEN PATERA: I was *furious*. I said, "I loan you my car and trust you to take care of it, and now it's all fucked up."

I didn't have much cash at the time, but I paid $500 to buy Dusty Rhodes an 18-karat gold money clip with a $20 gold piece in the center. Leslie and I were with Dusty at a country-and-western place when I pulled him aside and gave him the present. It was my way of telling him, "Thanks for taking me under your wing and helping me become part of the business."

In this book, you're going to read some great stories about Dusty Rhodes, and some bad stories about Dusty Rhodes. Yet despite all the tension we'd have between us later on, whenever I think of Dusty, the good will always outweigh the bad.

Angelo "King Kong" Mosca once predicted, "Ric, if you live past thirty, you'll be overstaying your welcome." And I was doing my best to make his words come true.

Ray Stevens and Harley Race were both great wrestlers whose performance between the ropes was never affected by their lifestyles. Stevens had been wrestling since he was a teenager in the fifties. He was known as the Blond Bomber, and was a genuine legend. Race and I would end up trading the NWA title back and forth.

The first time I ever met Harley, he could tell I was a huge fan. We were in Grand Island, Nebraska, and had to go over the Rocky Mountains—about four hundred miles—into Denver. He and Stevens

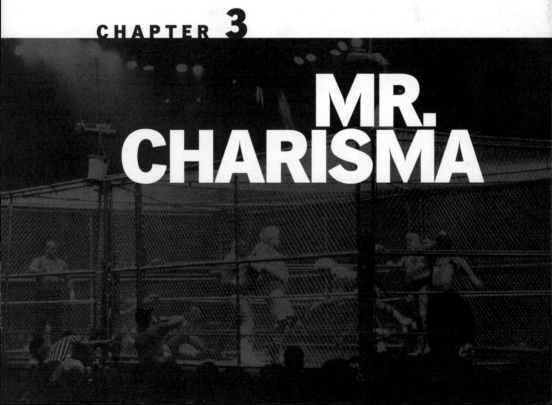

CHAPTER **3**

MR. CHARISMA

were in this station wagon, and they had bet Greg Gagne and Jim Brunzell that they could beat them to the hotel. Harley asked me, "Do you want to ride with us, kid?" Of course, I jumped at the chance.

At first, I was really enjoying myself. Harley was driving as fast as he could, and Stevens was screaming, "I'm a fucker and a fighter and a wild bull rider, with a pretty fair windmill hand!" But as soon as we got into the mountains, the snow really started to come down. The two of them pulled out two quarts of Southern Comfort and began passing it around. Every time the bottle came to me in the back seat, they'd turn on the interior light and check the rearview mirror to make sure I was drinking.

Being a station wagon, the car wasn't going that fast up the mountain. But when we went downhill, Harley made up the time—he was really gunning it, probably going about a hundred miles an hour down these snowy, winding roads.

HARLEY RACE: I look in the rearview mirror and notice that Flair's slapping Stevens on the shoulder, pointing at the speedometer. Eventually, Stevens looks over at me and says, "You're gonna kill us."

I tell him, "Have another drink. We're gonna win this thing."

Stevens says, "If you don't slow down, I'm gonna knock you out."

I answer back, "If you're so worried about getting killed, that'd be a good way of assuring it."

Now Flair starts to heave out the back window, and the snow's coming down so heavy that the back of his head is one big snowball. We pull him back into the car, keep going, and beat Gagne and Brunzell to the hotel by about forty-five minutes. I know that Ric enjoyed himself because he's told this story himself a million times.

Larry Hennig loved to pull jokes on me in the ring. Larry was a man among men who'd put fans in front facelocks and squeeze until they were unconscious if they dared imply that wrestling was "fake." His son, Curt Hennig, used the name Mr. Perfect in the World Wrestling Federation, and would also become one of my good friends.

In a match, Larry would hit me real hard and say, "Don't sell it." So I'd act like I didn't feel the blow. He'd turn to the referee and sneer, "Look at this young punk. He thinks he's too good to sell for me." Then he'd hit me really hard again and say, "You better sell this one." I'd go down on the floor, but he'd complain to the ref, "What's the matter with this kid? He's selling too much."

I was terrified that I was doing the wrong thing. He'd keep beating the shit out of me while I'd be asking the referee, "What did he say?" And this would go on for ten minutes, until the match was over.

When I'd get backstage, though, I got the impression that the older, wilder guys saw something in me that the other rookies lacked. Hennig once told me, "You already have all the fucking around down. Now all you have to do is learn how to *wrestle*."

THEN WAHOO CAME to the AWA, and my life changed forever.

When Ed "Wahoo" McDaniel played for the New York Jets in 1964, the public-address announcer would declare, "Tackle by . . . guess who?" And all the fans in Shea Stadium would chant, "Wa-hoo! Wa-hoo!" He even had his nickname, not his last name, on the back of his jersey.

Wahoo was part Choctaw and part Chickasaw, and wore an Indian headdress to the ring. Even when he wasn't around, people were telling Wahoo stories. One of my favorites was about the time he ran thirty-six miles in six hours for a hundred-dollar bet with Bill Watts.

I liked Wahoo instantly, the same way I liked Dusty. He was a man's man. He hunted and fished and partied and could wrestle. With the exception of Mad Dog Vachon, he was the only wrestler I knew who'd get sewn up without novocaine. He was also a phenomenal athlete who played golf with people like Charlie Pride and Mickey Mantle. I remember hearing a story about Wahoo losing $5,000 to Lee Trevino. Why would he be playing golf with Lee Trevino, a tournament pro? Because he was so competitive. Wahoo was the man, brother. He rocked.

He didn't take shit from wives,

Ed "Wahoo" McDaniel, the single greatest influence on my wrestling career.

either; he was married five times. If a woman didn't like his lifestyle, he'd tell her not to let the door hit her in the ass on the way out. He was bad to the bone.

In Atlanta, it was common knowledge that the wrestlers hung out at a place called Dee Ford's on Stuart Avenue. Crazy fans would come in there and hassle the boys. Tommy Rich, who was NWA champion for a week in 1981, occasionally got drunk and egged them on. One night, about three guys had Tommy down in the parking lot and were beating the hell out of him. Wahoo saw it and got his gun while Dick Slater, another wrestler, started coming from the other direction. Wahoo got to where Tommy was and hit one of the guys in the head with the pistol. It went off and shot Slater in the leg.

Wahoo and I started to become close. He invited me along one day on a trip to Fargo, North Dakota. Red Bastien—one of my childhood favorites who impressed me even more when I knew him as a peer— went along, too. The plan was to fly to Fargo in wrestler Lars Anderson's plane. "I didn't know Lars is a pilot," I said, to which Wahoo responded, "Well, he can fly, but he doesn't have a license."

We got into a single-engine 182, and Lars followed the highway from Minneapolis to Fargo in the daylight. I didn't think anything about it. On the way home, though, it was dark and snowing, and Lars had smoked a joint before we left. If that didn't disorient him enough, he, Wahoo, Bastien, and I began drinking Boone's Farm apple wine on the plane. Lars was trying to find the highway, but lost it in the blizzard. We ended up landing on a football field instead of at the airport, but I was relieved to be on the ground.

I'll always associate Wahoo with the birth of my oldest daughter, Megan. We were in Minneapolis at a bar called the Left Guard with Greg Gagne. Someone had asked if I wanted to go to a party, and for some reason I didn't feel like it. I went home around one-thirty in the morning, and at about two, Leslie went into labor. There were no cell phones back then; if I hadn't decided to call it a night, I would have been with Wahoo when my daughter was born. Clearly, I had a long way to go before I got my priorities straight.

I was pretty much willing to do anything that Wahoo asked. At one stage, he insisted that I buy two pairs of well-crafted wrestling boots from a guy named Clifford Mocias in Houston, who a lot of main-eventers used. The problem was, even though I wanted to look like a star, I wasn't getting *paid* like one. I ended up spending $400—$200 a pair—when I was making about $120 a week.

Still, I'll never have any regrets about taking Wahoo's advice. While we were in the AWA, he told me about the wrestling promotion in Charlotte, North Carolina. He was heading there when his stint with Gagne was over. His friend, George Scott, had just started in Charlotte as the booker—the man who makes the decisions on storylines and talent—and Wahoo promised to drop my name. "Keep working hard up here," he urged, "and I'll call you from Charlotte."

True to his word, Wahoo phoned me a few weeks later. "They want to book you," he said. "I think you should come down."

I left for Charlotte in 1974. I've been there ever since.

"MEAN" GENE OKERLUND: I'd known Ric since he was a bouncer at George's in the Park. I later announced his first televised match in Minneapolis against Kenny Jay, who had the moniker the Sod Buster because he used to lay sod in front of Verne Gagne's palatial estate out on Lake Minnetonka. Ric's charisma, that square jaw, his demeanor in the ring–that body language–told you that he was going to be the best. And he was pretty assertive. While some of these other guys were just enamored with being seen on television, Ric Flair appreciated his own self-worth. If Verne wasn't going to take Ric where he needed to go, Ric was going to get out from under Verne and go elsewhere.

Verne understood that I needed to keep learning the business. Back then, guys would travel from one wrestling territory to another, picking up the different styles. Charlotte seemed like a logical next step.

Just before I left, I went to see Verne and thank him for everything he'd done for me. "By the way," I asked, "could I borrow four hundred dollars? I'm broke."

"No, I can't do that for you," he said. "You have to learn to handle things on your own."

I shook Verne's hand and started to leave. "Oh, one more thing," he said, slipping a document across his desk. It was a contract, guaranteeing that Verne would receive ten percent of my earnings for the next five years.

Believe it or not, I wasn't offended by the gesture; Verne was the one who had taught me how to be a professional wrestler. I was ready to sign the document right there, but Verne said, "Take it with you, have a look at it, and send it back."

When I got down to Charlotte, I asked the promoter, Jim Crockett Jr., if this was standard practice in the wrestling business. "We don't give out contracts like that," he replied, sounding a little shocked, as he read through the document. "Nobody owns five years of your life."

Crockett recommended that I tear up the contract and send it back to Verne, but I couldn't do that. He had put in time and effort to train me. He had certainly earned *something.*

Eventually, Verne called to see if I'd signed the contract. I told him how I felt—"I don't think it's right," I explained—but I was willing to pay him a still-substantial flat fee of $2,500 (Crockett's advice as well; "Send him a check for what you think he deserves").

That seemed to be okay with Verne. We remained friendly, and even when I was touring the world as NWA Champion, I occasionally returned to the AWA to make special appearances on his shows. I don't think the Iron Sheik signed his contract, either, though Patera told me that the ten percent was taken from his paycheck when he left.

I headed to Charlotte with a new look—before leaving Minneapolis, Billy Graham's wife, Bunny, had bleached my hair blond, just like the Superstar, Dusty, Murdoch, and Ray Stevens. I got a pair of tie-dye trunks and started wearing a headband like Graham as well. I didn't have his physique, but I knew—if given the chance—I had the gift of gab.

WAYNE COLEMAN, AKA SUPERSTAR BILLY GRAHAM: It was time for Ric to make the transition, so we got it done. He ripped me off, but not as bad as Jesse Ventura. That's all right, though. It's a great compliment when they take your stuff.

I landed in Charlotte and was picked up at the airport by Johnny Heideman, an old-timer whose days in the ring were pretty much over. He still wrestled on occasion, but most of the time, he worked in the office for the promotion. Johnny brought me over to the Orvin Court Hotel—the fee was eight dollars a night—checked me in, then drove me to the Charlotte Coliseum, where I wrestled another aging veteran, Abe Jacobs, and got the win.

Leslie was still in Minneapolis with Megan; with only about $200 to my name, I couldn't afford to bring them with me. I don't think my parents were completely sold on the idea of me leaving my family behind to advance my career below the Mason–Dixon line. Deep down inside, though, I knew I was making the right move.

THE CHARLOTTE WRESTLING territory was started in 1935 by Jim Crockett Sr., or "Big Jim," a businessman who also ran restaurants, promoted concerts and Harlem Globetrotters games, and owned the Baltimore Orioles' AA affiliate as well as their stadium, Crockett Park. Like most wrestling companies at the time, this was a regional operation, affiliated with the gigantic National Wrestling Alliance. Every year, the various NWA promoters held a convention where they debated over whether to keep or change their world champion. Whoever had the title would then tour, defending his title in one territory after another.

The Crockett family's territory—also known as Mid-Atlantic Championship Wrestling—was based in Charlotte but extended through the Carolinas and into Virginia. Even when the NWA champion wasn't around, fans still filled arenas in Greensboro, Spartanburg, Roanoke, and other cities, where the territory's own United States and Mid-Atlantic titles were defended. It was different than the AWA, where you could count on the occasional night off. In Charlotte, we worked every single weeknight, twice on Saturday, and twice on Sunday.

When I arrived, the Crocketts were in the middle of a power struggle. Big Jim's son, Jim Crockett Jr., was a quiet guy who hadn't really planned on going into the wrestling business. When Big Jim died in 1973, his wife, Elizabeth, decided that her son-in-law, John Ringley, would run things. Then Ringley got caught having an affair with a beauty queen, and the Crockett kids—Jim Jr., David, Jackie, and Ringley's wife, Frances—voted him out. Jim Jr. was only twenty-four, but everyone thought that he'd be the best replacement. That is, except Ringley, who didn't want to leave.

DAVID CROCKETT: My brother Jimmy was not that outgoing. My brother-in-law Johnny was a good salesman and had the ear of a lot of the talent. You have to remember, too, that Johnny started working for my dad a lot earlier than anybody else in the family. But he was having an affair with this woman out in Memphis, and just was not thinking straight. This was a family business, and he was throwing it in the family's face, plus disrespecting my father with what he was doing. We could only have one person dealing with the talent, with the Harlem Globetrotters, with the concert promoters and with the bank. This *had* to be a dictatorship. It couldn't be Jimmy *and* Johnny. So Johnny had to go.

This presented a challenge for Jimmy, since the other NWA promoters looked at him as just Big Jim's kid. There was a definite vacuum, and he had to prove himself to everybody.

To the powers-that-be in the NWA, Big Jim was held in high esteem. But I could see that Jimmy was struggling for respect, and was ready to work hard to get it. He and I were from the same generation. We thought alike and became friends quickly. I had come to Charlotte to grow as a wrestler, and Jimmy was there with me, transforming into a smart promoter and successful businessman. He listened to his booker, George Scott, and let him bring in wrestlers who could take the company to the next level. Of course, you had to pay if you wanted a certain quality of talent; it all went hand in hand. And Jimmy paid.

DAVID CROCKETT: Having George Scott there was a necessity. Some bookers begin to think that they're more powerful than the promoter. They bring in wrestlers who are their friends and stop being innovative. George was *nothing* like that. He was creative. He knew how to get the most out of the talent. And, maybe even more importantly, he was no longer wrestling. So instead of consuming all the talent in order to build himself up as a star, he concentrated on the other wrestlers' strengths.

I felt that I had two people always looking out for me—Wahoo and George Scott. In the ring, Wahoo taught me the ropes, while George channeled all the wisdom he'd acquired during his years as a wrestler into booking. He took a territory that was known largely for its tag teams and started creating individual stars.

After the Orvin Court, I switched hotels to the Coliseum Motor Inn—where the fee was something like $36 a week—and began running up a tab at Valentino's restaurant, paying when my check arrived at the end of each week. I didn't have a car yet, so the promotion arranged for me to ride to the different arenas with Johnny Valentine, a major drawing card who was one of the first components in George's plan to make the Mid-Atlantic singles division stand out.

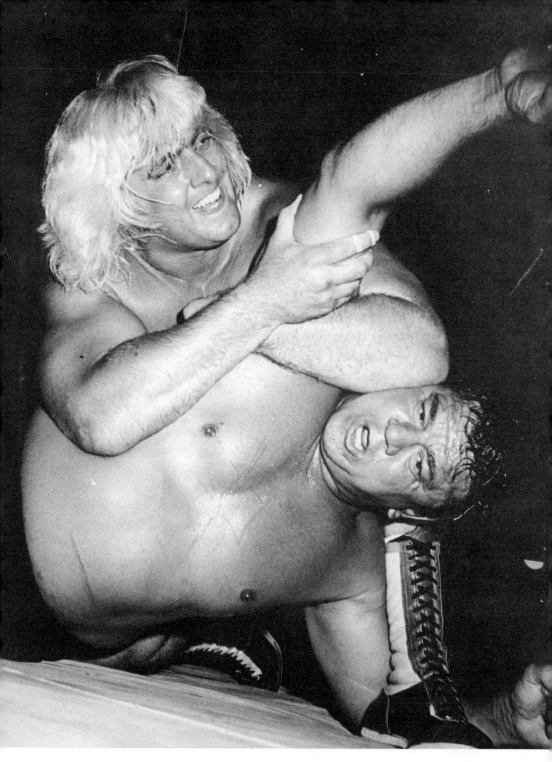

**Wrestling Wahoo gave me the skill and confidence
I needed to handle myself in the ring.**

Bleached blond, tanned, and fit, Valentine had been headlining shows all over the world for about twenty years, literally beating on opponents with a forearm to the chest. In Charlotte, the move was called the Brain Buster. When he'd worked for WWE owner Vince McMahon's father—Vincent James McMahon, or "Vince Sr."—in the northeastern-based World Wide Wrestling Federation (WWWF), announcer Ray Morgan labeled Valentine's finisher "the Atomic Skull Crusher."

Valentine definitely had a star presence—I'd been reading about him in wrestling magazines since elementary school—but he was an odd guy. Early in his career, George Herbert Walker Bush was campaigning for office in Texas, and was introduced at a wrestling show in Houston. He came into the ring, but when he turned his back on Valentine, Johnny gave the future president of the United States the finger.

In Charlotte, Johnny generally kept to himself, reading or playing chess without saying too much. To a kid like me, he was completely aloof. He also wouldn't pick me up anywhere, so I had to hitchhike to a mutually agreed upon spot. The first time we drove together, he put on a tape of bad Italian opera and blasted it. For the entire trip to Greenville, South Carolina, he didn't look at me or say a word. One side of the tape would finish, and he'd just turn it over and play more opera. It was the same on the way back. When we returned to the spot, long past midnight, he would drop me off without a word. It was too late to hitchhike, so I had to walk two miles or so through a bad neighborhood with bleached blond hair and a ring jacket slung over my shoulder.

In the ring, Valentine wanted everything to look legit. If he was asked to execute a move off the ropes, he either refused or did it grudgingly. He felt that those types of things cheapened the business, since you would never run backward and bounce off a bunch of cables in a real fight. He'd take a body slam once in a while, but never a high back-body drop. Johnny's way was to get a guy in a simple hold—like a hammerlock—cinch up on it, let go, beat the shit out of his opponent, then clamp on the hold again. This could go on for ten, even twenty minutes. But you know, the crowd got into it. They really believed that he was hurting the guy with that hold.

I learned a lot watching Valentine—the way that he made everything he did seem meaningful. Whenever someone hit him hard and repeatedly, he'd fall forward, right on his face. In time, I ended up doing the same thing, adding in a stumbling walk before I took the dive.

My first singles belt, the Mid-Atlantic Television Championship, looked good on me, though I wanted Johnny Valentine's Mid-Atlantic Heavyweight title.

After a few car rides together, Valentine began talking to me. But you always had to be careful whenever he was around. He was a terrible practical joker, playing very insensitive pranks. Jay "The Alaskan" York was asthmatic, and Valentine once put lighter fluid in the guy's inhaler. Jay came back to the locker room, winded after his match, grabbed the inhaler, and threw up all over the floor.

IF I THOUGHT riding with Valentine was strange, it was nothing compared to driving around with the Missouri Mauler and Brute Bernard. I hadn't spent a lot of time in the South, but these two quickly gave me an education. They'd have their country music blaring, drinking beer, while Brute would be eating his clove of garlic and raw onion.

"Hey, kid, you like country music?" one of them asked. I kind of nodded.

"Where you from, Flair?"

"Minneapolis."

"Minneapolis? What do they think about niggers up in Minneapolis?"

"Pardon me?" I'd become a pretty jaded guy, but these two really shocked me. I considered Minneapolis a tolerant city. And even on his worst day, I had never heard my father speak like that.

"Well, down here, we hang fuckin' niggers from trees."

They were even worse whenever they were with their manager, Homer O'Dell, who always carried two pearl-handled revolvers with him. Once, at a baseball park show in Richmond, Virginia, a group of fans attacked Professor Boris Malenko (whose son, Dean, would end up in the Four Horsemen with me in WCW) and "The Big O," Bob Orton Sr., grandfather of WWE Superstar Randy Orton. They stabbed Malenko, cutting him from the neck all the way down to his groin, and hit Orton with a baseball bat. O'Dell came running into the crowd, shooting off his guns, and the mob scattered. I have no doubt that Malenko and Orton owed him their lives.

In the car, Bernard and the Mauler would fire each other up, talking about "niggers" and "coons" and "spooks," and what they'd like to do to the whole race. One day, we were driving across a bridge and saw a bunch of black guys fishing off the side. Bernard and the Mauler pulled over, jumped out of the car, and flipped one of the poor guys into the water! Thankfully, no one was hurt, but the experience kind of made me pine for Valentine's opera music.

MY FIRST CHECK in Charlotte came out to $1,000—a fortune in my eyes. I then approached Jimmy Crockett with a request: "You know, I'd really like to have my wife and daughter down here, but I don't have the money yet." Jimmy lent me $3,000, and advanced me some more cash to move my family to Charlotte. I made all the arrangements for Leslie and Megan to join me and, once they were settled in, took the money that was left over and bought my first Caddie, a used black Fleetwood from Art of Arnold Palmer Cadillac.

That's the way my wrestling career went for the next fifteen years—if I made $3,000, I spent $4,000. If I made $5,000, I spent $10,000. The image people would later have of Ric Flair throwing around money was absolutely true. The difference was that in the real world, there *wasn't* always more where that came from.

IN CHARLOTTE, I finally took the "k" off the end of my first name, changing "Rick" to the catchier "Ric." I told audiences that I had "blond hair that Elke Sommer likes to run her fingers through, a body that looks like it was carved out of granite by Michelangelo, and that Raquel Welch would give her right arm to rub suntan lotion on."

George Scott decided to team me up with Rip Hawk, a sharp-dressing older guy who was a fairly good speaker. He and "Raw-Boned" Swede Hanson were a well-established tag team, but they'd recently broken up and were now feuding. Swede had taken on a young African-American named Tiger Conway Jr., as a replacement. As Hawk's partner, I was expected to counter Conway's fan popularity with youthful arrogance.

"You got Mr. Charisma, Mr. Excitement, Ric Flair," I trumpeted on television prior to clashing with Conway. "I'm gonna leave you with an Excedrin headache, baby, bleeding, messy, crying, begging for your mammy."

George figured that Hawk could mold me as a wrestler, while I'd help him stay contemporary. I found him to be an intelligent guy who had a lot to offer someone with my relative inexperience, but when we went out at night, he wasn't as loud or boisterous as Wahoo or Ray Stevens. In fact, sometimes I felt that he looked at me with a bit of astonishment. "He'd be all right," he once said about me.

I was feeling more confident every time I stepped into the ring, and I was learning against a whole variety of opponents. One night I'd be in there with Wahoo, the next night with Andre. For the first time in my life, I'd found a forum where both my athletic ability and my personal eccentricities were held in high regard. I knew that George and Jimmy had gotten word from guys they respected—tough, hard ring vets like Stevens, Larry Hennig, and Red Bastien—that I was dependable. And the fact that I could put up with their jokes only enhanced my position.

On July 4, 1974, I won my first championship, the Mid-Atlantic Tag-Team title, with Rip Hawk in Greensboro. We dethroned Paul Jones and Bob Bruggers, the former NFL player I'd trained with in Verne Gagne's camp. It would be two years before fans started calling me "Nature Boy," but my on-air persona was definitely developing. While driving to WRAL Studios one day to cut promos, I heard Jerry Lee Lewis on the radio and decided that I liked the way he screamed "Woooo!" in the middle of "Great Balls of Fire." Not long afterward, I gave it a try. "Everywhere I go, the people are shouting, '*Woooo!* There goes the big boss man'" I declared (unaware that some fifteen years later, Ray Traylor would be using that name in the World Wrestling Federation). The "Woooo!" started out short and clipped. It would later grow longer and louder.

Because of my upbringing in the Minneapolis area, I found myself in a lot of six-man tag-team matches alongside the "Minnesota Wrecking Crew," Gene and Ole Anderson. The Andersons weren't really brothers— Ole's name was actually Alan Rogowski—but they both came from Minnesota, and the promotion began billing me as their cousin.

To me, Ole was the consummate wrestler—he was tough, he could talk, he looked good in the ring, and he really knew how to wrestle. Then Arn came along. He was like Ole but better, because his interview skills were more creative and his offensive wrestling was far superior. When the Andersons needed to make someone look good, they did it better than anybody. There were stretches when they worked hour-long tag-team matches every night—something you rarely see today— and kept fans captivated the entire time. They'd confine an opponent

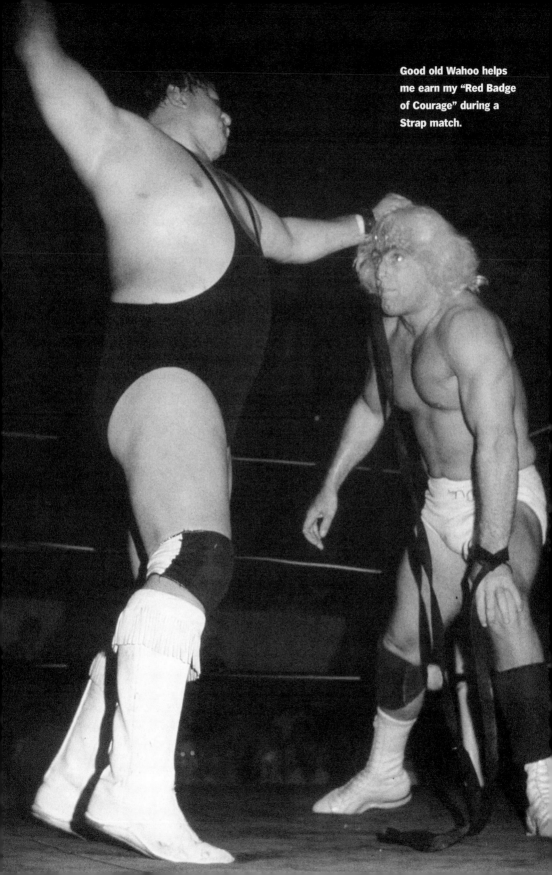

Good old Wahoo helps me earn my "Red Badge of Courage" during a Strap match.

to their side of the ring, tagging in and out and working him over as he struggled to get back to his corner. The exhausted wrestler would move a few inches, getting the people excited over the possibility that he might tag his well-rested partner. Then the Andersons would pull him back, and the collective emotions of the audience would sink. They utilized crowd psychology in ways so many of today's wrestlers can't comprehend. It's not their fault; they never learned. That's why they get into the ring, do a few moves, high-five the guy in the corner, and step out, eliminating all the drama that should be associated with a tag.

I was also getting an education on the "Red Badge of Courage," or bleeding. When you walked into the dressing room and looked at the rundown of matches, a little check next to your name signaled that it was your turn to "get juice." Sometimes I'd cut myself anyway, just like Dusty would, if I believed that it was going to add something to the confrontation. For example, if somebody hits you in the head with a chair, there should be blood. We didn't use chair shots as freely as today, so when you got smashed, it had impact.

An older wrestler named Art Neilson taught me the importance of bleeding. It adds so much more emotion to a match when the fans see me up close, taking a beating, with blood staining my platinum-blond hair. I've gone out of my way to whip my hair around so that little droplets of blood land on the fans. I picture some kid going home with blood on his clothes and showing it off to his friends. It's like catching a foul ball at a baseball game, only more exciting. These people pay for their tickets, and I want to give them something they'll remember.

Despite all my bleeding, I don't look as carved up as Dusty or Carlos Colon or so many other guys I've wrestled. I've used a lot of Neosporin, and have just two white scars on my forehead. Everybody's skin heals differently. I guess I'm lucky.

IN THE AWA, there were always hostile cities. The Chicago Amphitheater had a rough crowd. The fans in Milwaukee were hard on bad guys, but at least there was security. In most of the arenas in the Carolinas, we didn't even have cops. And Southern fans were very different from the Danes and the Swedes who attended Verne's cards in Minneapolis; people would throw penknives, or shoot pennies at us with slingshots. One night in Asheville, a guy ran up to the ring apron with a bag and threw a rattlesnake through the ropes!

If we wrestled seven nights a week, we had to be prepared for fanatical fans jumping into the ring during at least four of the shows. Some of the boys would encourage this kind of behavior, getting on the microphone to challenge spectators and hurting them if they accepted the offer. In Columbus, Georgia, one night, a two hundred eighty-pound man sucker-punched Tim "Mr. Wrestling" Woods and pulled off his mask. Woods got his mask back, took the fan down, and began toying with him on the mat. With the guy flat on his stomach, Woods crouched behind him and pulled back his head with a crossface submission. The man opened his mouth and bit off one of Tim's fingers, putting an end to open challenges in that town.

In the WWWF, Blackjack Mulligan was sliced in the leg down to the bone by a fan during a match against Pedro Morales in Boston Gardens. Jack wound up with a staph infection, which spreads through the body and can cause pneumonia or heart damage if it goes untreated. In the middle of the night, he knocked on Crazy Luke Graham's door, soaked in sweat. Luke looked down at Jack's leg, saw that it was flaming red, and rushed him to the hospital. The doctors said that the attacker probably worked in a butcher shop, because there was pig fat bacteria inside Mulligan's wound. They had to reopen his leg and scrape all that shit out.

GEORGE SCOTT IS the one who came up with the idea of naming me Nature Boy, just like the first Nature Boy, Buddy Rogers, a former NWA titleholder who became the WWWF's inaugural champion. Rogers was a blond wrestler with a silky walk and a cocky, sophisticated style. Whenever you saw him in street clothes, every hair was in place and he looked like a million bucks. George was his friend and admirer, and thought that I could project the same sense of cool.

I knew that Rogers used to strut in the ring, so I started doing the same thing. That doesn't mean that I did the same strut—*no one* could strut like Buddy Rogers, just like no one can swagger to the ring like Vince McMahon. I just developed a "Ric Flair strut," sometimes breaking into it in the middle of the action. Like Rogers, I used the figure-four leglock as my signature move. When people told me that he used to smoke cigars, I went through my own cigar-smoking phase . . . and burned holes in all my clothes.

I was definitely starting to stand out. On February 8, 1975, I won my first singles title, the Mid-Atlantic TV Championship—originally conceived as a title to be defended exclusively on television—from Paul Jones. The notion seemed ridiculous at the time, but I was telling audiences that I was put on Earth for only one reason: to be the world champion one day.

Before a visit by NWA kingpin Jack Brisco to the Mid-Atlantic territory, I did an interview about my alleged encounter with a fortune-teller. "She looked at a line on my hand," I began, "and she said, 'You're going to beat Paul Jones, you're going to beat Wahoo McDaniel, you're going to beat Jack Brisco—*Wooooo*—and you're going to be the world's champion!' She said, 'There's only one Nature Boy, and you are the greatest wrestler in the world today, Nature Boy. Know it for a fact.'"

I never thought about my interviews until I arrived in the studio, but I could whip myself up and set fire to the crowd. I claimed to be bigger than Elvis—a *huge* insult to Southerners, who held a special place in their hearts for "the King"—and that the mere mention of my name could get people high. I also told a story about seeing myself on television and looking so good that even *I* got aroused.

DAVID CROCKETT: When Ric was a bad guy, the women loved to hate him. But when the show was over, they loved to be with him. He had a bad habit of taking his clothes off. He'd often come out of the bathroom, walk up to a female sitting on the couch, and tap her on the head. Only he wasn't tapping her with his finger.

COWBOY LANG WAS a midget wrestler. He'd walk around the dressing room in his cowboy hat and boots, with his dick hanging practically below his knees. He was a good guy, and loved to party after the shows. But he always expected me to get him laid.

"You know, Cowboy," I'd explain, "it's hard to get a midget like you laid. Not all girls are attracted to midgets." But I had a friend in Charlotte, Sarge was her nickname—because of her National Guard obligation. She always hosted the best parties and, if pressured, would always find a girl for Lang. As the night went on, I'd often find myself asking a lady, "Hey, what do you think of my friend Cowboy Lang over there?"

"Oh, no," they'd usually say, "I'm not gonna do that. I'm not gonna screw a midget. I won't blow one. I won't do anything."

"Okay," I'd answer, "but you don't know what you're missing."

At some point, I would manipulate things so that Cowboy Lang could take the girl to the side and show her his dick. Afterward I'd see them walking out of the bar, hand in hand, with his big cowboy hat coming up to just above her elbow.

Thinking back, I honestly don't know how Leslie survived her marriage to me. I wasn't a real stable partner. We lived well, but I was so irresponsible. The territory was just wide open, and you couldn't pay me to be home. Not because of anything Leslie ever did, but because I didn't want to miss a party. I was having too much fun being Ric Flair.

As it was, even a wrestler with the most honorable intentions would have a difficult time maintaining his family life. The holidays were huge wrestling days in the South. We wrestled twice on Thanksgiving, twice on Christmas and twice on Easter. You went to work if you were hurt. You went to work if your wife was sick. You went to work if your kid had to go to the emergency room. You went to work, or you didn't get paid—or, even worse, you lost your spot.

Given my concerns about building my name, both in the ring and in the bars, I never would have considered taking a night off. What no one knew was that there was a long layoff ahead—a sabbatical that nearly flamed out the career of "Nature Boy" Ric Flair years before it hit its peak.

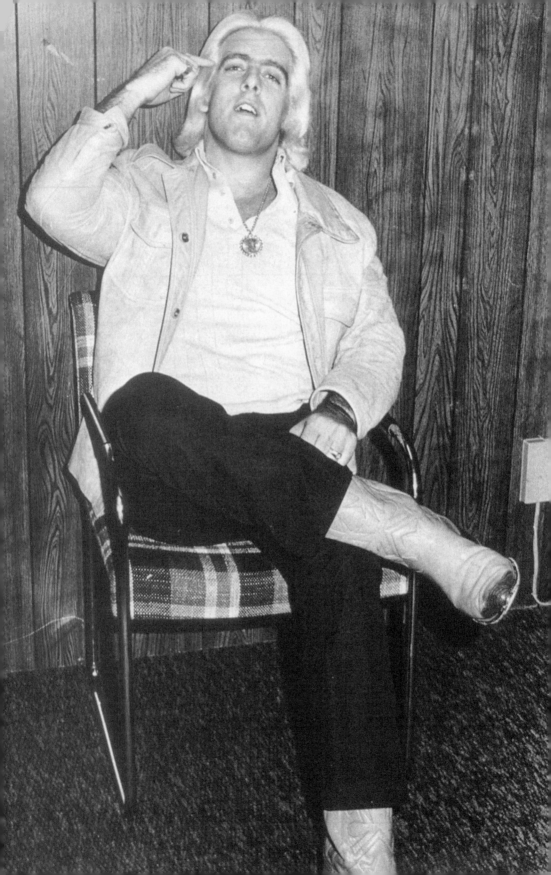

Mike Farkas was a Vietnam vet who was looking to make a couple of extra dollars. We started talking one night in a bar, and he told me that he was a pilot. At that stage, the wrestlers in Mid-Atlantic were making some pretty long driving trips—about three hundred miles to Richmond, even farther to Norfolk—and Farkas made me a proposition: how about I get a bunch of the boys together, and have him fly us instead?

The first wrestler I approached was Johnny Valentine. He liked the idea of commuting forty-five minutes by air instead of five hours by car. If we loaded up the plane with five or six guys, it would only cost about a hundred dollars apiece. No one had bothered

CHAPTER **4**

THE MAN WHO SAVED WRESTLING

investigating Mike's background or qualifications, so in no time at all, he was the official pilot of Mid-Atlantic Championship Wrestling.

On the afternoon of October 4, 1975, five of us piled into his yellow and white Cessna 310, a light twin-engine, to fly from Charlotte to Wilmington, North Carolina, where we had an outdoor show at Legion Stadium. This was a tiny plane, so the guy with the most stroke got the largest seat, next to the pilot. That was Valentine. Because of our size, the rest of us were really crammed in there. I was in the middle with Tim Woods. The guys at the bottom of the pecking order, David Crockett and Bob Bruggers, were in the last row. Originally, Wahoo was supposed to join us, but he had decided to drive at the last moment, and Bruggers had taken his place.

We were something like 1,400 pounds over gross, and Farkas couldn't figure out how to distribute our weight properly. To lighten the load, unknown to us, he dumped some fuel out of the gas tank.

DAVID CROCKETT: When I got to the tarmac, I saw the pilot outside the plane, checking the fuel. I said, "Make sure we have enough fuel in there." I was just joking. I'd never flown with him before.

I wasn't even supposed to be on the plane. My brother Jimmy was going to travel with the boys, but he was sick with the flu. He called me up and asked if I could go to Wilmington instead. I said, "Sure."

It was an easy flight. No headwinds. I guess around Lumberton, which is about the halfway point, the left engine started to sputter, then shut down. We were all concerned, especially as the plane dipped some. In retrospect, I never figured out why we didn't just land in Lumberton or someplace close. But Farkas said that a twin-engine plane was designed to carry us on a single engine, so we continued on.

Valentine pointed at the gas gauges and started laughing. "Heh-heh-heh, we're out of fuel." The left engine was on empty, but we all thought we had reserve gas. There was something major going on, and Farkas was yelling to the control tower over the headphones. But it was loud on the plane, so I couldn't hear what he was saying.

We had just crossed the Cape Fear River when the right engine died. I was thinking, God, when are we going to activate the reserve tanks? Then I heard a boom, and it scared the shit out of me.

DAVID CROCKETT: We were making our approach to New Hanover Airport, but the plane was too low; we almost hit a water tower. The pilot tried to pull up, but the engine stalled. There wasn't enough power. Had we been flying higher, we would have made it to the clear area of the runway. That's how close we were.

Farkas began to panic, and Valentine tried bringing him to his senses the only way he knew how—by slapping the guy. It didn't work. We were sputtering and spinning the whole time.

It's strange how your mind works during a crisis. Tim Woods later said that he was nervous because he wasn't wearing his shoes. Austin Idol, another wrestler, had told him that when he was in a plane crash, he had taken his shoes off and, as a result, tore his feet down to the bone. Tim didn't have time to grab his shoes, but he got hold of the pilot's briefcase and stuck his feet inside.

DAVID CROCKETT: I remember it becoming quiet on the plane. At a time like that, you get into yourself and wonder if you're going to survive. I didn't want the wind knocked out of me, so I bent over and grabbed my knees, controlling my breathing. Out of the corner of my eye, I remember seeing a light flashing on the dash and hearing a buzzer. I was later told that it was probably the stall warning. That was just before the crash.

I have no memories past the point where the second engine conked out, but I know what happened. The plane cut across several treetops, and a wing collapsed against a utility pole before we nose-dived, crashing into a railroad embankment. If we'd gotten past the trees, we would have ended up on the runway.

On the ground, the pilot managed to stall the plane enough to reduce our sliding. We still crashed hard, going at close to a hundred miles per hour, but it could have been a lot worse.

All the seats broke loose, and guys crumpled into each other. David's head crashed through the seat in front of him, cracking and bruising Tim Woods's ribs. (David received a concussion and a slight compression fracture in the collision.) Tim remembered because he was the only passenger who wasn't knocked unconscious.

When I woke up, I was being pulled off the plane and placed in an ambulance. "We better hurry," I heard one EMT say to his partner, "We might lose this one." I thought they were talking about me, but they were actually referring to Bruggers. Both he and Valentine had gone into shock.

I blacked out again, and when I came to, I was on one of those old steel X-ray tables. As disoriented as I felt, I still recognized the voice asking, "You all right, kid?"

It was Wahoo. I'd just beaten him for the Mid-Atlantic title, and we were supposed to wrestle that night. When he barged into the hospital, the orderlies tried to restrain him. On TV, we hated each other, and they actually thought that he was coming to finish me off while I was lying at death's door; that's how real it was to the fans. Wahoo pushed past everybody, breaking all the protocols of our business, to be there for me the way he always was.

Thank God Wahoo had driven to Wilmington. What would the fans have thought if he'd been pulled out of a small, intimate plane with me? It could have killed the territory. As it was, there was still a serious concern that the promotion had to address. Like Wahoo, Tim "Mr. Wrestling" Woods was regarded by fans as someone who'd never kick back with the likes of Ric Flair and Johnny Valentine—particularly since Valentine had supposedly broken his leg in a recent TV storyline and was supposed to defend the U.S. title against him in the main event in Wilmington.

Before the show began at Legion Stadium, the ring announcer informed the crowd that there had been a plane crash earlier in the day, and that Valentine and Flair were injured. The spectators were also told that in an unrelated incident, Tim Woods was lost and wouldn't be there, either.

Even as he checked into the hospital, Tim was protecting the business. He identified himself by his given name, George Burrell Woodin, and claimed to be a wrestling promoter. Because he wrestled under a mask, there was the possibility that no one would make the connection. But rumors started fast, and if Tim's actual whereabouts ended up in the press, it would have been a huge hit to the industry. So the next day—on his own—Tim checked himself out of the hospital. Two people propped themselves under each arm and literally deposited him on a commercial flight back to Charlotte. Amazingly, the brakes failed when the plane landed, but at least this time there were no injuries.

Immediately, Tim began making appearances all over the territory to dispel any speculation that he had been hospitalized. Then, two weeks after the crash, he stepped into the ring in unbearable pain and wrestled Superstar Billy Graham. I believe they had a relatively short match, but Tim was more than "Mr. Wrestling" that day. He became the man who *saved* wrestling. Mid-Atlantic wrestling, anyway.

Mike Farkas, the twenty-eight-year-old pilot, lingered in a coma for about a year before he died. He truly was beyond negligent and incompetent, but I still felt badly for him. On two occasions, I visited him in the hospital.

Bruggers and Valentine both suffered broken backs. After ten days at the hospital in Wilmington, Jimmy Crockett chartered a plane and had them flown out for more specialized treatment in Houston. Bruggers had a steel rod inserted into his spinal column and was released three weeks later. I believe that he could have wrestled again, but he just wasn't into it. So he took the $70,000 he received in the insurance settlement, retired, married a flight attendant, and bought a bar in West Palm Beach.

I heard that Valentine had virtually the same injuries as Bruggers, but by the time surgery took place, the nerve endings were apparently calcified and the damage could not be repaired. As a result, this forty-seven-year-old superstar, who'd been selling out arenas and stirring up shit for nearly a generation, was paralyzed from the waist down.

Understandably, he was pretty miserable. When I resumed my wrestling career, I would occasionally pick him up and drive him to the different arenas. Wahoo, Red Bastien, and I would also bring him to our homes for meals. A lot of the other guys stayed away from him. With all the mean-spirited jokes he'd pulled, he got less sympathy than most people in his position.

Even Bastien didn't forget. After a show in Columbia, South Carolina, Valentine got drunk and fell out of his braces in his front yard. With Valentine's wife standing right there, Bastien pulled out "the Bishop"—his own personal name for his dick—and pissed on his friend. "That's for all the years you pissed on me," he taunted.

Valentine was lying there helpless, going, "Uh, uh, uh, uh." But he was also smiling, like he enjoyed it.

He was still one of the boys.

MY BACK WAS broken in three places, yet remarkably, I didn't need surgery. I just had to wait to heal. It was all a matter of where we were positioned on the plane and how our bodies fell.

My weight had dropped from 255 to 180. Whenever I'd ask about when I could wrestle again, I'd hear, "Only time will tell."

Some doctors, including my own father, believed that I would never be able to perform at a high level in the ring with the injuries I'd endured. The more optimistic ones predicted that I wouldn't be wrestling for at least two years. But, hell, I was twenty-four years old; I couldn't wait that long! I loved wrestling and everything about it, and I believed with all my heart that I would recover sooner. I just wouldn't be denied.

SUPERSTAR BILLY GRAHAM: I walked into Ric's house in Charlotte. He was flat on his back with all the hospital equipment around him. I thought, This guy's been in a plane wreck. How's he going to come back? But there was never any doubt in his mind; his confidence just seeped through as he lay there with that Ric Flair smile. There was just *zero* negativity. All positive vibes coming off this guy. Totally positive.

Jimmy took care of me, making sure that I had money coming in besides the $35,000 I received in insurance. The first day I could get out of bed, I went down to the office wearing this huge body brace. I was looking for a pat on the back—*Wow, you just got out of bed, and you're here already. You're the man!*

Instead, George Scott glared at me. "Take that fuckin' thing off," he said.

"What?"

"That fuckin' back brace. Jesus Christ, don't you know it's holding up your recovery time?"

"It is?"

"Yeah, it fuckin' is. When you wear those damn things, the rest of your muscles atrophy. You gotta let your muscles build themselves back. What the fuck is wrong with you? You're gonna be out an extra six months now!"

George was giving me some old-school wrestler's home remedy, though he did kind of know what he was talking about. It's true that, with a back brace, the muscles can atrophy. But I also needed it to keep myself intact. What a heartless bastard he was for saying that, but it served me right for searching for compassion in such a callous profession. So I wore my brace in the house, when no one from the wrestling business was around, and never went back to the office until I recuperated.

That meant that I had to spend a lot of time at home. Obviously, I never enjoyed being idle, but I loved being with Megan. She was taking her first steps, so we learned to walk as a team. One of the fondest memories of my life is holding her hand and toddling up and down the street with her.

Another high point was when I finally received medical clearance to make my comeback. I was elated, and called everyone I knew. In early 1976, I strolled into WRAL Studios in my suit and sunglasses, to an audience that really didn't want to boo me. Announcer Ed Caperal handed me a stack of get-well cards and letters from fans. I contemplated the pile scornfully, said that I was only going to keep the cards from Raquel Welch and Joey Heatherton, then threw everything else on the floor.

The crowd turned on me instantly, and that got the ball rolling again, baby. I had them just where I wanted them, just where they were supposed to be—looking at Ric Flair and wishing it was *me* who died in the plane crash.

Greg "The Hammer" Valentine and I had different styles, but we worked well together.

Greg Valentine was brought in to replace his father. Greg resembled Johnny, both facially and by the fact that he was a good, solid performer who worked a rough, believable style. He was called "The Hammer" because of the way he'd lean an opponent backward over the ropes, then smash him across the chest with a forearm. The blow would come down so hard that sweat would fly everywhere. If anyone doubted the authenticity of wrestling, I'd have liked to see them get in the ring and take that move. His opponents believed, that's for sure.

Backstage, we called Greg "The Turtle" because he moved at his own pace, at his own time, even if it meant getting to the arena

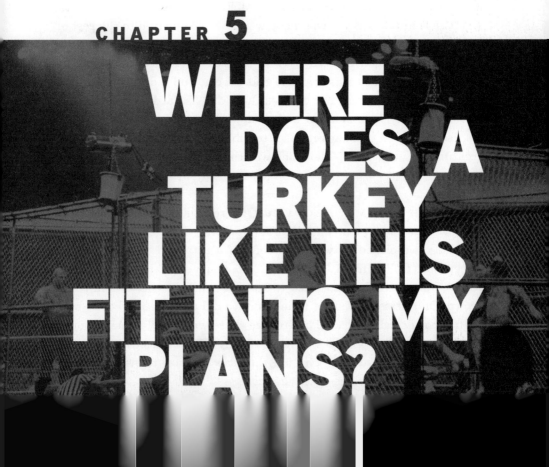

CHAPTER **5**

WHERE DOES A TURKEY LIKE THIS FIT INTO MY PLANS?

late. When we teamed together, I did most of the talking, while he was the quiet guy who definitely carried a little bit of that Valentine mystique. We were a good pair. He dressed nicely and knew how to represent the business. And he was accepted in the dressing room not because of his name, but because he established his own identity. In 1976 and 1977, we were NWA tag-team champions twice, trading the title back and forth with my "cousins" in the Minnesota Wrecking Crew.

Both of us had these long, elaborate ring robes made by Olivia Walker, whose husband, Johnny, was Mr. Wrestling II—Tim Woods's tag-team partner. George Scott had introduced me to Olivia while I was convalescing, and her work was awesome. In addition to ring attire, she had created sequined outfits for Charo and other entertainers. Among her creations for me was a green robe that looked like it had a boa sewn along the lapels, and a sparkling blue robe with "Nature Boy" in white glitter across the back. At one point I had twenty-two robes, but I've since given some to charity, had others stolen, and even lost two that had hung in the Nitro Café that WCW opened in Las Vegas. When the restaurant closed, the robes disappeared. Today, I have only seven left.

The last two robes Olivia made were lousy compared to the rest of her work; the quality just wasn't there. I must have sounded a little harsh when I asked her why. "Well, I haven't been feeling well," she answered. The truth was that she had cancer, and didn't tell me. She was bravely going about her business, working as hard as she could.

To this day, I think about how disappointed she must have been by my reaction, and it makes me feel terrible. Olivia played a big role in creating the aura of Ric Flair. She was the best.

THROUGHOUT MY RECOVERY, I remained the Mid-Atlantic heavyweight champion, and Wahoo was still the number-one contender, so we picked up where we left off. I returned to action at the Greensboro Coliseum on January 31, 1976, resplendent in one of Olivia's robes. Wahoo grabbed it, rolled it up in a ball, and threw it into the crowd. On television a short time later, we did a segment where I beat Wahoo with a table leg. I didn't realize there was a nail sticking out of it, however, and I opened him up so badly that he needed forty-two stitches. I'll tell you this—any fan that saw *that* on television wasn't thinking about the plane crash anymore.

Years after the plane crash, I still won't fall flat on my back properly, not even while wrestling guys I trusted implicitly, like Sting.

Wahoo and I in an
Indian Strap match.

Unfortunately, I still was. I was nervous about taking a backdrop, so George Scott came up with his own kind of therapeutic solution—he put me in the ring with Tim Woods for an hour, for fourteen straight days, until I took one. Nonetheless, I couldn't get myself to fall flat. If you watch me in the ring now, I still land on my left side after a backdrop—never the center of my back, like people are taught in wrestling school.

Other aspects of my in-ring repertoire also developed around this time. My opponent would whip me into a corner and I'd flip over the turnbuckles, land feet-first on the ring apron and stumble forward. From the opposite end of the ropes, my opponent would meet me with a clothesline or chop, sending me hurtling to ringside. In the same match, I'd climb the ropes to jump on my opponent, but when I got to the top, the guy would position himself underneath me and throw me across the ring. As soon as I landed, I'd tense up my body and let out an agonized *"Aaarrrgh!"*

The knife-edged chops that have become such a big part of my routine were largely inspired by Wahoo and Terry Funk. Wahoo was an incredibly physical wrestler who worked in a very rugged style. It was never his intention to deliberately hurt his opponent; he was just Wahoo. Sometimes he'd get tired and hit you in the mouth, or he'd throw you off the ropes and you'd come back to a chop in the nose or ear. Wahoo also kept his blade taped in his wristband, and the thing would come loose. In Norfolk once, he grabbed me by the hair and went into his Indian war dance while his blade pierced my eyelid.

"Jesus Christ, Wahoo!" I yelled. "Hold still! Hold still!"

"Fuck," he muttered, pulling me closer toward him, not realizing that the blade was now penetrating my eyebrow, and leaving a large flap of skin dangling over my eye.

"Wahoo, you motherfucker, you just cut me up!"

"Quit complaining," he said. "I've had more stitches in my foreskin than you've had all over your fuckin' body."

Wahoo enjoyed laying into me with loud chops that echoed through the arena and brought a feeling of authenticity to the action. He loved it even more when I gave it right back to him. A lot of guys don't like getting chopped; it stings and it hurts. Some guys don't like getting slammed. But there were no limitations in my matches with Wahoo as long as the crowd was into it. I'm flattered that today, in any arena in the world, when any wrestler gives his opponent that hard, slapping chop, the fans scream *"Wooooo!"*

As much as there's a lot of Wahoo in those chops, someone else deserves credit, too: Terry Funk. When he was the NWA World Champion, I watched him wrestle Paul Jones in Raleigh one night. Jones grabbed Terry's arm, and Terry started backhand-chopping the guy. A short time later, I began doing the same thing in my matches. I also copied Terry's habit of holding onto the ropes with one hand and chopping his opponent with the other.

Whenever Terry came to town, I knew it was going to be a fun night. Once, after a show in Raleigh, the two of us drove back to Charlotte with Jimmy Crockett and Greg Valentine, who was behind the wheel. Along the way, I picked up a fifth of Everclear—100-proof clear alcohol—and poured some into Terry's beers. Terry was completely hammered—so was I, by the way—and he was pissing off Greg, trying to light his hair on fire with a cigarette lighter while he was driving. When we got back to Charlotte, Terry took off all his clothes except for his cowboy boots and the NWA championship belt, and started directing traffic. Every wrestling fan that drove by had a story for the rest of his or her life.

Next, Terry decided to pay a visit to my house. As he was stepping—naked—onto the property, I warned him to be careful because I had a pit bull. Rising to the challenge, Terry stood in my front yard and dared the dog to take a piece of him. The pit bull leaped over the fence, jumped on top of Terry, and bit him through the nose. Leslie was out with her friends, but we had a babysitter watching Megan, and the poor girl was hiding in the closet.

Funk was furious. He pulled my shotgun off the wall and started screaming like a maniac. Then he got a knife, put it between his teeth like a pirate, and began crawling around the yard, trying to get the dog. By that point I felt sick, so I vomited and fell down on the kitchen floor. A few minutes later, Leslie came home, surveyed the scene, and uttered, "My God." She turned to one of her girlfriends and pointed at me, lying in my own puke in the kitchen. "I want you to meet my husband," she said sarcastically. "And that's the world champion, Terry Funk, crawling around in the backyard on his hands and knees, naked."

Leslie gathered up Terry's clothes and threw them out into the front yard. The next morning, I woke up in his hotel room. To this day, I don't know how I got there.

THE YEAR AFTER the accident ended up becoming a good one; in 1976, for the first time ever, I made $100,000. On interviews, I'd periodically tease the fans and call myself the "People's Champion," acting oblivious to the fact that the crowd was shouting for my dismemberment. The Rock uses the same term, but goes out of his way whenever he sees me to say that I was the original "People's Champion."

From time to time, Jimmy Crockett would exchange talent with other promoters for special shows. Although Vince McMahon Sr. had originally started the WWWF—the company that later became the World Wrestling Federation and then WWE—because of a conflict with the NWA, by 1976 the wounds were healed enough that I was flown to New York twice for appearances at Madison Square Garden. The matches were hardly classics; in one confrontation, I beat Pete Sanchez, in the other, Frankie Williams—both wrestlers who lost on television every week. But it was cool to be at the Garden, the place that was known as the mecca of professional wrestling, and I invited my father to New York to see it for himself.

After the show, the two of us went to dinner at Mama Leone's, the big Italian restaurant in Manhattan, with Superstar Billy Graham. This wasn't Minnesota, and my father couldn't help but be impressed. Whether he fully approved of my career choice, I'll never know, but he definitely knew that I was making it as a wrestler.

I was actually backstage at Madison Square Garden on the night that Stan Hansen broke WWWF champion Bruno Sammartino's neck. In reality, Hansen was pretty green at the time, and he dropped Bruno the wrong way. The promotion claimed that Stan put Sammartino out of action with a running clothesline called "the Lariat" and held their rematch in Shea Stadium—the same night they simulcast Muhammad Ali's "Boxer vs. Wrestler" bout with Antonio Inoki from Japan.

Bruno definitely generated intensity, and the fans in the Northeast went crazy for him. I have to admit, though, that I was far from overwhelmed. He was a tremendous draw, a great spokesman for the guys, but not a good in-ring performer. Sammartino could put an opponent in a bear hug or lift him over his back, but he was limited—especially compared to versatile NWA champions like Harley Race, Dory Funk Jr., and Jack Brisco. The wrestling magazines all came out of New York, so Bruno was always number one in the rankings. But after seeing him wrestle, I thought, How could anyone rate *him* ahead of Harley? Christ, how could this guy be champion of *anything*?

I recognize that Bruno was loved in New York, Boston, Pittsburgh, Philadelphia, and other WWWF cities where people were very conscious of their immigrant roots and enjoyed seeing an ethnic champion. But in my opinion, Pedro Morales, who held the WWWF title from 1971 to 1973, was better. That's why he was able to work in different territories. When Sammartino came to St. Louis, where the NWA was headquartered, nobody cared because he was so far below the standards of the wrestlers they knew as champions.

With all the fond memories his fans have, Bruno should still be regarded as a hero, even though he's become a bitter man who has spent much of his retirement burying the business that gave him money and fame. It's just ludicrous. I've told my second wife, Beth (more about her later), that if she outlives me, I never want her criticizing professional wrestling. It's because of professional wrestling that we've been able to travel around the world together, expose our children to people who are the best in their fields, and live a lifestyle that most Americans could never imagine. Bruno should be able to enjoy the things that this industry gave him and become a frequent visitor in the dressing room, like the late Freddie Blassie, with the boys coming over to listen to his stories. Unfortunately, he hasn't been able to change with the times and accept that wrestling will never be the same as it was in 1965.

Nonetheless, a lot of older fans continue to characterize Bruno as "great," a term that is thrown around much too liberally. When I was starting out, "great" applied to Harley, Jack Brisco, the Funk brothers, Ray Stevens, Dick Murdoch, Red Bastien, and Nick Bockwinkle. I never saw him in his heyday, but from everything I've heard, Verne Gagne was a great performer. The same applies to Lou Thesz, who was the NWA Champion from 1948 to 1956, except for one eight-month period.

Ricky Steamboat was a great in-ring performer. Triple H, Eddie Guerrero, and Chris Benoit are great in-ring performers. Austin is great, Arn was great. Shawn Michaels was the very best performer the World Wrestling Federation had to offer and the first guy that made me aware that even greatness can be challenged. He was much better than Bret Hart. There was really no comparison. Even today, after all his back problems, Shawn can still be the best performer on any given show. Then you have Undertaker, who I admire not just for his ring work, but because he's been a household name for over a decade.

Kurt Angle is great because he can wrestle with anybody, but he's still relatively new to the business, so he needs longevity. Curt Hennig, Terry "Bam-Bam" Gordy, and Barry Windham were great performers in their prime, like Angle, but Hennig didn't always mentally show up, Gordy developed a drug problem, and Barry just stopped taking care of himself as he got older. Let's not forget the referees. Earl Hebner and Tommy Young are great. There were a lot of nights I couldn't have made it for an hour without Tommy.

To make a baseball analogy, Ken Griffey Jr. may have been a great player for a few years, but that doesn't make him the greatest of all time. Jose Canseco was going to be the next Mickey Mantle, and instead, he ended up a disgrace. I have every reason to believe that Kurt Angle won't fall into the same trap, but right now he's Alex Rodriguez, the young player with the potential to be the greatest. If A-Rod stays healthy, he's going to break all the records. If Angle stays healthy, he'll be one of the very best ever.

THREE YEARS AFTER moving to Charlotte, I was still learning the secrets of becoming great. I prided myself on my cardiovascular conditioning. I never wanted to tire out in the middle of a match. From the time I started in wrestling, I did five hundred free squats a day until 1986, when I bought my first Stairmaster.

The really good in-ring performers can speak to each other during a match—"Hey, how about this?" or "Let's try that." If they do things properly, even the referee barely notices that they're having a conversation.

Today, my fans insist that I could have a great match with a broom. At times, I honestly think a broom would be easier; at least a broom can't mess things up. Over the years, I've worked with wrestlers who actually had less ability than a broom—guys who played politics or who had the right cosmetic look, but didn't deserve to wear a pair of wrestling tights.

I was determined to wrestle a classic every night, and willing to sell my heart out to make it happen. If a guy had a big move, I'd react huge to it, making him look like a legend. I discovered that once you showed that type of good faith, most opponents would sell all your stuff, too.

The important thing was how the fans felt when the night was over. You have to make them think that they are part of it. That's what Steve Austin and The Rock have been able able to do—reach into the audience and touch the people. Every great drawing card has had that skill, in his own way—Wahoo, Dusty, Hulk Hogan, and, yes, Bruno Sammartino.

CHARLES ROBINSON (REFEREE): In the 1970s, I'd be front-row every single week in Charlotte. Before the Charlotte Hornets and Carolina Panthers turned up here, Ric Flair and professional wrestling were the deal. I was different than other fans because I liked Ric Flair; in fact, I made some life-size posters of him. I'd draw a picture of Ric, and sew sequins and rhinestones on the paper. I was so obnoxious; I was trying to be like Flair. Every time I was at the arena, I got into an altercation with fans trying to tear up my posters. It got so bad that my grand-father, a Charlotte police officer, arranged for another policeman to escort me everywhere, so that the other fans didn't beat me up.

It didn't happen all at once, but I periodically noticed that some people thought my style of riling up the crowd was cool. I can't recall exactly when I started getting heated reactions just by pointing at chubby guys in the crowd and screaming, "Shut up, fat boy!" But I did it so much that by the 1990s a sizable amount of the audience would cheer whenever they heard this catchphrase. Some people even held up signs with an arrow pointing down at them under the inscription, FAT BOY.

What mattered most was that the crowd was entertained. I appreciated that attitude in other athletes like Joe Namath and Wilt Chamberlain, two guys I enjoyed as much for their flamboyance as for their accomplishments. On television, I began improving myself, trying to project the same image. I'd come out for interviews in a long black mink, just like the one Dusty Rhodes owned. Whatever Dusty bought, I bought, too.

Jimmy Crockett was looking for more talent, and contacted the Atlanta territory. Richard Blood was a muscular kid with a strain of Asian ancestry that gave him a handsome, exotic look. Under the name Rick Steamboat, he was billed as a native Hawaiian and the son of veteran Sam Steamboat. We had a 400-pound wrestler named One Man Gang who Atlanta promoter Jim Barnett wanted, so he and Jimmy made a trade. Crockett believed he was getting a talented prospect, but from the moment we met, I knew Steamboat had magic.

Like me, Steamboat had been trained by Verne Gagne, so we were automatically friends. I also understood that anybody who survived Gagne's camp had to be good. On June 15, 1977, we introduced him to the territory in dramatic fashion: he walked into the TV studio in Raleigh and pinned me clean in the middle of the ring, winning my Mid-Atlantic TV title. The upset established Ricky as a serious force, and did nothing to hurt my momentum. On July 9, I won my first U.S. heavyweight championship, unseating one of my childhood favorites, Bobo Brazil (I'd promised to streak through the Richmond Coliseum if I lost).

Whenever I thought about Steamboat, I imagined the two of us headlining and blowing the house away. So I went to George Scott and

asked, "How about letting me work a main-event program with this guy?" Admittedly, it made a lot of guys in the back sick to see a kid like this being elevated. Most of the heroes in Mid-Atlantic were thirty-five or older, and dubious about whether Steamboat had earned the right to headline. But George obviously respected me enough to give it a shot.

The title went back and forth a couple of times, but we weren't drawing the kind of money I had anticipated, so we tried something different. On April 9, 1978, I appeared on TV, offering to put up my U.S. championship against the newcomer right there in the studio. Steamboat came over to the interview area wearing an open robe and Hawaiian

My rivalry with Ricky Steamboat always brought the fans to their feet.

necklace, and was apparently surprised by the gesture. I walked up to him and shoved him. "Perhaps you didn't hear me," I yelled. "Get in there and wrestle me right now!"

I was the first one in the ring, laying down the U.S. title on the mat and holding my arms open as Steamboat advanced toward me. As soon as he bent to step through the ropes, I charged—as anyone who listened to my interviews knew, I *was* the dirtiest player in the game—pulled him into the ring, and rubbed his face on the mat. I seemed crazed now, and threw Steamboat back to ringside, where I ground his face into the studio floor. The referee tried to stop me, but I shoved him aside and continued the attack, snapmaring Steamboat, then dragging his face across the ground and sticking it into the television camera.

"There's your pretty boy!" I shrieked, reminding anyone who hadn't noticed that Steamboat was a sex symbol. "Now, he's ugly!" To underscore my point, I rubbed the championship belt into Ricky's face and eye.

RICHARD BLOOD, AKA RICK STEAMBOAT: While the beating was going on, Ric put me in a position where I was sitting on my butt. He pulled back my head, put his face close to mine and said, "Rick, I'm really sorry I have to do this." Then he gave me a hard-way shot to swell up my eye.

We wanted Steamboat to look beaten up when he went on the road for our grudge matches, so we took him upstairs into the dressing room and really administered some torture. Harley Race was like a doctor in situations like this. He wanted to hit him real hard and break his eyebrows open, but after some discussion with Wahoo and myself, he simply cut Ricky's face in five places with folded sandpaper, poured iodine into the wounds, and rubbed sandpaper across the scars.

RICK STEAMBOAT: Harley sent David Crockett to get the sandpaper, and David came back with what I call the "variety pack." At the top was a very fine sandpaper, and then you went through the other varieties like a deck of cards until you got to the end, which looked like there were granite rocks glued onto the paper. A couple of guys were holding my arms when Harley said, "Kid, this is gonna hurt."

He started to sandpaper my face up around the eye, literally taking

the hairs of my eyebrow completely off. When my skin dried, it looked . . . creased. Even after I healed, my face was discolored for six to eight months. I remember walking into a 7-Eleven, and people kept looking at my face and going, "Oh, my God! That was real?"

As great as this looked, it didn't open the door I had wanted. But we were getting there. I just needed one more creative hook to make it work.

I'd purchased a 1974 Lincoln Continental limo that looked brand-new. I traveled all over the territory in it with my friends and my chauffeur, Terry Brown. He was in high school when I first met him, working at his parents' Texaco station about a mile from my house. I don't remember exactly what I paid him, but I do know that because of our association, he got laid every night.

On November 1, 1978, Terry drove me up in front of WRAL Studios with two girls who worked for a local modeling agency. (By coincidence, one of them, a pretty blonde named Bonnie, would later become Rick Steamboat's wife.) With a lady on each arm, I strolled up to the interview area, all dressed up, and announced, "Everybody knows that Ric Flair lives a life that makes guys like Joe Namath and every average human being in the world today go dizzy. Ask these girls, 'Who is the number one man in the whole wide world?' Tell them, girls."

"Nature Boy," they swooned, leaning into the microphone.

Holding up a photo of a freshly bruised Steamboat, I continued, "Where do you figure that a turkey like this fits into my plans, huh? Ricky Steamboat's probably sitting in a corner somewhere, sucking his thumb, while Nature Boy Ric Flair stands before the whole world with two of the most gorgeous human beings on the face of the earth."

Apparently feeling emasculated, Steamboat stepped onto the set. "Check out the turkey, girls," I said, swaggering as the future Bonnie Steamboat twirled her hair. Steamboat slapped me and ran my head into the ring post, then dragged me—by my tie—through the ropes. He slung me into the cables, delivered a double thrust to my neck, and tore off my jacket. Lurching forward, I swung at Steamboat, but he ducked under the blow, got me on my knees, and pulled my dress shirt over my head. Now I was bare-chested, except for my tie. After a knee drop to my chest, Ricky tore off the waistband of my pants and the upper portion of my left trouser leg. With the fans shouting in disbelief, he kept

tearing, leaving me in nothing but my tie, dress shoes, socks, and tiny briefs. I like to say that I was one of the first television personalities to model a thong years before it became popular.

Finally, everything clicked. We went back on the road, and from day one we sold out everywhere. More significantly, the feud transformed Steamboat from an up-and-comer into the superstar he deserved to be.

RICK STEAMBOAT: George Scott would ask us to go twenty or thirty minutes, and we'd go sixty. At the fifty-nine-minute mark, the announcer would be on the public-address system: *"One minute to go! One minute to go!"* Everybody in the house would be standing up. At fifteen seconds, we'd go to the finish. Maybe Flair would go over. Maybe I would. It didn't matter; we gave them such a good match, they really didn't care who won that night.

DAVID CROCKETT: The rivalry was a great thing for the company. Ric Flair had all the moves, the talk, the walk of a veteran at a young age. And now, instead of dealing mainly with fans between thirty-eight and sixty years old, we were drawing a younger audience. Suddenly, we had teenagers coming to the matches to see Ricky Steamboat.

Steamboat had everything—charisma, work rate, intensity, and one of the best bodies in our business. He was training for the Mr. North Carolina contest at one point while wrestling me for a minimum of thirty minutes a night—on *sixty* carbs a day. He was just amazing. If he had any drawback, it's that he never played the bad guy. Unlike wrestlers who could get the crowd to either love them or hate them, he only knew how to be the hero. But he's the greatest hero I've ever wrestled.

Steamboat was the antithesis of everything the Nature Boy represented . . . and one of the greatest guys I've ever known.

After the Steamboat series, Jimmy Crockett was aggressively pushing me for national recognition and—a few years down the line—a possible run as NWA champion. He'd been picking up syndicated stations outside of our traditional base in the Carolinas and Virginia. In time, the Charlotte territory would expand into West Virginia, parts of Tennessee, and as far away as Buffalo and Ontario, where promoter Frank Tunney's Maple Leaf Gardens cards sometimes featured NWA, AWA, and WWWF talent, along with Canadian regulars like Billy "Red" Lyons and Angelo Mosca.

I was also being flown into the Atlanta territory, where I would work Friday-night shows at the old City Auditorium, then stay overnight and tape the promotion's television show for WTCG—the

CHAPTER **6**

I AIN'T STUPID ENOUGH

UHF channel Ted Turner was turning into a cable "SuperStation"—on Saturday mornings. As a result, fans—as well as the power brokers that sat on the NWA board—could turn on their televisions and see me regularly.

But St. Louis was the deal! It was the flagship city of the NWA, the place where promoters from all over the country sent their top guys to show off their skills. A typical show would be loaded, with Dick the Bruiser, Pat O'Connor, and other legends appearing alongside rising stars like Ted DiBiase and David Von Erich. If you were working the main event in St. Louis in the late 1970s, you were guaranteed to make $3,500. It was big-time.

The promoter, Sam Muchnick, was a former sportswriter and NWA president who presented wrestling as pure sport. He hadn't changed the ring since Ed "Strangler" Lewis won the title from Joe Stecher there in 1928. It was big, and hard as concrete. Former NWA champion Dory Funk Jr. once told me, "If you want to get over in St. Louis, take big bumps, 'cause the other guys don't want to do it in that ring. That's how Harley got over so well." And that's what I did—taking suplexes, getting slammed off the top rope, and enduring every other imaginable hit or fall. It was brutal.

Still, the guys couldn't wait to get to St. Louis, since Muchnick was one of the best payoff men in the business. Paul Boesch in Houston had the same reputation and tended to better compensate everyone up and down the card. Don Owen in Portland, Oregon, was also charitable, even though he was paying big money on small gates.

In 1978 I also took my first tour of Japan since my AWA days. In a Tag Team match, I actually scored a pin on Shohei "Giant" Baba, the promoter for All Japan Pro Wrestling and a man-god in that country. It made me in Japan, but after the three-week tour I came back to Charlotte and said, "I'll never go again."

It just seemed too far to travel to make money. Vince McMahon hadn't kicked the business open yet, so Charlotte was a mecca, with Steamboat, Greg Valentine, Wahoo, Paul Jones, Mulligan, and the Andersons appearing on virtually every big card, and Dusty and Andre frequently coming in as special features. The payoffs were good. Why would I want to leave? The answer was that I had to. When someone like Baba is generous enough to lie down for you, he expects you to return.

Some Americans loved going to Japan because they could be big stars there and get paid better than they were in the States. Bruiser Brody and Stan Hansen would earn in the neighborhood of $15,000 a week, working something like sixteen weeks a year in Japan. Then they had the rest of the time to go home and pick and choose whether they worked in Puerto Rico, the WWWF, the AWA, or somewhere else. They didn't want the steady grind of working in one territory.

Both Brody and Hansen were great performers and good guys. Brody was too independent to work for one company for an extended period of time. Sometimes a promoter would want Brody to come in and wrestle their top attraction. If he didn't like the finish for his match, he'd leave and infuriate the promoter. That's why Brody never came to Charlotte; Jimmy Crockett wouldn't have tolerated that.

But Brody and I were friends and never had a problem anywhere. I worked with him in New Zealand, Georgia, Texas, and Florida, and we always made it happen in the ring. My favorite match against him took place at the Checkerdome in St. Louis in 1983. It was two out of three falls, and Giant Baba was there with his whole entourage, taping the encounter for Japanese TV. Brody was huge in St. Louis; he, Dick the Bruiser, and Harley were the three biggest stars I worked with there. We split the first two falls, then wrestled to a draw. There were 19,000 fans in the building, and none of them sat down for sixty minutes. It was a big deal, and *the* match that established me internationally.

In 1988, Brody was killed in a dressing room in Puerto Rico. He'd been there a few months earlier, working a tag-team match with the Rock's father, Rocky Johnson, against Kendo Nagasaki and Mr. Pogo. Nagasaki and Pogo were the local tag-team champions, but in their home country of Japan, no one considered them anywhere near Brody's level. Because there were some ringside photographers covering the match for Japanese publications, Brody didn't want to look bad in the country where he made most of his money. So instead of making the champions look good like he was supposed to, he tossed Nagasaki and Pogo around like they were nothing.

Obviously, the promotion wasn't happy about this, but when Brody came back, everything seemed okay. On July 14, he was scheduled to wrestle another American, Danny Spivey, at Juan Lobriel Stadium in the city of Bayamon. I heard that Brody didn't like the proposed finish, so he went into the backstage bathroom to have a discussion with Jose Gonzales, the booker who also wrestled in Puerto Rico as the masked Invader #1. Not long afterward, some of the wrestlers heard a scream.

When they rushed into the bathroom, Brody was clutching his bloody stomach. He'd been stabbed through the lungs, liver, and arteries, and died a few hours later.

Gonzales insisted that he'd acted in self-defense, and he was eventually acquitted of murder. A lot of people claim that given the corrupt nature of the Puerto Rican legal system, the verdict was inevitable. I wasn't there, so I'll never be sure. I do know this, though: Brody was a pretty stubborn guy, but so were the Puerto Ricans. And it was their island.

Out of deference to Brody, none of the upper-echelon NWA wrestlers—the Road Warriors, Terry Funk, Harley, and myself, among others—ever returned. I feel bad about it because the guys who ran the promotion, Carlos Colon and Victor Jovica, were good friends of mine.

Stan Hansen was a different type of guy than Brody. I always thought of Stan as a good ol' boy from Texas who was street-smart and very ring-savvy. He and I became close, more because of the time we spent together in Georgia than Japan. Once, before a match at the Omni in Atlanta, he asked, "Do you mind bleeding when I hit you with my Lariat?"

"No," I joked. "Are you sure you'll be able to see me?" I asked because I think Hansen was legally blind without his glasses.

"Don't worry. I won't hurt you."

Unfortunately, as I predicted, Stan hit me so hard that the blade broke through the strips of tape on my fingers, went into my forehead, and snapped in half. For the rest of the match, I tried to dig the blade out of my skin while Hansen laughed, "I told you not to move, stupid."

Another time, we met up with two girls at Billy's, one of our favorite hangouts in Atlanta back then. One was in love with me, the other with Hansen. (I still can't figure out what she saw in the big bastard; I guess it was that rugged, tobacco-chewing cowboy image.) At the end of the night, I somehow ended up driving Stan's rental car and decided to show off. I floored the gas, not realizing that there was a cement median about fifty feet in front of me. I think I was shouting my old Ray Stevens slogan, "Circle the wagons and hold Old Blue," but just before I got to the part where I'd scream, "I'm a fucker and a fighter and a wild bull rider"—*bam!*—we hit the barrier hard enough to knock all four wheels off the car.

God, Hansen was pissed. Still, I know that he got over it, because two weeks later he said, "Hey, Flair, call those two girls again." Once again, I ended up behind the wheel of Hansen's vehicle. And, believe it or not, while leaving the Ramada Inn parking lot on Central Avenue, I couldn't resist gunning the car another time. On this occasion, I hit the median at a mere thirty miles per hour, so we only lost the two front wheels.

"How the fuck could you do that *twice?*" Hansen yelled. I could only look at him and laugh, hoping that he wouldn't slap the shit out of me.

FOR ME, THE wrestling lifestyle definitely led to a certain recklessness with automobiles. In the Mid-Atlantic territory, we were always in a rush and had to cover 120,000 miles a year. In 1978, on Christmas Day, we had a double shot—Greensboro *and* Charlotte. I made it to both shows, but received two tickets for driving in excess of eighty-five miles per hour.

Ultimately, I got dragged into traffic court. This was something new to me. In South Carolina, we usually paid the cops twenty dollars and kept going. In North Carolina, we'd pay a lawyer to make everything go away. But this time, the judge had a large printout in his hands; he looked at me and said, "Do you realize that you have *eighty-two* moving violations?"

"No, sir," I responded nervously.

"You have eighty-two moving violations in four years, most of them in excess of eighty miles an hour. I think that sounds like thirty days in jail. Maybe that will slow you down."

I was scared to death. The deputies cuffed me and put me in a cell for a few hours before my lawyer got me out. We had to appeal the case in superior court, where murderers, rapists, and armed robbers were also being tried. This judge had a different attitude. He looked at my record and said, "That'll be $2,500."

Here I was, expecting a jail term. Thank God I ended up in front of the right judge. Nonetheless, the ordeal cost me $2,500, and the experience slowed me down . . . for a little while, anyway.

IN 1979, LESLIE gave birth to my son, David, back in Minneapolis. He was born late on a Tuesday, and the next night I was supposed to appear at a television taping in Raleigh. I called George Scott and said, "We just had a baby boy. Is it okay if I miss TV?"

"If that's what you want to do," he answered, "go ahead. But when you start driving south, keep going until you hit Memphis." That was the *last* territory anyone wanted to work; the promoter, Nick Gulas, was the cheapest man in the industry.

George's message to me was explicit: Stay in Minneapolis, and lose your job. And George was a hero compared to most of his peers. It was just the way the business was run. The word *compassion* did not exist.

ALTHOUGH LESLIE AND I were both thrilled to have a new child, the birth of David did nothing to help our marriage. I was still really wild, and she had run out of patience. The decision to get divorced and to give Leslie whatever she wanted was very easy. When the case was over, I looked at my lawyer and said, "This judge must think I'm Rod Stewart." In 1979, $3,000 a month for child support and alimony was a lot of money.

Not once had I stopped to ask myself, "How could you cause someone so much anguish?" I can't pinpoint anything that Leslie ever did wrong. I could have been married to Raquel Welch and it wouldn't have made any difference. I wanted to be Ric Flair, the character the fans saw on television, every minute of every day of my life.

I had so much energy and needed someone to bounce it off—all the time, without a break. One person couldn't possibly have filled that role. Plus, Leslie had the responsibility of taking care of two kids. Twenty-five years later, Leslie still hasn't forgiven me, and I haven't forgiven myself for putting my Ric Flair persona before her and two beautiful children.

For anyone out there who cares, you can never take things like this back. You can never replace the moments you've lost. Trust me, money and time cannot mend all the wounds that you've inflicted by being so selfish.

Still, Leslie managed to hurt me worse than anyone before or since when she called one day and said, "We're leaving. We're going back to Minneapolis."

"Leaving?"

"Yeah, I'm selling the house. I'm gone."

I was floored. I had just bought a beautiful new home and was giving it to her in the divorce settlement. I was hoping to have the best of both worlds—my career and my children close by. Leslie was an independent woman who'd made friends in Charlotte and fit into the community. Minneapolis was AWA country. I worked every day for the NWA, and we never went there. That meant that I'd never see my kids.

David was only a baby, and it makes my heart sink, thinking about all those years together that we could have had. I should have been there with him, encouraging him to play football, to wrestle, to do the things that he needed. But I just failed.

When I'd driven around Charlotte during the day, Megan sat next to me on the armrest (that was before anyone told me about children's car seats). I brought her everywhere. Now she was being taken away from me. Whenever I came home, she wasn't there for a kiss and a hug. It was horrible.

MEGAN FLIEHR KETZNER: My dad had a blue Cadillac with little arm-rests that folded down. He'd take me all over Charlotte, but also to the studio when the wrestlers were doing their interviews. These big guys would yell into the camera, then come over to me and smile and shake my hand. I could tell that my dad liked showing me off. I also kind of realized that there was something a little different about his life.

I was five when my parents divorced and we moved back to Minnesota. We lived with my mom's aunt and uncle during the transition—her parents had both died by that time—and she took a job as a dental technician.

My brother David and I spent a lot of time on airplanes. We flew by ourselves. We'd try to meet my dad in Chicago or another city close to Minneapolis where he was wrestling. He did the best he could do. Sometimes on Christmas,

One of my favorite pastimes was driving around Charlotte with my little girl, Megan.

I'd stay with my dad's parents in Minnesota, even if he wasn't there.

I found my grandparents to be a little standoffish. My grandfather was an ob-gyn and had to take calls in the middle of the night, so they had separate bedrooms. My grandmother and I used to make Christmas cookies, but she liked having control of the house. They were very prominent in the community, and they enjoyed their friends. I mean, it's not that they didn't love us. They just weren't kid people. They were so different from my dad, who was always warm and very emotional.

DAVID FLIEHR, AKA DAVID FLAIR: I hardly ever saw my dad. As I got older, I was able to travel with him in the summer from Charlotte to Greensboro and Florence, but there were always people around him. And then, before we really had a chance to do anything, he'd have to leave and wrestle somewhere else.

He always protected the business around me. I wasn't allowed to go into the babyface [good guy] dressing room. If he saw one of his opponents at the airport, he wouldn't talk to him. This was his life, and he sacrificed everything to be the best.

Eventually, he told me his thoughts about the business. "It's not about you," he said. "It's about you and your opponent having a great match. You *both* have to look good. Because if you're the only one who looks good, no one cares."

In the course of a few years, I felt that I'd taken the Buddy Rogers character that George Scott had suggested and brought it to a different level. Rogers had defined the style of grabbing a hold, working high spots around it, then going back to the hold. I took a little bit from him, a little from Ray Stevens, a little from Harley, and a little from Dick Murdoch and Terry Funk. Those were my favorites. To this day, when I'm in the ring and can't think as fast as I used to, I remember what they did in similar situations.

On Jimmy Crockett's recommendation, I began leaving the dressing room in my long sequined robe with white light flashing behind me and *Also Sprach Zarathustra*—the theme to the film *2001: A Space Odyssey*—playing as I crossed through a cloud of smoke. The song, written by German composer Richard Strauss, projected the exact image I wanted—classical, yet futuristic.

In 1979 George brought Buddy Rogers to Mid-Atlantic for a feud with me. He'd been out of wrestling for several years, had lots of money, and was bored. Now, according to the storyline, he was going to reclaim the title of "Nature Boy."

I was excited as can be. We were in Greensboro when I first saw him. He was moving through the backstage area with that unmistakable strut—Buddy never walked; he just strutted 24/7—tanned, fit, and elegant. Even from a distance, I noticed a big diamond sparkling on his hand. I went over and introduced myself, and as we shook hands, he actually said, "Kid, there's only *one* diamond in this business, and you're looking at him."

He got no argument from me. In fact, pretty soon I began doing a variation of his remark in my interviews: "Diamonds are forever, and so is the Nature Boy! *Wooooo!*"

On television, Rogers began belittling me: "You know, I find you well balanced. You're light in the feet, and light in the head." He claimed that he'd invented the name "Nature Boy"—it actually came from a Nat King Cole song—the strut, and the figure-four leglock.

During a match I had with Len Denton, Rogers critiqued my performance to announcer Rich Landrum. When I locked Denton in the figure-four, Rogers sneered, "You don't even have his leg on the right side." Then he came into the ring and began stomping me.

Rogers was fifty-eight years old and nowhere near the caliber of athlete he'd been at his peak. He couldn't take a lot of shots or hard falls. But when we wrestled, he wanted to be the ring general. He had to call the shots in our match.

Like Johnny Valentine, Rogers wasn't held in the highest regard by some of the old-timers—not because of his ring work, but because of his attitude. He had a history of double-crossing people in the ring and refusing to lose to opponents after agreeing beforehand. Over and over again, I was warned not to lose to Rogers. "Ric, whatever you do with him," I was told, "you'll never get it back."

It was kind of sad. Rogers had beaten Pat O'Connor in two straight falls for the NWA title in Chicago's Comiskey Park in 1961. Two years later, he'd been chosen by Vince McMahon Sr. and his partner Toots Mondt to become the first WWWF champion. But to a lot of Buddy's peers, it hardly mattered. To them, Rogers was a self-serving prick who wouldn't elevate worthy opponents. I thought about myself at Rogers's age, and how I never wanted to be perceived as a guy who was uncooperative.

I don't think Rogers himself realized what an awful legacy he had. Regardless, he kept his word to George Scott. On July 21, 1979, he submitted to my figure-four after a three-minute match. Not only did he do the honors for me, he did it with blood.

Sometimes a guy can have a terrible name with everyone else, but act nice to you. You know what, then? It's not your problem. If I listened to what people said about Vince McMahon, I would have thought that he was the biggest asshole in the world. Instead, he turned out to be a wonderful guy to work for, and right now, he's my mentor. I'm sure a lot of the stories about Buddy Rogers are true. But I'm glad to say that *that* Nature Boy did the right thing for *this* Nature Boy. The one thing I learned from the experience was to judge people by the way they treat you.

IN 1980, DON Owen called Crockett from Oregon. "I got a guy here who's a *great* talker," Don said. "I think you'll like him. They call him 'Hot Rod.'"

I fell in love with Rowdy Roddy Piper the day I met him.

As much as I enjoyed wrestling Piper, I may have had even more fun interviewing against him. When we were feuding, there were times when we'd go at it on the microphone at the announcer's table. Nothing was scripted. I'd say something, and he'd try to top me. David Crockett was announcing for the promotion, and he would practically laugh out loud. Once Piper got going, he was tremendous.

DAVID CROCKETT: I never knew what they were going to say, and I didn't want to. I wanted to be a fan. At that time, an interview would go like thirty or forty-five seconds. With Piper and Flair, we were going two, three, four minutes because the banter was so entertaining. And it was all ad-libbed.

Roddy and I used to ride down the road together. He'd be constantly reading and listening to the radio and writing things down to use in his interviews. He was a true student of the business, but I think the reason he worked so well with Ric was that they're both nuts.

I was going through a "good guy" phase when Piper won the Mid-Atlantic TV title. Then, on January 27, 1981, he defeated me for the U.S. championship with the aid of a foreign object. The next time we appeared on television, he strolled up to announcers David Crockett and Bill Caudle dressed in a tuxedo and kilt with the U.S. title strapped around his waist.

"Let me tell you something, Mr. Ric Flair, the Mae West of wrestling," he began. "I have a little something for you here, you see." He held up a gift-wrapped box. "Here's just a little something that I have had for a long time that I know you could never have."

He placed the box on the announcers' table and challenged me. "Go ahead. Open it."

I unwrapped the box and removed the Mid-Atlantic TV title belt.

"So that's yours," Piper gloated and giggled. He pulled open his tuxedo jacket and displayed the U.S. title. "And this is mine."

Since I was the good guy, I was obligated to act offended by Roddy's audacity. I spoke about the prestige attached to the television championship, adding, "And Ric Flair, whether a punk like you realizes it or not, doesn't wear anything he doesn't win." Furthermore, I had proof that Piper had used devious means to take my U.S. title—a piece of metal, allegedly procured by a fan after Roddy tossed it into the audience during our match.

"That's a lie," Piper insisted.

"You keep your mouth shut!" I hollered indignantly. "Now, I'm gonna tell you something. I don't wear *rented* tuxedos." Going for the cheap shot, I pointed at Roddy's kilt. "I don't run around in a skirt. I'm a man, and I'll always be a man." Getting more animated, I removed my jacket and ripped it. "Just as sure as I can take a four-hundred-dollar sports coat and tear it up, I'm gonna grind you up and spit you out!"

My action prompted Piper to pull off his own jacket. "I'll tell you something," he yelled, practically hyperventilating. "You think you can do things? Well, I'll show you up." He made a gesture to tear the garment, then—seemingly realizing that it was a rental—had a change of heart.

"I ain't stupid enough," he spewed.

I DIDN'T NEED Piper to get into trouble. But when the two of us were together, we were incorrigible. In Puerto Rico once, Roddy began imitating Stan Hansen—he was walking through the lobby of our hotel, clotheslining the potted plants one by one. Of course, everything was on the hotel's surveillance camera, so a group of cops and police dogs turned up at Roddy's door. He had to take a couple of the hundred-dollar chips he'd just won in the casino and stuff them in everyone's hands to avoid a night in lockup.

The night before I lost the NWA title to Kerry Von Erich in 1984, I wrestled Piper in Portland, with Red Bastien as special referee. My

Bantering with Rowdy Roddy Piper was even more fun than wrestling him.

most vivid memory of that night, though, is of Piper in his kilt outside the Red Lion in Jansen Beach. I was in my robe while Don Owen was in his boxer shorts and knee-high socks. And Bastien was throwing up in a planter. It's the only time I ever got to Red Bastien. (Red, if you're reading this, you and the Bishop keep pounding 'em, buddy.)

One of my nicknames for Piper was John Wesley Harding, according to legend the fastest gun of all time. Whether alcohol or drugs were on the table, Piper could put anyone to bed. Kevin Sullivan once bragged that when it came to partying, the Purple Haze, Mark Lewin, "could tuck Piper in and kiss him on the lips good night."

We resolved this issue when Wahoo and I hosted a party at my house. We dubbed the event "The Great Shootout—the Hot Rod vs. the Purple Haze," and bought a thousand bucks' worth of seafood, steak, and liquor. All the boys in the territory were invited.

The shootout commenced. In the course of the night, I poured Piper and Lewin each about thirty shots of Crown Royal. I'm sure that there are different opinions about who won, but since this is my story, I'm telling it the way I want to. The nod goes to the Hot Rod. Around six-thirty in the morning, I sent everyone out. Piper walked upstairs into my guest room, lay down, and went to sleep. Lewin was carried from the house. In my eyes, Hot Rod will be the fastest gun of all time, forever and ever.

WHEN I WAS the NWA Champion, I always flew first-class. On one flight back from Japan, I paid the stewardess two hundred dollars so Piper and Dick Slater could join me in the front. This is not an exaggeration—we finished *every* drop of booze in the first-class cabin between Tokyo and Chicago.

During our trips to the Caribbean, Piper and I often found ourselves with Jack Brisco and his brother, Jerry. Although they acted sportsmanlike in the ring, the Briscos were crazy, especially when alcohol was part of the equation. Like Wahoo, the Briscos were fiercely proud of their Native American ancestry. But their friends loved to tease them—"Keep those Indians off the firewater."

When Mike Rotunda started in wrestling, the Briscos looked after him. The pairing seemed natural enough—Jack, an NCAA wrestling champion, and Jerry had both wrestled at Oklahoma State, and

Rotunda had been a wrestler at Syracuse University. But to the Briscos, "mentoring" meant manhandling the poor rookie, once making him down twenty Budweisers in a single sitting. One night, they got him so screwed up that he started climbing over a chain-link fence and got his balls stuck on the metal barbs. He pretty much tore his nut sack off, and Rocky Kernodle had to rush him to the hospital.

One Christmas season, Piper and I were going through customs in Miami after a trip to the Dominican Republic when we saw the Briscos in the terminal. We sneaked up behind them, tackled them, and started wrestling Jack and Jerry on the floor. The other passengers just stood there, looking on in disbelief.

None of this seemed to bother Jim Crockett. Piper, myself, and everyone else in the territory brought that same exuberance to our matches, and Crockett Promotions was pulling in millions of dollars a year. The promoters who had written him off were rapidly being humbled—to the point that in 1981, Jimmy was ready to pull the power move that would launch both of us to the apex of the NWA.

In June 1981, Dusty Rhodes—now an extremely charismatic fan favorite calling himself "The American Dream"—beat Harley Race for the NWA title. And I received my first education about the political side of the wrestling trade.

The process of picking an NWA champion was not so different from the UN Security Council deliberating over a resolution, or the College of Cardinals choosing the Pope. It was highly political, with every single board member having his own agenda. There were nine members on the board of directors, to ensure that their negotiations never ended in a tie. Although active wrestlers weren't allowed to sit on the board, each promoter had a favorite. Bob Geigel in Kansas City liked Harley. Fritz Von Erich in Dallas lobbied for his

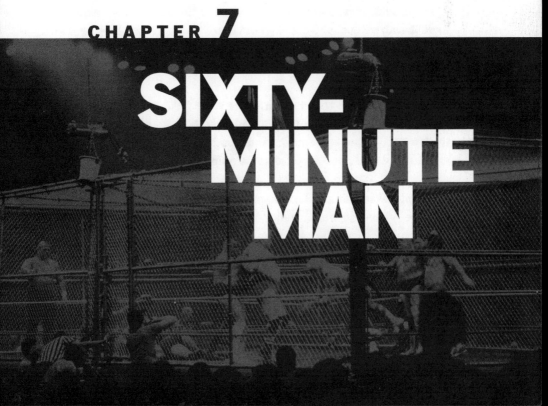

CHAPTER 7

SIXTY-MINUTE MAN

son, David. Eddie Graham in Florida was loyal to Dusty. Jimmy Crockett was pushing me hard.

The NWA had never had a champion who came from Crockett's territory, and the old-school guys didn't want to give him anything now. Jimmy hustled to line up allies—among them Jim Barnett in Georgia and Vince McMahon Sr., who had repaired his relationship with the NWA so much that he actually sat on the board in 1981. Graham headed the opposition. There were grumblings that, at six feet and 245 pounds, I was too small to hold the title. Of course, Buddy Rogers and Jack Brisco were about the same size, but the argument was that wrestlers had gotten bigger and stronger since Rogers's time, and I didn't have Brisco's amateur credentials. One thing was obvious, though: the board had thrown Graham a bone when they gave Dusty the title. Dusty may have thought that he was going to hold the title for life, but very few members envisioned him as a long-term champion.

HARLEY RACE: First off, an NWA champion had to be a class of wrestler who could wrestle any human being at any time for an hour, if it was determined that he do so, and have a good match. It didn't matter if your opponent was Ricky Steamboat or [Tennessee promoter Nick Gulas's son] George Gulas, who was pushed as a main attraction, but as a worker was very, very limited.

Flair could wrestle anyone on the face of the earth. Dusty was able to do it with people who could go out there and work and hold up their end. But the sad truth is that he'd have some problems doing it with everybody.

DAVID CROCKETT: It was a major honor to be NWA champion. Some of these guys slept with the championship belt. Dusty really didn't want to give it up, so the agreement came about that Ric would win the title, and Dusty would get it back at some point.

If the title was going to be taken from Dusty, he didn't want to lose it in a place where he was a major name. So on September 17, 1981, I defeated him at Memorial Hall in Kansas City, Kansas. Having an NWA title change take place on his turf raised promoter Bob Geigel's esteem, but Dusty wasn't a big star in Kansas City, and neither was I. The crowd was a little lackluster, and the building itself was very small. My parents were there, but because everything was kept so secretive in wrestling back then, I couldn't tell them why. My current wife, Beth, was just my girlfriend at the time, so I wasn't allowed to bring her, or even let her in on what was going to happen.

What made me feel even worse, however, was the animosity that I detected from Dusty. He was a guy I idolized, and the whole atmosphere was weird. The NWA title meant so much to him, and he was struggling over losing it—especially to a friend who also happened to be a big Dusty Rhodes fan. It was the first time that there'd ever been tension between us.

The match itself was terrible. Dusty didn't want to be there. Lou Thesz was the referee. I climbed the ropes, and Dusty followed me up the turnbuckles, attempting a suplex. Because I'd been working over his leg earlier in the match, it buckled and I landed on top of him. It was an absolutely terrible finish.

After one minute as champion, I was already feeling the pressure. Dusty was unhappy, Geigel didn't want me to have the title, and I was uncomfortable walking around backstage with the championship belt. Not being wrestling fans, I don't think that my parents realized what I had just accomplished. My friend, Harley Race, wasn't there. Celebrating at the arena was out of the question, so Jimmy Crockett and I just went out quietly by ourselves, like two actuaries on a business trip.

Over the years, Dusty and I learned to work around personal issues when we were in the ring. We'd go on to have great title matches and realize that, regardless of who was winning or losing, we owed it to both the fans and ourselves to deliver.

JIM BARNETT: In addition to being the promoter in Georgia, I was the treasurer for the NWA. When a wrestler won the NWA championship, he was required to put down a $25,000 deposit on the championship belt. When he lost the title and returned the championship belt, I gave him a check for $25,000. If he didn't want to lose the championship, he would forfeit the deposit, and no one else would use him on their shows.

I also handled the champion's bookings. You book your arenas two years in advance, and the promoters wanted to be sure that they had the champion for certain big dates. Roy Shire ran the Cow Palace in San Francisco. Jim Crockett had his big dates in Greensboro. At the NWA meeting in August, the promoters would bring me the dates that were very important to them, and I would weave a schedule for the

champion. Sometimes champions would want to be off a couple of days a week. Ric Flair, God bless him, worked every day, and double-headers on the weekends. He put the business first.

Outside of the territories where I was established, the fans didn't know me very well. If they felt a connection to my opponent, they were excited to see him have his shot at the NWA champion. If they weren't interested in my opponent, we weren't going to draw money.

The week after I won the title, I was scheduled to defend my title in Florida. Eddie Graham—the promoter there and supposedly the most creative mind in wrestling—disappeared. No one knew where he was. When Dusty resigned as the booker in Florida, I quickly figured out what was going on. They were mad about being outvoted. They wanted Florida to bottom out, so when I came down there, no one would turn up at the arena. Then they could say, "This guy Flair isn't over and doesn't draw."

J. J. Dillon was sworn in as the emergency booker. I spent a lot of time that week pouring him rum and Cokes. He didn't have any opponents for me. The Briscos weren't working in Florida at the time. Mike Graham, Eddie's son and a popular wrestler, quit. So I was booked with Charlie Cook, a mid-card guy who no one believed could win the championship. He tried hard, but the fans didn't care. I wasn't popular in Florida, and he wasn't popular, period. It was a horror to watch.

I was seeing a new side of the wrestling business. Dory Funk Jr., the former NWA champion, was the first one who told me that winning the title was not as glamorous as it seemed. You came back to the dressing room at the end of the night in some godforsaken city. Everyone else on the card had left, so you were the only one there. Nobody was around to say, "Good match, bad match, mediocre match." You showered, got dressed, walked into an empty parking lot, started your rental car, and either went back to the hotel or the next town.

But the actual wrestling part of the job gave me life. Since I was a bad guy most of the time, I'd win a lot of my matches with my feet on the ropes, or holding a handful of tights—reinforcing my standing as "the dirtiest player in the game" and leaving fans convinced that their local hero almost had me. This was important because my opponent couldn't lose his status as the number-one guy in the territory. He'd still have to draw fans to his matches after I packed up and left.

A lot of my matches would end in a one-hour draw. My opponent would have me trapped in his finishing hold or tied up on the canvas. The referee would raise his hand, slap the mat—one-two- . . . and the bell would ring just as the ref's hand hit the canvas a third time. As the fans erupted, sure that they'd just witnessed history, the ring announcer would inform them that the sixty-minute time limit had expired.

I did this so much that when I called myself a "sixty-minute man" in my interviews, part of me really *was* referring to wrestling. During my nine NWA title reigns, I can't count the number of guys who worked sixty-minute draws with me—Tommy Rich and Butch Reed and Jimmy "Superfly" Snuka, "Bullet" Bob Armstrong and Dick Slater and Harley, the Funks and Wahoo and Steamboat, Austin Idol and Dick Murdoch and Bulldog Bob Brown, Billy Jack Haynes and Dino Bravo and Ricky Morton, Dusty Rhodes, and Jack Brisco. (The Rock's dad, Rocky Johnson, under a mask). In 1987, I wrestled Ricky Morton in eleven one-hour draws in nine days. Then there were times when I did *two* sixty-minute draws in a single day. I once wrestled in Tampa early in the night, got on a chartered plane, and appeared last on a show in Raleigh.

Three hundred and eighty matches a year. And I loved it. I couldn't get enough of it.

SHORTLY BEFORE I won the title, Blackjack Mulligan and I had purchased a territory in Knoxville, Tennessee, from another wrestler, Ron Fuller, for $150,000. Jimmy Crockett gave us Roanoke and a bunch of towns in northern Virginia that he was too busy to run. Jim Barnett in Georgia was going to share talent with us. In our minds, it seemed like a pretty good deal, but what did we know? We were just a couple of dumb wrestlers.

JIM BARNETT: **Before Flair bought Knoxville, I owned the promotion for a while with some partners. We had a lot of problems. Our television station insisted on having us do a live show Saturday mornings. Well, we already taped the *Georgia Championship Wrestling* show in *Atlanta* on Saturday mornings. It was very difficult to have guys who were doing a program in Atlanta appear in Knoxville at the same time. And since I was busy with a lot of things in Atlanta, I just couldn't go to Knoxville all the time. We ended up giving it back to Ron Fuller. Actually, I think we ended up selling it back to him at a loss. I guess that's when Flair got involved.**

Blackjack Mulligan and I had tremendous matches and drew lots of money.

Like Wahoo McDaniel, Blackjack Mulligan had played for the New York Jets, though under his real name, Bob Windham. But while Wahoo had an Indian schtick, Mulligan became a cowboy, with a black hat and handlebar mustache. When we first met in the Charlotte territory, we became instant friends, buying a van to travel to shows together and homes on the same block. There was only one house separating us; that's how close we were. Jack's son, Barry Windham—my future tag-team partner and opponent—spent part of his childhood playing in my yard.

It was harder running a territory than I'd realized. And once I became NWA champion, I could only wrestle in Knoxville three or four times in a six-month period. That left Mulligan as the only marquee player. He was frustrated because he wanted more out of me, but I was on a calendar run by the NWA.

This is a typical wrestling story—within a year, we were out of business. Mulligan believed that Ron Fuller had set us up, and he was mad enough to kill him. He wanted me to be mad at Fuller, too, but Ron had a lot of power in the NWA, and I knew that I needed his support if I wanted to protect myself as champion. Needless to say, our relationship was never the same. To this day, I miss Blackjack Mulligan, and wish that the two of us could relive those years when I got on TV and called him "my main man . . . my best friend in wrestling."

I EARNED JUST about $200,000 during my first year as champion—far less than most fans thought. The only thing promoters paid for was my airfare; everything else—hotels, meals, rental cars, health insurance—was on me. So it wasn't a ton of money, and I was working really hard for it.

Every day, the pressure was on. Although I had the championship belt, I wouldn't be the main guy until I proved, night after night, that I was capable of wearing it. Later on, whenever I shouted, on interviews, "To be the man, you've gotta beat the man," I wasn't only addressing my opponents. I was talking to those other people in wrestling who couldn't wait for me to trip over my own feet.

Over time, the fans in the different territories accepted me as champion and got into my matches. Ted Turner's WTCG was now SuperStation TBS, where I appeared regularly on Saturday nights. In 1981 and 1982, the show was drawing a 6.6 rating, and was the most-watched program on cable television. I also traveled more than any

champion in NWA history, staying in a territory for a week at a time. In Kansas City, I'd check into the Crown Plaza and spend more on room service than I made that week. In Oregon, it was the Red Lion in Jansen Beach, in Dallas the Hyatt, and in Tampa the Hall of Fame. Throughout the week, I worked the promotion's big cards and appeared on the local television show. Every fifth week or so, I'd come home and work for Mid-Atlantic Wrestling.

The WWWF had changed its name to World Wrestling Federation, and on July 4, 1982, I had a Champion vs. Champion match against their title-holder, Bob Backlund, in Atlanta. I respected Bob as an amateur wrestler and as a guy who was a fanatic about conditioning. In his personal life, Bob was a great person, and every bit as clean-cut as the character he played on television. There was also a lot of political turmoil in wrestling at the time, so Vince McMahon Sr. knew that with a champ like Backlund, no one could double-cross him and take his title. (By contrast, when I wrestled Jumbo Tsuruta in Tokyo in 1983, Harley Race was sent over as my manager, just to make sure I walked out of the building as the NWA champion. I remember watching Harley sit in the corner for an hour; every time I landed near him, he'd bark, "Will you hurry up! There's cold beer waiting for us on the bus!")

In my match with Backlund, there was another issue—the World Wrestling Federation title didn't mean anything in Atlanta, just as the NWA championship didn't excite people in New York. When you've been repeatedly told that your guy is the only real champion, someone coming in with a different championship just doesn't hold much value.

In Puerto Rico, it was entirely different. The local World Wrestling Council (WWC) promotion was part of the NWA, and its owners, Carlos Colon and Victor Jovica, were big advocates of mine. When I came down to Puerto Rico, it was a major event. The fans there

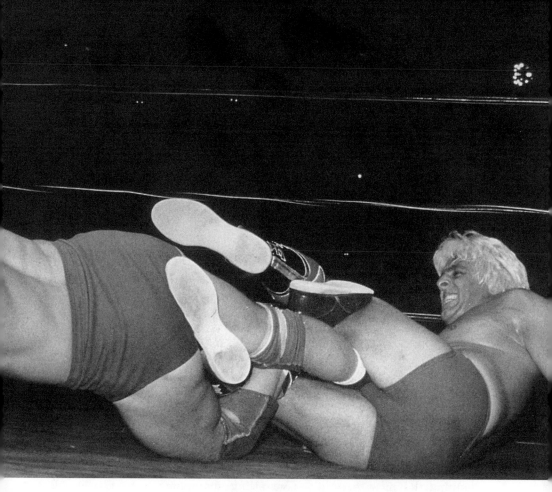

Atlanta's Omni was the spot for a rare Champion vs. Champion match with Bob Backlund.

were even more obsessed than Southerners. Outside Hiram Bithorn Stadium, vendors sold rocks for spectators to throw.

I had great times with Carlos Colon. After big shows in San Juan, he would rent out the best restaurants and play host to me. At one NWA convention in Reno, he and Victor Jovica lost $100,000 between them. In a gesture of goodwill, Jimmy Crockett bought them each a first-class ticket home . . . but not before treating Carlos and Victor to a trip to the Mustang Ranch, a legal brothel in Nevada.

Carlos was a first-class guy who ran a first-class territory and took good care of me. If he had one disadvantage, it was that—like wrestlers who ran promotions everywhere—he had to be the number-one attraction. In early 1983, when he was the WWC champ and I had the NWA title, we had a special match to determine a new "Universal" champion. My title wasn't at stake, so when I lost, it had no impact on the NWA championship. But—in Puerto Rico, at least—Colon could one-up the NWA by claiming that since he beat their champion, his Universal title was bigger.

A more unusual situation occurred in the Dominican Republic, where Colon and Jovica promoted with a fellow named Jack Veneno. The first time I traveled there, I didn't realize that I needed a passport. Since I didn't have one with me, people had to get paid off to get me into the country.

I checked into the Sheraton Hotel in Santo Domingo feeling a little disoriented because nobody spoke English. I was just settling into my room when George Napolitano, the wrestling magazine photographer, called. "Hey, Ric," he said in his Brooklyn accent, "look out the window."

Pulling open the window shade, I saw about 30,000 people going wild in the street. A guy who looked like a midget was jogging over a bridge, with the crowd cheering and jogging alongside him. It was like a scene from *Rocky*.

"Who the hell is that?" I asked George.

"That's the guy you're wrestling tonight."

Apparently my opponent, Jack Veneno, was training for the biggest match in his life—a chance to bring glory to the Dominican Republic by winning the most prestigious wrestling championship in the world. People had poured into the streets from all over the country. My God, it was unbelievable.

When I arrived at the arena, hordes of people were battling police outside; the promoters had oversold the building two or three times over! If the capacity was 10,000, there were 20,000 fans in the street, people who had purchased tickets and couldn't get in. In Santo Domingo, Ric Flair vs. Jack Veneno was bigger than the Super Bowl *and* the World Series. This was life and death.

Our finish was an example of what wrestling people call a "Broadway." Veneno had me in a sleeper hold. The referee picked up my arm, and it wilted. He picked it up a second time, and it flopped again. He picked it up a third time, and—just as my arm fell to the side, indicating that I was truly unconscious and Veneno had won—the bell rang.

What followed was a full-scale *riot*. People were throwing chairs and fighting with the military police. And they didn't know the actual finish. The spectators believed that Veneno had become the NWA champion, and they were jubilant. I can't imagine what it would have been like if they were *upset*. Everyone wanted to get into the ring to congratulate him. I didn't want to spoil anybody's fun, so I just left the championship belt in the ring. If Veneno felt like holding it over his head and pretending to be champion, that was fine with me.

HUGO SAVINOVICH, WWE SPANISH-LANGUAGE ANNOUNCER: I was working for the WWC and knew that if the ring announcer told the truth—that Veneno hadn't won—people would die. No one had any idea that this was showmanship. Everyone, even the athletic commissioners, believed that they had seen a legitimate wrestling match. The clock we used had stopped twenty seconds too early, and the commission wanted to see it, because if the match had gone twenty seconds longer, of course, Veneno really would be champion. El Puma, a wrestler who worked with Jack Veneno booking the matches in the Dominican Republic, took a hammer and broke the clock. He had to destroy the evidence, or there would have been riots in the country that even the military couldn't control.

I decided to leave the championship belt in the Dominican Republic; Jack Veneno tried to give it back to me in the dressing room, but I said, "Forget it. I'd rather leave alive."

No one in the United States knew about the apparent title switch, and it was never acknowledged in the NWA records. But the house had been so good that Colon and Jovica asked me to return. "Don't worry," they swore, "we'll secure you. Nothing like that will ever happen again."

"Okay," I said, "but I want to bring Piper with me."

HUGO SAVINOVICH: Flair and Piper created hell everywhere. If they were together, you were going to have combustion, whether it was in South Carolina or Santo Domingo. And these generals who ran the country, they thought wrestling was real. They were at the arena, and didn't want to see anything that would hurt their national pride. It was a *very* delicate situation.

The fact that our first match had been a no-decision was never reported in the Dominican press, so Veneno entered the ring wearing the NWA championship belt. Roddy Piper came out with me, waving the American flag and singing "God Bless America" in a high, obnoxious voice. The crowd was *screaming,* cursing the United States. It was even louder than the last time I was in that building. It was absolutely fuckin' crazy.

Veneno and I had worked out a finish where I would screw him out of the title. He began crisscrossing the ropes, and when he moved too close to the apron, Piper stuck his hand into the ring and tripped him. There were soldiers all over the building, and a good half-dozen of them picked up their rifles and pointed them at Piper's head. This was the spot where I was supposed to cover Veneno and steal the win, but I got so scared that I pulled him on top of me and yelled, "Pin me!"

"Qué dice?" Veneno was confused and began pulling away. I tugged him back toward me and held him over my body so he couldn't move. Then I looked at the referee.

"Count!" I screamed.

Taking note of the soldiers at ringside swinging their billy clubs at Piper, the ref got the picture and quickly slapped the mat three times. Veneno stood up, a little perplexed, while I kept shouting, *"Put on the belt! Do you hear me? You're the fuckin' champion! Wear the fuckin' belt!"*

Both uniformed and civilian personnel were hurtling through the ropes to go after me. I'm not sure how this happened, but in the middle of the mayhem, Invader #1—my friend Jose Gonzales, the WWC booker later accused of killing Bruiser Brody—ran into the ring and managed to rush both Piper and myself to the dressing room.

According to Dominican wrestling fans, Jack Veneno not only defeated Ric Flair for the NWA World Heavyweight Championship, but he retained the gold in a rematch. I don't know what local viewers were told the following week when Veneno came out on television without the title, because this time, when he offered me the championship belt backstage, I took it.

Piper and I waited until the crowds disappeared and, in the middle of the night, left the arena in an ambulance. For my effort, I was paid $5,000; Piper got five hundred bucks and a spittoon full of cocaine. The two of us retired to a nightclub, where I spent half of the money I'd just made. A few hours earlier, we were afraid for our lives, but now I was laughing out loud, watching Roddy shovel that shit up his nose—like Al Pacino in *Scarface* as the guerillas attacked the mansion—mumbling, "This is what I get when I travel with you. You get all the money, and I get this."

VICTOR JOVICA WAS considered an average wrestler everywhere in the Caribbean but Trinidad. Over there, for reasons I could never figure out, he was worshipped. It was strange—the audience was almost 100 percent black, and they loved this guy from Croatia who relocated to Puerto Rico. When we wrestled at the Jean Pierre Complex, the place was immediately sold out. But they do a lot of walk-up business in the Caribbean, and people were pissed off after they showed up with money and still couldn't get inside. I saw taxicabs being tipped over in the street. Cops were riding around on horseback, trying to break up the crowd, and someone shot a horse.

> **HUGO SAVINOVICH:** Flair and Jovica had their rematch at the national soccer stadium, and it was the same situation—people rioting because there weren't enough tickets. They shot at some cars, and one of the baby-faces from Trinidad—a big black wrestler named Thunderbolt Williams—actually went outside, punched one of the riot leaders, and knocked him out. Then he looked at the crowd as if to say, "You follow *me*, not him."
>
> Since there was no other way of knowing what was going on inside the stadium, about 20,000 people sat down outside and waited for information. After each match, some guy would stand up on the announcer's table, face the walls and shout out the finish over a microphone, just to keep the people outside at bay.

After the second Jovica match, I was asked to come back to Trinidad and wrestle Bruiser Brody. "I won't do it," I said. "Enough is enough."

The first time I saw Beth Harrell was around noon inside a restaurant at the Hilton Hotel in Raleigh. She was wearing a tube top, satin shorts, and a pair of knee-high socks. "Man, look at her," I told Blackjack Mulligan.

"You don't stand a chance," he scoffed.

"Watch me."

I tried taking up the challenge the next time I saw her. That was at the Embers, a club inside the Raleigh Hilton that was named after the local beach band. Beth and I talked a little bit, but I kept

CHAPTER 8

YOU'VE BEEN HERE BEFORE, AND WE'VE NEVER BEEN THE SAME

getting distracted by friends and fans. At the end of the night I left, assuming that this was one friendship I was not going to consummate.

BETH FLIEHR: I thought Ric was a pimp. There were about seven women with him, and he didn't look like a normal person. He had bleached-blond hair and was covered with jewelry. His suit was orange and blue, the colors of my football team at the University of Florida. But somehow, he didn't seem like a Gators fan.

"Who is that?" I asked my friend.

"Ric Flair," she said.

"I don't want to sound ignorant, but who's Ric Flair?"

"He's a wrestler."

At this point, Ric turned around, looked at me, and said something like, "Love of my life." He tried to make small talk, but didn't do a very good job. "Are you from around here?" he asked.

"No, I'm from Florida."

"Oh, Dusty Rhodes is pretty big in Florida. Do you like Dusty Rhodes?"

I didn't know who he was talking about. Ric asked me out. I told him I had a boyfriend. Ric really wasn't my type.

I fell in love with Beth the moment I first laid my eyes on her.

The Embers was one of my favorite places, and I ended up running into Beth whenever I was there (she was friends with the owner's wife). We were acquaintances for a long time, so I got to know her. She was from Tallahassee, and was modeling in commercials locally while trying to figure out whether she'd stay in North Carolina or go back to Florida.

At the time, Beth had dated a couple prominent business guys. I wasn't impressed then, nor am I now. Sometimes when we've argued, she's mentioned that she could have had a different kind of life with one of them. "Well, obviously, they were missing something," I've replied. "You tell me."

These former boyfriends are wealthy, successful guys, and fairly well known in Raleigh. But if they ever travel to Europe or Australia—

or even just out of North Carolina, for that matter—they'll need their American Express cards before anyone identifies them. And I'm not sure how well their DVD sets would sell, either.

BETH FLIEHR: Every time I would see him, Ric would say, "Hello, love of my life." It became a joke, and I began to think of him as a nice, funny guy. One night I was sitting with my friend, Barbara Davis, and she said, "You know, my kids are really big wrestling fans, but I'm embarrassed to go over to Ric Flair and ask for an autograph."

I told her, "No problem. I know him," and got the autograph.

Ric asked me to sit down at his table. I hadn't seen him for a while, and I noticed that he was tan. "Where were you?" I asked.

"Oh, I've been in Hawaii, shooting for *Playgirl* magazine."

I've used this line a lot over the years. Beth didn't even flinch. "Oh, when is it coming out?" she asked.

It was April, so I told her that I'd be in the November issue. That seemed to make sense.

"Did you really do that?" she said.

"Of course I did. What do you mean?"

"You're kidding. You posed naked in it?"

"Yeah. It's kind of embarrassing."

BETH FLIEHR: I really believed him. I mean, Ric's a good-looking guy and a pretty famous wrestler, so I guess *Playgirl* would be interested in someone like that. I was laughing about it with my girlfriend when Ric said, "You know, after the bar closes, a bunch of the guys are having a party in one of the hotel rooms. Would the two of you like to join us?" I thought, "Why not?" So we joined the party.

Beth and I ended up living together for a while. We were married in 1983 and, of course, we wanted to have children.

Jimmy Crockett was my best man, not Wahoo or Piper or either of the Briscos. Since I arrived in Charlotte nine years earlier, Jimmy had taken me under his wing and made me his franchise player. Now I was the NWA world champion, and it was all because of him. I honestly believed that I would be close to Jimmy forever.

As far as I was concerned, Beth and I had a happy life. She traveled with me to Japan, Singapore, Hong Kong, all through the Carribbean

and Europe. Once I flew Beth and two of her girlfriends to Hawaii for a week, while I was in Singapore and Japan. We always stayed at the Sheraton Waikiki in a suite, compliments of my good friend, hotel manager Dick Wood. I came back early, unannounced, walked out to the pool to surprise Beth. Guess who she was sitting poolside with? Tom Jones and Frankie Avalon. I was out of my mind and power-walked over to their side of the pool. I snapped my fingers and demanded to know what was going on. Beth replied, "Oh, they are such nice guys, they have been really friendly to us. Susan (Beth's friend) went out with Tom, but nothing happened." For the first time, Beth sounded like me talking to her! On the same trip, we met Tom Selleck and to this day, Beth will remind me of the fact that Magnum, P.I., must have made eye contact with her ten times.

MEGAN FLIEHR KETZNER: Beth didn't have any children of her own, and when we came to town, she'd have to nurse these two kids. If my dad wasn't around, we'd go roller-skating together. She'd make dinner for us. We just had a lot of fun.

Beth and I would sit together in the arena whenever my dad wrestled. You have to remember that most of his matches weren't these little ten- or fifteen-minute confrontations that they do now; these were full-out brawls for sixty minutes. He'd be getting backdropped, having his head smashed, and bleeding all over the place. I'd bite my nails and have to get up to go to the bathroom like three hundred times. Beth would sit next to me, hold my hand, and tell me that he was going to be okay. I didn't want him to get hurt, but everyone else there did.

On Christmas Eve, when I stayed over their house, they'd make me take a nap in the middle of the afternoon. They'd tell me that Santa came while I was sleeping, since he knew my dad had to wrestle that night.

There were no cell phones or pagers, so when it was Father's Day or my dad's birthday, I'd have to call Beth, and Beth would have to call him. If he was in the midst of traveling here or there, it could be a day or two before he got back to me.

I had some stepdaughter-stepmother issues—you know, wanting to be with my dad, and wondering why my dad wasn't home with us and my mom. I saw my mother working and living in a town house, and Beth with my dad in this nice, nice home. In my mind, her life looked good. Of course, I never thought about what it was like from her point of view, to have your husband traveling all the time and never be sure what he is really doing.

I lost my driver's license around the time that I married Beth, so she had to drive me everywhere. What happened was that I was drinking with Roddy Piper—who else?—and we began racing each other through downtown. Piper stopped as we came to a red light, but I pulled in behind him and pushed his car through the intersection. Neither of us noticed that the cops were parked right there. They told Piper to go home, and placed me under arrest.

Piper beat us to the police station, banging on the walls and screaming in that distinctive voice, "Let him out! Let him out!" The police let me have my one phone call, and I called my wife.

"I got arrested," I told her. "They got me on a DUI with Piper."

"Oh, you're with Piper?"

"Yeah, Beth, I'm under arrest."

"You have to come up with something better than that."

"What do you want me to come up with? I'm in jail."

I put one of the officers on the phone to explain my situation, but Beth wasn't buying it. "Who's that—another wrestler? It's three-thirty in the morning. Get home now."

For two years, from 1983 to 1985, I had to get rides with guys on the road. But when you lived the way I did, these kinds of things came with the territory.

ROBERT REMUS, AKA SERGEANT SLAUGHTER: We had a big show in Greensboro. Me and Don Kernodle wrestled Ricky Steamboat and Jay Youngblood in a cage, and Ric Flair had some kind of grudge match against Greg Valentine. It was jam-packed; something like 6,000 people were turned away at the door. The traffic was backed up out of town, on the highway. We lost the tag-team titles that night, and I was bleeding, Kernodle was bleeding, everyone was bleeding.

After the show, Flair decided that because of the turnout, he wanted to have a party. We went to about three different hotels and asked to rent the banquet room. And in each place they said, "No, Ric, we know who you are. You've been here before, and we've never been the same." Finally, I think it was the Hilton that allowed us to come in. Wrestlers were there, and we invited fans. Everyone was having a good time and drinking when Flair gets up and says, "It's time for this party to get rolling." He left and came back with his robe, and started doing quite a dance. I started to laugh so hard that the stitches busted open on my head. I lost my breath. If you've never seen Ric Flair do his dance, it's something you should pay to see.

Being the Nature Boy meant a lot of things, including not taking care of my business. I just went through life so fast. I bought whatever I wanted—a private plane, three condos in Florida, two condos in South Carolina, three Rolexes, a three-carat diamond ring, two hundred custom-made suits, and three hundred pairs of alligator shoes. At one stage, I even purchased two oil wells that I was told would soon yield a huge return in Texas. And I've already told you about the Knoxville territory I purchased with Blackjack Mulligan. From 1976 to 1991, I estimate that I bought one hundred kamikazes a week; that's nearly 80,000 kamikazes, in addition to all the beer, liquor, and wine that went on my tab.

Unfortunately, throughout the course of my career, I've also paid a million dollars in late penalties and interest to the IRS. I just hired one accountant after another. If one told me something that I didn't like, I'd say, "You're wrong," and fire him. I looked at myself as being invincible. I also suspect that—because I kept such poor track of my assets—at least one accountant embezzled money from me. But I couldn't prove anything.

I had just been sent a $130,000 tax bill before I was booked on a foreign tour. I'd already been away from home for five weeks, and now Giant Baba wanted me to work a series of three hour-long matches for his promotion in Japan. I got on the plane and just flipped. I was drinking the whole way and thinking to myself, I'm Ric Flair. I'm bigger than the business. Screw it. I'm not working.

I drank some more to confirm my thoughts, and when I landed at Narita Airport in Tokyo, I asked one of the ticket agents, "When's the next flight back to Chicago?"

"There's nothing to Chicago till tomorrow, but there's one going to Seattle right now."

Baba's wife, Motoko, was having me paged—"Flair-*san,* Flair-*san,* please report to baggage claim." I just boarded the Seattle flight.

On the way back, I turned to the guy next to me and poured my heart out. I told him my whole life story. I wish I had remembered his name, because I'd like to thank him, big-time, for being such a patient man. He felt so bad for me that I received Christmas cards from his family for about five years afterward.

In Seattle, I switched to a flight to Chicago. In Chicago, I transferred to a plane to Charlotte; I actually managed to get some sleep on that flight. Meanwhile, the wrestling world was in an uproar because the NWA champion was MIA.

As soon as I got to the terminal in Charlotte, I saw Beth and Jimmy Crockett waiting for me. Jimmy took me gently by the arm and turned me around. "Come on, Ric," he said. "We're going to Japan. I'm coming with you."

I didn't utter a word of protest. I kissed Beth good-bye and flew all the way back, over the continental United States and Pacific Ocean to Asia—and actually arrived at the building just before my first match.

Dick Slater was standing in the dressing room. "Dick," I told him, "I am completely flipped. Just come with me to ringside and talk to me, in case I have a nervous breakdown in the ring. I'm gone, man. Fried."

Once the bell rang, though, everything was fine. In time, Jimmy helped me solve my tax problem. Here's how: I literally sold myself to him, David Crockett, and George Scott. They each owned 10 percent of me, like a fuckin' racehorse. I paid them back the money I owed out of my checks—with 10 percent interest.

Eventually George left Crockett Promotions to work for Vince McMahon when Vince began expanding the World Wrestling Federation out of its northeastern territorial boundaries and putting other companies out of business. Jimmy needed a new booker, and I had the perfect guy: Dusty Rhodes.

Whatever rift we had over the 1981 NWA title change had passed, and we were close again. The stuff Dusty was doing as the booker in Florida was very innovative. I wrestled there one week a month, and we were always sold out. He was the hottest good guy in the country, and his presence was unreal. He could exhilarate the crowd by talking the working man's rap, telling tales about being the son of a plumber and digging ditches. "I've wined and dined with kings and queens," he said with poetic cadence, "and I've slept in alleys and dined on pork and beans."

Jimmy was a little hesitant; he had problems with Dusty for once missing a couple of dates. I went to his defense. "Dusty Rhodes sees wrestling shows as spectacles," I explained. "He can take us further than we've ever been."

With that, Dusty became our booker, and we were working together. But that didn't buy me any kind of guarantee with the NWA board. If you were champion, you had to be drawing—not just in the Carolinas, where we were selling out like crazy, but in Georgia, Dallas, and everywhere else.

Still, Harley Race had been playing this game a lot longer than I had. He owned a piece of the wrestling offices in St. Louis, Kansas City, and St. Joseph, Missouri, and had a lot of stroke. And in June 1983, he wanted the title back.

HARLEY RACE: That was when Vince McMahon was taking over the earth. Once the World Wrestling Federation branched out of the Northeast, the first place where he got television was St. Louis. This had been the NWA's headquarters since the mid-1900s, and now Vince was attacking the organization inside its home base. The decision was made that if we were going to be fighting a war, we had to put the title on someone who represented that part of the country. And that was me.

Whenever you lose the championship, you wonder, "What have I done wrong?" But if I had to drop the title, it was an honor to do it for Harley Race. Harley is the toughest man I've ever met, and he's afraid of no one. I've watched him wrestle hurt, yet never show it in the ring. He's the first guy I ever saw do a vertical suplex. When his opponent was sprawled out on the mat, Harley would go to the top rope and deliver a diving headbutt—every day for twenty years. That's a 250-pound man hurling himself through the air! The human body is *not* supposed to land that way.

Once, Harley and I were partying in a hotel room with Greg Valentine, Blackjack Mulligan, and Wahoo. Suddenly—and I don't remember what precipitated this—Mulligan sucker-punched Harley. The two began fighting and fell between two beds, and it took eight of us to break it up. Afterward, Jack, Harley, Wahoo, and myself got into a van and drove to Charlotte. It was the longest 110 miles of my life. No one uttered a sound. I kept waiting for Harley to spring on Mulligan, but they shook hands and made up, and Harley was man enough to take that kind of gesture seriously.

If a promoter wanted to put a bunch of athletes from any other sport into a room with a team of wrestlers, with the stipulation being that the first squad to fight it out gets paid, I'd send Harley in there with Mulligan, Dick Slater, Mad Dog Vachon, and Wahoo McDaniel. I guarantee you that, when it was over, the wrestlers would be counting the money.

We did the title change on June 10, 1983, in St. Louis. Harley lifted me up for a suplex; I shifted my weight in midair, rolled over his shoulder, and landed on my feet. Then I got Harley from behind and executed my own suplex. We crashed onto the canvas with our shoulders simultaneously pinned to the mat. As the referee counted, Harley lifted his arm at two, and became a seven-time NWA champion.

ALMOST IMMEDIATELY, JIMMY Crockett began planning for me to win back the title, and he wanted it done with style. He held a press conference for the local media and announced a rematch at the Greensboro Coliseum for November 24, 1983. Taking advantage of Dusty's grandiose imagination, the company staged something that went beyond being a show. It was an *event: Starrcade '83*. The card was stacked with matches like Carlos Colon, coming in from Puerto Rico, against

Harley Race tries to stop me from slapping on my finishing move, the figure-four.

Abdullah the Butcher; Rick Steamboat and Jay Youngblood against the Briscos for the NWA tag-team title; and Roddy Piper against Greg Valentine in a dog-collar match. Two years before the first *WrestleMania*, *Starrcade* was broadcast around the South on closed-circuit TV.

We spent a lot of time building up the card. I was portrayed as a straight-out good guy, representing the Carolinas. I've always been more comfortable as the antagonist, but this was an easy role to play.

In my eyes, Charlotte's the place that gave me my success. When I moved there in 1974, it was still a small southern city; you couldn't even buy liquor by the drink. We had auto racing and wrestling, and that was it. Since 1980, the city has almost doubled to a population of about 600,000, and—this comes from the Chamber of Commerce—140 people move to Charlotte every day. Throughout my life, I've had offers to relocate to other places, but once I got to Charlotte, I had no reason to leave. I raised my two youngest kids there and grew with the city. I remember promoters who wanted to announce my hometown as Minneapolis because Charlotte sounded "too small-market." Not to me. It's my home, and I love it.

Harley played the battered champion who was afraid of being unseated by the dynamic upstart. Like Triple H before his *Survivor Series 2003* match with Bill Goldberg, Harley appeared on TV holding a suitcase full of money and offering a bounty to the first person who took me out. The only difference between the two instances was that, in 1983, the dollar figure was $25,000, as opposed to $100,000 twenty years later. "Somebody take the money," Harley ordered in his raspy voice. "I want rid of Ric Flair."

Not long afterward, the two of us were wrestling in a televised match. I had Harley in the figure-four leglock when Bob Orton Jr.—Randy Orton's father—stormed the ring and jumped on me from the top rope. Dick Slater joined in, and the two of them gave me a spike piledriver. The attack was made even more emotional because Orton had been depicted as my intimate friend; a short time earlier he had even appeared on TV, holding Megan and David!

Fans were reminded of my plane crash and informed that my neck had been injured again. I announced my retirement, but then appeared to have second thoughts. While Slater and Orton were in a tag-team match one week, I flew out of the dressing room in my neck brace and street clothes, brandishing a baseball bat. I ran them off, then looked into the camera and shouted, "If you guys are gonna walk around telling the world that Ric Flair's done, you're out of your minds!" I tore off the brace. "You see, nothing matters to me! Yeah, the neck hurts, and I've paid the price, but I'm gonna stay. . . . And I promise you, Race, for paying those guys $25,000, I'll have a piece of you, and it's gonna be your gold belt."

The day of *Starrcade,* we had a major snowstorm throughout the Southeast, from Savannah all the way up to Charlotte. It killed us at the closed-circuit locations because people didn't go out. Spartanburg only had 1,000 fans, Greenville and Savannah about 2,000 each. In better conditions, all of those places would have drawn 8,000 or 9,000 people. In Greensboro, we still had 16,000 fans and a $500,000 gate, but we should have done a million dollars, total.

That wasn't the only crisis. The night before, Harley had a meeting with Vince McMahon in New York. Vince made Harley a proposal: skip *Starrcade* and jump to the World Wrestling Federation with the NWA title. Do you know what this would have done to the NWA and Jim Crockett Promotions in 1983? We would have collapsed.

HARLEY RACE: Vince offered me a quarter of a million dollars to work for him. I was drinking martinis, he was drinking Scotch. Pretty soon, we both had to go to the bathroom. There was a big mirror on the wall, and I asked Vince, "What do you see?"

Vince said, "I see you in the mirror."

I said, "Tomorrow morning, I have to get up and look at the same reflection."

Vince nodded his head. "Well, evidently, you've answered my question," he said.

"I hope so."

I was ready to lose the NWA title one last time. Truthfully, I was tired. I told myself, "I'm not going back out on the road anymore. I'm going to stay home and watch out for St. Louis and Kansas City. I'm going to protect it from Vince."

Everyone backstage was nervous until Harley came in around five o'clock. I knew that he would. Yes, he didn't want to lose the NWA title, and he realized that this was probably the last time he would have it. But he was such a man, and he didn't have it inside him to stand up the NWA.

I know that Jimmy Crockett offered him an extra $25,000 to show up and do the honors for me, so he took it. Good for him. He ended up with an extra twenty-five grand, and he was still Harley Race.

The theme of *Starrcade '83* was "A Flair for the Gold." It was so different than the first time I had won the championship. Now it was *my* night. The fans were into everything I did. We fought in a cage, with former NWA Champion Gene Kiniski as the referee. Harley wanted a bit of an out when he lost, so we had Kiniski fall on all fours in the ring. At that moment, I came off the ropes with a flying body press and hit Harley, and he tumbled over Kiniski's body. Gene crawled around and counted, "One . . . two . . . three!"

Several of the other good guys—Ricky Steamboat, Angelo Mosca, Jay Youngblood, Rufus R. Jones, and Johnny Weaver—ran into the cage and picked me up on their shoulders. The moment was planned, but I think a lot of these guys were genuinely happy for me. So were the fans. They stood up on their chairs and chanted, "Two! Two! Two!" in tribute to my second reign.

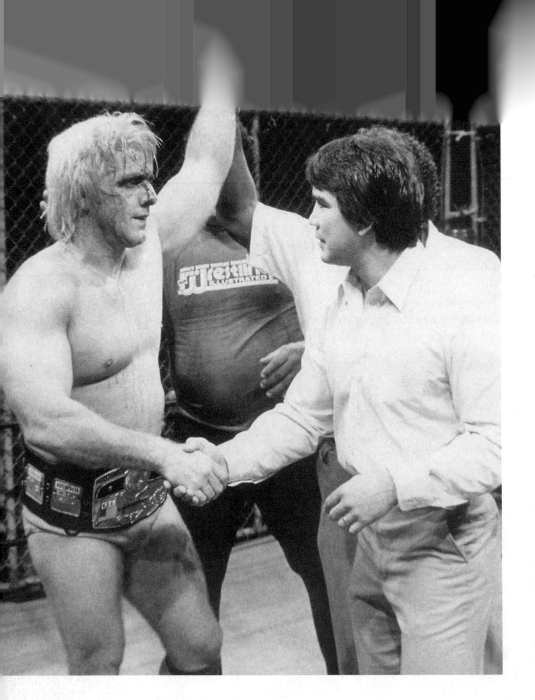

I have to admit, I was touched. Beth was brought into the ring, and she gave me a hug. There were tears mixing with the blood on my face when I told the fans, "This is the greatest night of my life. And thank you, *thank you* very much."

This was *real* to me.

"I'm the kind of guy you could put the whole world around, and I can support every part of it," I'd brag in an interview before flying into Dallas to wrestle Chris Adams or Gino Hernandez; Portland to work with Rip Oliver or "Playboy" Buddy Rose; or Mobile to battle Robert Fuller or Jimmy Golden. "I'm not a movie actor—better looking than most of them. I'm not a rock star, but I can dance and sing my fanny off. I just happen to be a kiss-stealing, wheeling, dealing, limousine-riding, jet-flying son-of-a-gun that you know to be—*Woooo!*—the World's Heavyweight Wrestling Champ, customly called Slick Ric Flair."

CHAPTER 9

ANY KIND OF HEAT I CAN GET

MICHAEL HICKENBOTTOM, AKA SHAWN MICHAELS: I've stolen a bunch from Ric Flair. It's very simple: if you want to be the best, you need to go to the best and take from the best. When Ric was around, I asked. When he wasn't, I just took what was fantastic about him—his delivery, the hair, the clothes. It was intoxicating. I wanted to become that guy. So I stole it. Blatantly stole it.

JIM "J.R." ROSS, MID-SOUTH, WCW, AND WWE ANNOUNCER: If all wrestlers were artists, Ric Flair would be Picasso and everyone else would be using finger paints. Ric was a gourmet chef, and the other guys were short-order cooks. When Ric came to your territory, he'd elevate your resident stars to a higher level through their association with him. You'd get a better TV rating and—as my old boss, Bill Watts, used to say—an ass every eighteen inches.

In Quebec City one night, Rick Martel and I headlined a twelve-match show and didn't get into the ring until just after midnight. Most fans are pretty close to exhausted by ten-thirty and don't appreciate being forced to stay in their seats past a certain hour. But the local promoters didn't want a French boy to lose in his hometown, and no one could agree on a finish. So you know what we did? We gave the people a phenomenal sixty-minute match.

Unfortunately, for every Rick Martel, there's a Rufus R. Jones.

Rufus, aka "The Freight Train," was a large black wrestler. When we worked together in the Carolinas in the 1970s, I'd get the crowd riled up by calling him "a big, ugly, black bear" or a "big, ugly dummy." Rufus particularly thought it was funny when I'd refer to him as "Kunta Kinte," the character from *Roots*. Could you imagine if we did something like that now?

Jones came from Dillon, South Carolina, and once, when we were in the area, he got a whole jug of moonshine and challenged Piper, "How would you like to get drunk on some *real* liquor?" The next morning, Piper walked into the TV studio to tape our show—slightly hungover, but ready to go. He looked around the dressing room; no Rufus. We later found out that the cops were called to a spot where the wrestlers met alongside the highway, and they found Rufus passed out on the hood of his Cadillac, at the Kentucky Fried Chicken!

I loved Rufus as a person—and he was a huge regional star—and it was fun to wrestle him for twenty minutes. Beyond that, though, there was very little that you could do with him. There were a staggering two hundred fans in the arena one night in Hutchinson, Kansas, when I was asked to wrestle an hour-long draw with him. I was running out of ideas on how to make the match entertaining, so I put Rufus in the figure-four and had him reverse it. When I got up, I acted like my legs were all wobbly. The referee then said something to piss me off, and I shoved him. The ref shoved me back, and because my legs were supposed to be weak, I fell backward. It got the biggest reaction of the night.

Buck Robley, the booker in the territory, was fuming backstage. "You're the NWA champ!" he yelled. "You don't bump for the referee! That's cheap heat!"

"Tomorrow, you try wrestling Rufus R. Jones for an hour!" I shouted back. "I'm taking any kind of reaction I can get!"

And that's exactly what I kept on doing. In Hayes, Kansas, I defended my title against Mark Romero for an hour in the parking lot of a Pontiac dealership, in the rain and while people walked around looking at used cars. In the same territory, I wrestled in a cow pen at three in the afternoon, changing in an outhouse, slogging through the mud to the ring, and literally showering in a horse stall. The match was part of a carnival. Once you paid your admission, you had several choices: go on the Ferris wheel, knock someone in the dunking tank, or watch Ric Flair defend his NWA World Heavyweight title.

After another match with Rufus, I came back to the dressing room, and everyone was gone. I looked all over the place, but couldn't find my robe. I began pacing around the backstage area, wondering if one of the ring attendants had misplaced it, when I heard some noise coming from the parking lot. Peering out the window, I spotted some kid modeling my $4,000 robe for his friends! Before I could say a word, he looked me straight in the eye and gave me the finger.

What was I going to do—run downstairs in my trunks and start chasing a bunch of laughing teenagers through the streets? There had been zero security in the building, and predictably, promoter Bob Geigel never offered to reimburse me for the theft. How could I have expected anything more? He was one of the cheapest men of all time.

PROTOCOL DICTATED THAT, as NWA champion, I would be announced to the crowd *after* my opponent. This system of etiquette was based on the notion that the champ was the most important guy on the card. Now, it's a different universe. In 2003, I was teaming with Randy Orton and Triple H in some type of Six-Man Tag match. Triple H was the world champion, but we came out first. When one of our opponents, Shawn Michaels, entered the ring, we stepped through the ropes so he could strut to his entrance music. I can't even imagine what Harley Race would have done if somebody suggested, "Hey, Harley, leave the ring. Shawn needs to parade around in his chaps." It's just one example of how wrestling has changed.

Today's fans don't value the importance of the world championship as much as they used to. Truthfully, though, the erosion was beginning when I first held the title. A few times in Alabama, I remember local stars like the Fuller brothers and Bob Armstrong suggesting that they be announced last, or they'd want the hour-long draw reduced to thirty minutes. I'd have to tell them, "Sorry. That's not the way we do it."

Prior to Sam Muchnick resigning as NWA president in 1975, a local promoter wouldn't dare screw around with the champion. If he did, all it took was one call to St. Louis. Sam wielded real power and would unequivocally state, "Absolutely not. You do it our way, or the champ doesn't wrestle tonight." Before you even had the champion lose via disqualification, there first had to be written approval from the board.

By the early 1980s, Bob Geigel was NWA president. I'd arrive in a town, and the promoter would want to play with a finish. I'd call Geigel, who would be somewhere in his shower shoes with a toothpick in his mouth. "Well, what do you want to do, Ric?" he'd ask, throwing the thing back in my ballpark. He just didn't want to deal with the trouble, so I'd be forced to insist that the match either go to a draw or—if my opponent wasn't good enough to wrestle a full hour—I won. Still, I blame myself for making certain concessions only because I wanted to avoid a confrontation.

When Dusty was booking in Florida, you couldn't beat him there, so he'd have to go an hour in every championship challenge. Fritz Von Erich didn't want his kids losing in Dallas, or even in St. Louis because it was an NWA showcase. The more we caved in to these types of demands, the more diminished the credibility of the NWA title became.

There were some things that I didn't mind at all. When Dusty lost a "Loser Leaves Town" match in Florida, he returned as a masked man

Dusty Rhodes, "Midnight Rider," was the world's worst-kept secret, and a great storyline.

in a full bodysuit and called himself "The Midnight Rider." The Rider spoke and acted exactly like Dusty, so the fans believed that he was putting one over on his enemies. (Hulk Hogan did the same thing in WWE as "Mr. America" in 2003.) On February 9, 1983, the Midnight Rider beat me for the championship. But because of a purported rule that banned hooded wrestlers from holding the title, NWA president—and special referee—Bob Geigel ordered the Midnight Rider to either unmask or return the championship belt. As a result, the championship was surrendered back to me.

Without a doubt, Dusty's ego demanded that he beat everybody, including the champion. But he was so wildly popular, and the Midnight Rider was a really good concept. We both had fun with the character.

In March 1984, Harley and I were on an international tour when he and New Zealand promoter Steve Rickard came up with a more controversial idea. I'd drop the title to Harley in Wellington, New Zealand, then win it back three days later in Kallag, Singapore. Harley swore all the boys to secrecy because nobody from the NWA board knew anything about this. I was a little worried, but it was Harley's call. "What are they gonna do?" he reasoned.

HARLEY RACE: The NWA thing was kind of half-assed falling apart, and we wanted to draw the best we could in Singapore. Coming into Singapore with a new champion and giving the title back to Ric would be different than anyone expected. But nobody knew that [Houston promoter] Paul Boesch was going to be in Wellington. He ran right to the telephone and called the guys on the NWA board. By the time anybody got to us, the title was already switched back to Ric, so they all pretended that it never happened.

For most of his career, Fritz Von Erich played a Nazi. But by the early 1980s, he was a Bible-quoting born-again Christian who promoted in Dallas, using his sons—David, Kerry, and Kevin—as the territory's top good guys. He'd been taking them to NWA conventions since they were teenagers, and describing them as future champions. Years later, after the family suffered a chain of catastrophes, people accused Fritz of pushing his kids into the wrestling business. But I can tell you this—Kevin and Kerry weren't forced into anything; they were good athletes, and they wanted it. And David Von Erich would have been an NWA champion and could have carried it.

I first met David in Florida, where Fritz had sent him to work as a bad guy and learn his craft. He became a good performer very quickly, and we had a lot of great times.

I expected David to be part of my life for years, but on February 10, 1984, he was found dead in his hotel room in Japan. The official story was that David had been hit with a kick in the ring the night before—though in reality he had yet to wrestle his first match on the tour—and died of acute enteritis, a severe inflammation of the intestines. Everybody in wrestling believes that he overdosed, and that Bruiser Brody flushed a bunch of pills down the toilet before the police arrived.

This was the first of many drug deaths in wrestling that, unfortunately, continue to this day. A lot of people, including my good friend Roddy Piper, have blamed the wrestling business for this. They're wrong. Cocaine, uppers, and downers are recreational drugs that a lot of people in our society elected to do in the 1980s. Yeah, too many wrestlers got hooked. But not me.

I drank tons of vodka and Crown Royal and beer and wine. I could sit around a table and drink kamikazes until everyone else's head hit the floor. But I never smoked marijuana or experimented with pills, and three decades in the wrestling business couldn't change that. When I was growing up, my dad got it through my head that drugs were the end, so I stayed away from them. It was a matter of individual choice.

HUGO SAVINOVICH: Ric Flair never liked drugs, and I think there's a reason for this. You didn't need drugs when you were with Ric Flair. Ric *was* the drug.

In Fritz's promotion—World Class Championship Wrestling—the roster consisted of a group of young guys with money in their pockets who made bad choices. Sadly, Terry "Bam-Bam" Gordy, Gino Hernandez, and Chris Adams are all dead now. Everyone knew that the Von Erich brothers were messed up all the time. But Fritz wouldn't recognize the problem. He was in denial.

Once David died, Fritz worked to make Kerry into a champion. They called him the Modern Day Warrior, and he had a great look, with long, feathered hair and the best body I'd seen in our business to that point.

This is where writing a book like this becomes very personal and very touchy. Like most people in wrestling, I was very fond of Kerry. But the simple truth was that he was drug-impaired *all* the time, whether it was eight in the morning or after midnight. You'd talk over your match, and then he'd come over to you before you walked through the curtain, asking, "What are we doing, again?" He'd ask questions about things you never discussed. And in the ring, he'd give you his specialty—the Iron Claw—out of nowhere, when it made no sense to the story you were trying to build. It didn't matter; Fritz had so much stroke that all the rules were broken for Kerry. But it was much more serious than the issues of the relationships. Fritz just wouldn't accept the reality of Kerry and his brothers' personal problems.

In 1985, I wrestled Kerry for an hour at the Will Rogers Coliseum, a rodeo arena in Fort Worth, in a match for KTVT's Saturday-night show. In terms of excitement, we did okay; Kerry was so popular in Texas that the people pretty much reacted to whatever he did. Technically, though, I'd characterize this as the one of the worst matches of my life.

I got to the ring first and stood there about ten minutes, waiting for Kerry. Nobody knew where he was; it was embarrassing. Eventually, someone looked in the cattle area outside the Coliseum and found him passed out in his Lincoln. When he finally made it to the ring, I noticed that his boots were open. He wrestled for an hour with the laces untied.

The first thing Kerry did was look at referee Dave Manning and ask if he knew where a certain girl was sitting. "Hey, Kerry, get a grip," I said. "We got an hour to go here."

Next I had him shoot me off the ropes, lift me up, and press-slam me. My fear was that, in Kerry's state, he would drop me the wrong way, but to his credit, he was very safe. As the bad guy, I was supposed to beg off or roll out to ringside. But while I was lying on the canvas, I turned around and saw Kerry walking around in the front row.

"Where'd he go?" I asked Manning.

"He's looking for that girl."

"Well, fuck, get him back in here!" I yelled.

I'd estimate that things went that way for about thirty minutes, with Kerry completely distracted and me trying to get his head into the match. During an attempted hip-toss, my strategy called for him to stiffen up his body, then hip-toss me instead. But he just kind of stood there, trying to figure out what was going on, and the two of us tumbled onto the canvas like a couple of kids. Another time, I was facedown on the mat in a hammerlock, and Kerry was supposed to spring up and swing a knee into my arm. Instead he lost his balance, fell on his ass, and kneed me in the head. When he tried a sunset flip, he grabbed some imaginary person and rolled onto the canvas with him while I stood there, watching in astonishment.

It all became so pathetic that I actually put *myself* into holds. I placed Kerry in a figure-four, then turned over like he reversed it. I fastened on a headlock, then took his hand and clamped it on my arm while I ducked around, making it look like he was powering out of the maneuver.

When the time limit expired, I stomped into the dressing room and threw the NWA title at the World Class booker, Ken Mantell. But that wasn't enough to motivate somebody into having that long-overdue sit-down with Kerry. In fact, the enabling hit a ridiculous level—the next day, Fritz arranged a story in the newspaper about how his brave son fought a 105-degree fever and the NWA World Champion on the same night.

Regardless of Kerry's condition, the two of us always packed the house. In 1982, we drew the first $100,000 gate in Texas history, and also sold out in places like Hawaii and Japan. So when Fritz requested that Kerry beat me for the NWA Championship at a special David Von Erich memorial show, the NWA board went along with him.

The event, held May 6, 1984, at Texas Stadium, was called *The David Von Erich Memorial Parade of Champions*. We drew 32,123 fans who paid $402,000 for a card that included Fritz coming out of retirement to team with Kevin Von Erich and a younger son, Mike, against the Freebirds, an incredibly exciting trio with a rebel rocker attitude. The atmosphere was feverish. The sun was beating down so hard, it felt like it was 130 degrees on the field. All day long I stood there, watching EMTs pick people up off the ground and load them onto stretchers. There was genuine emotion over David's death, and when a local girl got into the ring to sing a self-composed song called "Heaven Needed a Champion," the whole stadium was in tears.

This was Kerry's chance to win the title that had been waiting for his brother, and no one wanted him to fuck up. So I told him to beat me with a backslide—a relatively simple move in which he'd hook my shoulders from behind and roll me onto the mat. Why lay out some elaborate finish, I thought, that Kerry's going to forget anyway? On this particular day, Kerry remembered my instructions, and the people in Texas were ecstatic.

Nonetheless, virtually every promoter understood that having Kerry as anything but a short-term champion was a liability to the NWA. From the moment he won the title, the plan was for me to take it back eighteen days later in Yokosuka City, Japan. For all his addictions, Kerry had a sweet-natured personality, and it hurt to see how sad he was about losing. There really was no other choice, though; in another time, a guy like him would have never been considered for the championship in the first place.

After Kerry's loss, the Von Erichs' misfortunes just steamrolled. Mike Von Erich, who had neither the body, the skill, nor the charisma to be in the ring, contracted a fever that rose to deadly levels through toxic shock syndrome. Fritz rushed him back into the ring much too fast; Mike was underweight and appeared to have some sort of brain damage, slurring his words in interviews. Like his brothers, Mike also had substance abuse issues, and after police pulled him over and discovered a variety of drugs, he felt terrible about embarrassing the family. On April 12, 1987, he wrapped himself in a sleeping bag and killed himself with an overdose of Placidyl.

The youngest Von Erich, Chris, had been hanging out in World Class dressing rooms since he was barely a teenager, wearing the same fringed outfits as Kerry and boasting about drug and sex exploits like the rest of the boys. He'd been billed as the future of the Von Erich family, but Chris had some limitations. He was short and chubby, and had to take an asthma medication that made his bones brittle and susceptible to fractures. In 1991, after World Class's fortunes had long faded, Chris—heartbroken over the loss of his brothers as well as the knowledge that his wrestling career was going nowhere—shot himself to death.

Kerry lost part of his foot in a motorcycle accident in 1986, but continued wrestling—showering with his boot on so the other boys wouldn't realize the severity of his injury. In 1990 he entered the World Wrestling Federation as "The Texas Tornado" and did all right for a while, even winning the Intercontinental Championship from Curt Hennig. Eventually, though, his problems caught up with him; he was suspended for missing dates and failing a drug test, then arrested for forging prescriptions. Kerry promised to go through rehab, but in 1993 he was busted again—this time for cocaine possession—and faced jail time for violating the terms of his parole. On February 18, 1993, he took his own life by shooting himself in the chest on the family ranch.

When Fritz died of cancer in 1997, Kevin was the only surviving Von Erich brother. It's easy for people to look at this tragedy and say that the Von Erichs died because they were professional wrestlers. That's not how I see it. *Drugs*—not wrestling—killed the Von Erichs. I also wish that Fritz had opened his eyes and held his kids accountable for their behavior. If he had, I think those boys would still be alive.

With the kind of houses that we were drawing, I never looked at Vince McMahon, or the World Wrestling Federation, as a threat to the NWA. But it seemed like everyone else did. In 1984, Jack and Jerry Brisco stunned the entire NWA organization by selling Vince their stock in Georgia Championship Wrestling, allowing him to take over their slot on SuperStation TBS. Vince now had national exposure, and he signed away wrestlers from established NWA promoters and began staging cards in their home cities. I heard a lot of wrestlers say they were going to kick the Briscos' asses. Twenty years later, nobody has yet, and I see Jerry every Monday at *Raw*.

CHAPTER 10
THINGS ARE TAKING PLACE

GERALD "JERRY" BRISCO: Jack and I wanted to expand Georgia Championship Wrestling to other parts of the country, but because of the NWA rules about where you could promote, we were limited. We were allowed to go into Ohio and Michigan because the promoter there—Ed Farhat, the original Sheik—had driven that territory into the ground, but we couldn't go anywhere else, and it was frustrating. Meanwhile, Vince McMahon was promoting shows anywhere he liked, and we concluded that if we didn't make a deal soon, he was going to put us out of business.

The World Wrestling Federation had gotten Paul "Mr. Wonderful" Orndorff from Georgia, Roddy Piper from Jim Crockett, and Hulk Hogan—along with announcer "Mean" Gene Okerlund and manager Bobby "The Brain" Heenan—from the AWA. A group of us were sitting in Crockett's office, talking about it, and someone mentioned that Piper had injured his finger. We heard that it was a severe injury, but we didn't know how severe. Finally, my brother Jack just said, "Hell, I'll call Vince myself and ask him." And that's what he did.

Jim was still sitting in the room when Vince asked Jack on the phone, "How would you like to sell me your Georgia stock?" Jack arranged to continue the conversation later, and Vince sent us a pre-paid ticket to New York for a meeting the next day at LaGuardia Airport. We told him that we could get most of the other stockholders to go along with us, and essentially we put TBS in Vince's hands.

It was treason. Jack had been an NWA champion, and both of us were NWA insiders. Before we left to work for Vince, we had a few commitments to finish out. I'll never forget that we were part of the card, a sold-out house at the old Cleveland Auditorium, and the match was Jack and I against the Road Warriors. There was a lot of uneasiness backstage, and we knew that we had to stick close together. About forty-five minutes before the match, Road Warrior Animal asked to talk with us, so we went off to a far corner of the building. "You guys better watch your backs," he said. "We've been offered $5,000 to hurt you, but we're not those kinds of business people."

Paul Jones warned us about a death threat. "I don't know how true this is," he said, "but I heard that somebody's been hired to shoot you guys."

At the body shop we owned in Tampa, my partner started receiving calls that the place was going to be burned down, and that he should watch the Briscos because they would screw him like they screwed the NWA. Meanwhile, my wife had been called by two young ladies who each claimed to be pregnant with my baby; I guess I had been a pretty busy boy. Both of the women suggested that my wife divorce me.

For about eight months, I just never knew what was waiting around the corner. To this day, a lot of people say that sale changed the course of history for the industry.

WHEN FANS TURNED on the Saturday-night wrestling show on TBS and didn't see any of the NWA wrestlers there, they were pissed, and began bombarding the station with phone calls and letters. As a result, Ted Turner allowed Ole Anderson to produce his own *Georgia Championship Wrestling* show for the network, but his slot was early in the morning, and really no challenge to Vince.

On March 31, 1985, McMahon presented the first *WrestleMania* at Madison Square Garden. *Starrcade* was a great concept, but this went even further. Liberace danced with the Rockettes in the middle of the ring. Pop star Cyndi Lauper managed Wendi Richter when she beat Leilani Kai for the women's title. In the main event, Hulk Hogan teamed with television hero Mr. T against Paul Orndorff and Roddy Piper. As with *Starrcade,* the show was offered to fans on closed-circuit television, but this wasn't just in one pocket of the country, it was all over North America. And for the first time, a wrestling card was available on Pay-Per-View, establishing the World Wrestling Federation as the leader in that brand-new field.

The public response to *WrestleMania* was enormous, and the press covered it like there was no other wrestling organization in the world. But I didn't even watch the show. Yes, I was happy for Piper, Bob Orton Jr., Greg Valentine, and other friends who were part of it, but I didn't see those guys as bigger than me. The World Wrestling Federation Champion was chosen by one man. To win the NWA title, you needed *nine* individuals to pick you. That meant that you *had* to be better than everyone else, and if you weren't, they took it away from you.

"When you talk about professional wrestling," I said in one interview, "there's only one man who you can legitimately look at your neighbor, look at your daughter, look at your wife, and look in the mirror, and talk about being the best. There's only one." I then held my

Partying in limousines–all in a night's work for
the World Heavyweight Champ.

championship belt up for the camera and said, "And this is it—the
World Heavyweight Championship. *Wooooo!* As I've said so many times
before, custom-made—Oleg Cassini, Ralph Lauren—that's what Ric
Flair's all about. You see, I'm gonna ride in that big Mercedes. And I'm
gonna live in that big house. And I'm gonna—*Wooooo!*—all the beautiful
women, as long as I am the number-one man. . . . I don't care if it's
Baltimore, Philadelphia, Charlotte, North Carolina, Greensboro, L.A.,
Chicago—you know that when *my* name's on the marquee . . . you're
stylin' and profilin'."

Back then, I didn't understand the World Wrestling Federation's
marketing and merchandising strategy. God only knows what kind of
money I could have made if I had left the NWA in 1985. Sure, Hulk
Hogan was on top, but in the ring, he wasn't my peer. How could he
have held me down?

**JIM CORNETTE, 1980S NWA MANAGER: There was no comparison
between Ric Flair and Hulk Hogan. Hulk Hogan may have been the big**

star and made a lot of fuckin' money. But Ric Flair was the man, and we were on the man's team.

We saw the publicity for the World Wrestling Federation. We watched the glitzy Pay-Per-Views. We heard about the action figures and the ice-cream bars and the toys and shit. But we were hard-hitting, gritty, and emotional. We'd tell ourselves, "We go in the ring and tear the house down, and give the people their money's worth. We're better at what we do." And we were.

Here's the fundamental difference between Hulk Hogan and myself: Hogan told his fans, "Train, say your prayers, and take your vitamins." *My* motto was, "Drink, party all night, and love all the ladies."

MIKE MOONEYHAM, PRO WRESTLING COLUMNIST: Any discussion of Ric Flair inevitably invites a comparison with Hulk Hogan. The two have been dominant figures in the sport over the past two decades and have helped shaped the course of the industry. Rick Flair is loved, adored, and admired by the wrestling public. Ric's not bigger than pro wrestling, as Hogan once portrayed himself. Ric Flair *is* pro wrestling, and he loves the sport with an undying passion. The word *icon* is loosely used in many circles, but it's no exaggeration in the case of the Nature Boy.

Occasionally I'd allude to the comparisons between us during my interviews, calling myself "the measuring stick"—as in, "You can't measure me. I *am* the stick, baby." I always had the sense that Hogan had to lobby to keep his spot every day—unlike Stone Cold Steve Austin and The Rock, who grew into their positions in a more natural way in the late 1990s. At one time, I believe Piper could have been as hot as Hogan; he was a better interview and a better worker. Had Vince decided to make him champion, they would have drawn a lot of money.

Other guys were just lucky to be working for the company. With Hogan headlining the show, anybody wrestling on the card shared his glory. Where would the Honky Tonk Man have been if he hadn't been employed by Vince McMahon? Jake "The Snake" Roberts was a very good worker, but when he wrestled in the Carolinas, the fans looked at him as a marginal guy. Vince had him chase Andre the Giant around with a snake, and now Jake was a superstar. In reality, he was just one part of the World Wrestling Federation machine.

Still, we were holding our own. Dusty Rhodes and I were the main event at *Starrcade '85*. The show was simulcast from two separate locations—Atlanta and Greensboro—and drew $936,000. Wherever I traveled, I did what I could to help Jimmy Crockett build the territory. For example, I persuaded two of the best tag teams in the business, the Midnight Express and Rock'n'Roll Express, to relocate to Charlotte from Bill Watts's territory in Oklahoma and Louisiana. My selling point wasn't just the money, but the quality of life. In Louisiana, the guys were making long, hard trips on two-lane highways—traveling 3,500 miles a week, by one estimation. In North Carolina, we traveled less and made more.

Jimmy also managed to wrest possession of TBS away from Vince. When Turner made his deal with the World Wrestling Federation, he expected original programming from the TBS studio. Instead, he got repackaged matches from other places, and was ready to sue Vince off the network. Before this could happen, Jimmy insinuated himself into the mix, offering to buy the slot from Vince. Reportedly, Crockett paid McMahon a million dollars, but got 80 million potential viewers—and the advertising revenue they brought along—in return.

Because of TBS, we were able to join up with the AWA and invade the Meadowlands in New Jersey, just across the Hudson River from McMahon's command center at Madison Square Garden. But the notion of the NWA and AWA working together wasn't a very sensible one. Vince once joked that the different promoters could agree that they hated him and wanted to put him out of business, but after that, they couldn't even agree on what to order for lunch. Still, I enjoyed wrestling against AWA champions like Rick Martel and Curt Hennig. Martel had a million-dollar look and could perform as smoothly as Steamboat when he wanted to; that's the best compliment I can pay anyone. And at one time, Hennig was one of the ten best performers in wrestling.

As the old NWA system began disintegrating, Jimmy filled the void, updating the look of the World Championship belt and making me available to different promoters only when he saw fit. In 1985, Crockett Promotions merged with Georgia Championship Wrestling, a company that—because of Turner's fear about sounding too regional—had been renamed World Championship Wrestling (WCW). The next year, he took over St. Louis. The year after that, Florida. Soon, Jimmy was promoting everywhere.

Many people in the wrestling business may have detested Vince McMahon, but Jimmy Crockett shared many of the very same traits. Both men were born into the wrestling business, clawed their way past the old-timers who wouldn't give them respect, and now had their former detractors coming to *them*.

HARLEY RACE: There used to be twenty-eight promotions throughout North America. No one particular person was in charge; the NWA was. When Crockett began taking over, the other twenty-seven promotions became the poor stepchildren to the people in Jimmy's home office. I had put so much money into Kansas City and St. Louis, but I could no longer keep it afloat. So I cut my losses and started wrestling for Vince.

In 1985, Arn and Ole Anderson, Tully Blanchard, and myself formed a bad-ass clique on Crockett's programs. Arn had replaced Gene Anderson in the Minnesota Wrecking Crew and was also billed as my cousin. He was a young guy with the same kind of roughhouse style as Ole, but he was actually a much better wrestler and talker. Tully, the son of San Antonio promoter Joe Blanchard, had been the quarterback at West Texas State on a team that included Merced Solis (Tito Santana) and "Million Dollar Man" Ted DiBiase. Blanchard was a gifted worker who dressed well, so he could style and profile with the Nature Boy. The four of us didn't have a name yet, but Dusty, as the booker, portrayed us as a violent gang, constantly getting involved in each other's business and beating down the good guys.

One night in Atlanta, I was in a cage match against Nikita Koloff, a pumped-up monster with a shaved head who liked his Russian persona so much that he legally changed his name from Scott Simpson. This was in the middle of the Reagan administration, when the Soviet Union was still the "Evil Empire," and I was getting more cheers than boos. When I won the match, Nikita's "uncle," Ivan Koloff, ran into the cage, and the two of them ganged up on me. Then a third Russian, Krusher Khrushchev—a fellow Minnesotan named Barry Darsow, who later worked in the World Wrestling Federation as Demolition Smash, and as Repo Man—held the door shut so I couldn't escape. During the melee, Dusty Rhodes came running down to the ring in his street clothes, hitting the Russians with bionic elbows and sending them scurrying back to the dressing room.

Dusty and I were now alone in the cage. Fans expected some type

Using the ropes for leverage is only one of many tricks that have established me as "the dirtiest player in the game."

of reconciliation. But instead of showing my gratitude, I lay on the mat, pointing up at Dusty in an accusatory way. As Dusty held out his arms to explain himself, Arn and Ole entered the cage. While I locked the door, they attacked, positioning Dusty's leg on the rope. I climbed the turnbuckles and jumped onto the limb. Dusty acted like his leg had been broken, but I pushed things even more, locking on a figure-four to apparently magnify the pain.

Other wrestlers on the show—guys like Magnum T. A., Terry Taylor, and the Rock'n'Roll Express—ran out and tried to rescue Dusty, but we punched them off the cage. At this point, the fans surged past security, pushing themselves against the enclosure. Then Jake "The Snake" Roberts's younger brother, Sam Houston, managed to reach the top of the cage, but Ole scrambled up from the other side and began beating the living shit out of him.

"Goddamn, Ole!" I yelled. "What are you doing?"

He looked over at the fans, now pressed fifty deep against the cage, and said, "Just letting them know that anyone who comes in here is getting his ass whipped."

MARTY LUNDE, AKA ARN ANDERSON: People were throwing bottles, batteries, bolts, nuts, whatever they could get their hands on. In those days, we didn't have a barricade around the ring like we do now, and the fans pushed the little metal barrier right up to the cage. God almighty, we couldn't get the door open. I'll tell you who saved our lives, and I owe them to this day: ten Atlanta police officers who came down with their nightsticks out. They beat back the people far enough for us to get out of the cage. They made a little clearance, and Flair, Ole, and myself were standing back to back, throwing punches and working our way down the aisle. It took us thirty minutes to get to the dressing room, and we were fighting the whole way.

We got our asses kicked by the fans. I had about twenty stitches in the back of my head. Once I realized that all my organs were still inside my body and I was still breathing, it was the biggest rush. I had never been in *anything* like that before, and I knew that there was big money going forward.

What made our group unique was that everyone held a championship. Tully was the U.S. Champion, Ole and Arn were the Tag Team champions, and I had the World Heavyweight title. Each member also had a particular style of punishing his rival. Tully would beat an opponent with a slingshot suplex, ricocheting him off the ropes before ramming him into the canvas. Arn used the spinebuster and DDT. Ole would wrap his body around a wrestler when he was face-down, then pull the guy's arm back to force a submission. Tully and Arn also had some great double-team moves, including a dual Brain Buster—holding a guy upside down over their shoulders before driving his head into the mat.

It was Arn who came up with a name for our unit at one of the television tapings. The four of us were being interviewed by announcer Tony Schiavone when Arn blurted out, "The only time this much havoc has been wreaked by this few people, you'd have to go back to the Four Horsemen of the Apocalypse!"

ARN ANDERSON: I put no thought into it beforehand. It just popped into my head. I was trying to think about all the negative things we represented and all the horror we were going to rain on the world. It was an interview line for one individual day that grew into a gimmick.

Whenever the Four Horsemen were together, we'd turn our hands toward our bodies and hold up four fingers. We were just missing the thumb, which was actually our manger, J. J. Dillon.

I was starstruck around Ric Flair, but he always treated me as an equal. As we got to talking, I found that we had a lot in common. Both of us had been an only child. He was adopted. I never had a father. The more we traveled together, the more our friendship grew.

Arn became as big a part of my life as the General, my high-school buddy who's my son Reid's godfather. There was no jealousy in the Four Horsemen. Everybody liked the idea and ran with it. We could all talk, and we could all wrestle. Every night, we made our foes, selling whatever they could throw our way. And J. J. was an experienced wrestler who could get in the ring and perform. The group will never be duplicated.

Everyone got so ramped up, trying to have the best match of the night. If Ole and Arn were putting up their titles, Tully would not only have to follow them later in the card with a U.S. title defense, but improvise a bit to outshine them. Then I had to follow him in the main event. It was a nightmare trying to outdo those guys, but I loved the challenge. It was the same with our interviews—if Jim Cornette came out with the Midnight Express and then Dusty cut a great promo, I wanted to go on next and blow them away.

"Now, Tony Schiavone, let's talk about real life," I began one interview. "You know, I've got a real big house on the big side of town in Charlotte, North Carolina. And you know why I let Arn Anderson and Tully Blanchard come over to my house, and work out in my gym, and swim in my pool, and dive off my five-meter board? Huh? You know why? Because they are *champions.* And I let only champions come to my home, or play golf at my country club, or sit next to my women, or whatever else they want to do with my private stuff. . . . That's why Dusty Rhodes can't get through the gate."

ARN ANDERSON: The Four Horsemen became a way of life. We bought five Mercedes. We'd pull them up on the ramp at Butler Aviation in Charlotte, the pilots would get our bags, and we'd walk up to one of Jim Crockett's private planes and fly out. When we landed, a limo would pick us up at the airport. We'd check into the hotel, go to the gym, go to work, kick some ass, head back to the limo, and party. If we had to wrestle on the West Coast, we'd stay in Vegas, fly to Oakland for a match, come back to Vegas, stay up all night, fly out to Los Angeles, wrestle, come back to Vegas, and not go to sleep. There was nothing fake about the Four Horsemen. It was a full-blown shoot.

CHRIS IRVINE, AKA CHRIS JERICHO: One time, the NWA came to Winnipeg, where I grew up. We used to hang out at the hotel where the wrestlers stayed, and we saw the Four Horsemen getting into their limousine. My friend and I got in my mom's car and started following them; we wanted to see where they'd go. They stopped at a vendor, went inside, bought a twelve-pack of beer, and got back in the limousine. **We were still following them when they just stopped in the middle of the street, put the limo in reverse, and started chasing us backward. This went on for about five minutes. They wouldn't stop. And we're like, "Go, go, go, go, go! The Horsemen are gonna kill us! Keep going!" They were probably howling, making these kids shit their pants.**

We killed some poor limo driver in Chicago—not literally killed him, but our hours didn't help, picking us up at three in the afternoon and dropping us off at eight in the morning. Poor Dave had been driving us around for three days when he had a heart attack and died in his sleep the day after we left town.

Jimmy Crockett didn't pay for those limos; I did. When the Horsemen were running heavy, I ran up an annual bill of $60,000 for limousines alone. If I bought a new suit, I showed it off during my interviews. I remember holding open my jacket for Tony Schiavone, displaying the label sewn onto the red lining, and saying "Read it, brother. It says, 'Custom-made for the World Champion'—*Woooo!*—'by Michael's of Kansas City.'"

On airplanes, the other wrestlers always wanted to fly with me. They said it made them feel safer. After all, I'd been in one plane crash. What were the odds that it would happen twice?

BEFORE WE ARRIVED somewhere, I'd announce our hotel and invite all the ladies. In Baltimore, St. Louis, Kansas City, Miami, and Fort Lauderdale, it was the Marriott. In Chicago, it was the Bismarck; in Richmond, the Holiday Inn. When we began performing regularly in the New York area, it was always the Helmsley Palace. In Georgia, I'd say, "To all the girls driving down I-85 toward Disney World, you needn't go any farther. Just pull into Atlanta. I'll be at the downtown Marriott, and you can ride 'Space Mountain' all night long!"

Before the Crockett Cup, a two-day tag-team tournament in Baltimore, we rented the penthouse at the downtown Marriott, and I cut an interview inviting all females between eighteen and twenty-eight to a party. No husbands, no boyfriends. And I wasn't joking. We hired a doorman to let the women in and turn their dates away. While the girls hung with us in the penthouse, dozens of irritated guys were downstairs, wandering around the lobby.

AFTER A VEGAS trip, I got to the airport and realized that I'd left a $10,000 ring—a three-and-a-half-carat diamond ring—on the tenth floor of the Tropicana. By the time I got back to the hotel, it was gone. In my career, I've lost two major rings, a twenty-dollar gold piece with diamonds around it, and three Rolexes. And if two of those watches weren't stolen by girls, I must have been handing out Rolexes as they left. Once, around four in the morning, Arn was going through the revolving glass door at the Bismarck and saw a girl coming out in my full-length coat. He spun back outside, grabbed my mink, and managed to confiscate Tully's wallet and ring, too.

In Norfolk, I hung out at a bar called September's. I was driving into town one day and caught a glimpse of the marquee: LADIES NIGHT AT SEPTEMBER'S FEATURING RIC FLAIR AND ARN ANDERSON. Arn shook his head. "Can't you keep me out of all of this shit? If my name's gonna be on the marquee, I prefer that it be at the arena."

There's a point that I need to make here: I'm not proud of this stuff. I don't want anyone to read one of these anecdotes and think that it's cool to do that to your wife and family. It's great that I've had a wonderful career and more fun than most people could experience in five lifetimes. But I was on such a mission to be Ric Flair that I neglected what was really important. Beth has always been my support system, and I'm lucky to be her husband. She didn't deserve to be disrespected by me acting like an irresponsible kid when I was already in my thirties. She's the greatest woman of all time, and it's a miracle that I didn't lose her through my own selfishness and stupidity. I was always there monetarily, but everybody—including my wife and kids—came second to the business.

It's even more important for me to emphasize this now because my younger son is still growing up. If he chooses to fill my shoes by having a strong work ethic, I'll be proud. If he tries to imitate some of my other behavior, I'll be disappointed. I know that my children are going to read this, and I want them to know that at the end of the day, it's your family that matters.

BETH FLIEHR: Ric and I really wanted to have children, but after two tubal pregnancies and four miscarriages, the doctors gave me less than a 10 percent chance. I thought about adopting, but with Ric's

schedule I didn't know if anyone would allow us to. It got so bad that I'd just given up on the thought of ever having a family.

Beth and I were in Hawaii when we found out that she was pregnant. We were celebrating. The Rock's grandmother, Lia Maivia, had started promoting there, and she had me booked against Kerry Von Erich. Beth started having problems during the matches, and we went to the hospital. I had to get on a red-eye to Kansas City to work for Bob Geigel, so I left Beth in the hospital. While I was on the plane, she miscarried.

The ticket to Kansas City cost $1,400, and Bob Geigel still hadn't reimbursed my transportation costs. He looked at me and said, "I thought Lia was going to pick that up."

"No, Bob," I argued. "When I'm coming into your territory, *you* pay the trans. When I leave, the promoter in the next place picks up the trans. It's *always* been that way."

"Well, Lia should have paid half of that. That's a lot of fuckin' money."

The fact that my wife was still in the hospital, traumatized about losing a child, wasn't even a factor to him. When people use the word *integrity* in reference to professional wrestling, I still laugh. Back then, in most cases, there was none.

Fortunately, I was there when my daughter Ashley was born in 1986. Beth gave birth in the morning. I worked an afternoon show, then headed back to the hospital. Beth was really happy, and so was I. But it was still a Ric Flair night. After a while, I left to have dinner with Arn and Barry Darsow and their wives. I bought thirty beers for Arn, put them on ice in a bucket, and he drank all of them. We were roaring. I remember holding back the hair of Arn's wife, Erin, so she could throw up. The next morning, everyone had another good story. This time, though, I offer no apologies for having a good time.

This time, there really was a reason to party.

BETH FLIEHR: The day after Ric's thirty-ninth birthday, I gave birth to our son, Reid. I had a healthy beautiful baby boy, but I almost lost the father. Ric was beside the bed crying as the birth of Reid was about to happen. He had just put a breath mint in his mouth, and while he was

crying it lodged in his throat. He ran to the bathroom, which was in my line of vision. I knew he was choking at the same time the doctor was telling me to push. I said, "But my husband . . ." The doctor insisted that I had to concentrate and push. I responded that a nurse needed to help my husband. So we had a baby and saved the dad.

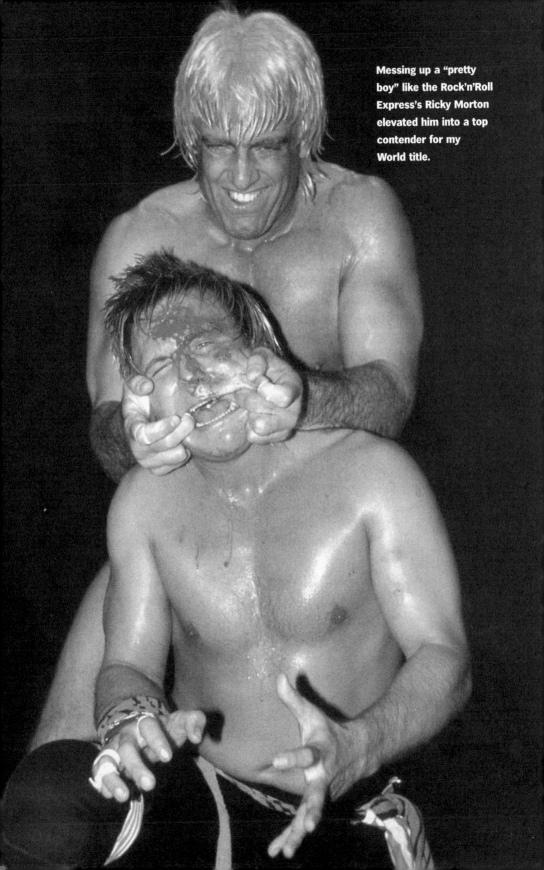

Messing up a "pretty boy" like the Rock'n'Roll Express's Ricky Morton elevated him into a top contender for my World title.

The Great American Bash was another spectacular conjured up by the fertile mind of Dusty Rhodes. The first one was staged in 1985 at Charlotte Memorial Stadium. I wrestled Nikita Koloff in the main event, and the crowd loved it. The next year, we had a series of outdoor shows with fireworks, skydivers, and—in the southern states—country music. In our traditional locations, we did really well; in other venues—and this was one of the first examples of Dusty and Jimmy Crockett overreaching and trying to be like Vince McMahon—we fell short. I don't know what anybody was thinking when they booked RFK Stadium in Washington, D.C., and Riverfront Stadium in Cincinnati. Even with TBS exposure and great lineups, there was *no* way that we were going to sell those places out.

CHAPTER **11**

I JUST HAPPEN TO BE YOUR MASTER

One of the best things about those *Bash* shows was that I got to work with guys who fans rarely saw in the number-one contender's spot: tag-team wrestlers like Road Warriors Hawk and Animal, and Ricky Morton of the Rock'n'Roll Express. The Rock'n'Rolls, who came to the ring with shag haircuts and bandannas tied around their outfits, got more women than anybody else. Robert Gibson, the dark-haired member of the Express, was a good wrestler and played well on the team, but his blond-haired partner, Morton, was the heart of the unit. Ricky was a fabulous performer, and probably could have been one of the top singles wrestlers in the business, but—unlike Shawn Michaels, who became a World Wrestling Federation champion after parting ways with his tag-team partner, Marty Jannetty—Ricky never broke up with Robert.

Teenage girls went wild for the Rock'n'Roll Express, just as they had for Steamboat nine years earlier, so I used some of the same tactics. Taunting Morton by waving a training bra, I yelled, "We like our women special. We don't like little girls in training underwear that think guys with Dippity-Do in their hair and scarves on their legs are men."

To establish Morton as a serious contender, we had him pin me in a televised non-title match. Then the Horsemen followed him into the dressing room, and I rubbed his face into the floor. Like Steamboat, Ricky got sandpapered. We also shot another segment where Tully, Arn, and J. J. Dillon held Morton while I dropped a knee from the second rope, "shattering" his nose.

All of these things created an extra sense of tension during our series of matches. For the first thirty minutes of a bout, I'd try vainly to pry Ricky's nose guard off his face. When I finally succeeded, he'd bleed. Then, for the last fifteen minutes of the match, I'd bleed, too. We'd send Arn to ringside to interfere, prompting Robert Gibson to come down and defend his partner. During one stretch, I wrestled eighteen hour-long matches with Morton in fourteen days. He was so good that it wasn't even like working.

During the 1986 *Bash* series, Dusty managed to squeeze in a brief title run. On July 26, we met in a cage in Greensboro. Early in the match, I went into my strut, and Dusty amused the fans by running his fingers through his hair and strutting, too. He knocked me down with two stylish right jabs, followed by two elbows, then entertained the people even more by sticking out his big ass in satisfaction.

Beating Dusty was tougher than most people realized–especially when the NWA World Championship was at stake.

Every test of strength and wrist-lock reversal seemed to hit a nerve with the audience. When I pointed at a fan and screamed, "You keep your mouth shut!" an entire section stood up to berate me. Another time I waved Dusty forward, shouting, "You come here, dammit!" But when he advanced, I backed up, fell into the corner, and begged for mercy.

We were both bleeding when Dusty tried dropping an elbow on me and I rolled out of the way. But when I bent down to give him a body slam, he cradled me and got the win.

Three years earlier, in the same town, in another cage match, the fans had reveled in my title win over Harley. Now it was Dusty's turn. Magnum T. A., Ronnie Garvin, Sam Houston, the Rock'n'Roll Express, and others piled into the cage to honor "The American Dream" while the fans danced and screamed with joy.

A short time later, we began setting up a plot leading to the inevitable title switch. On August 7, after Dusty beat me with a clothesline in Kansas City, J. J. Dillon stepped into the ring to protest. As Dusty watched the exchange, Tully Blanchard swung a chair into Rhodes's leg—the same leg, fans were told, that we had broken the year before in Atlanta—and I slipped on the figure-four. Sounding like a Pentecostal preacher, Arn Anderson predicted Dusty's doom: "They say a miracle is a brief moment of divine intervention. Well, Dusty Rhodes, for 1986, you've had your miracle. Now all things come back to the way they're supposed to be."

Two nights later, the premonition came true—Dusty showed up for our clash in St. Louis "injured," with his leg bandaged and braced. I spent much of the match zoning in on the limb. During Dusty's "courageous" rallies, his leg would invariably fail on him. At the end of the match, he covered me for a pin after a clothesline. At the final moment, though, I draped my foot on the ropes. Apparently believing that he'd won, Dusty rose from the canvas. But I was right behind him, clipping the bad leg and locking on the figure-four. Valiantly, Dusty squirmed, trying to reverse the hold. I turned him back, used the ropes for leverage, released the strands and appeared to intensify the pressure. Eventually, Dusty "passed out from the pain." His shoulders fell to the mat, and I became the NWA champion again.

I bled every night during the *Bash*es, and ultimately bled for forty-two consecutive nights. After the show, it was party time. A lot of the other guys tried keeping up with the Horsemen, but after seventy-two hours without sleep, their performance in the ring suffered. Inevitably, they'd have to face the cruel truth: they weren't the Four Horsemen.

I was running on vitamins and nutritional supplements. Only in my most private moments did I worry about neglecting my health. I remember a muscle pull in my rib cage that caused a spasm all through my back. I'd heard that major back pain could be an indication of a heart attack, so I went to the emergency room with Beth. At the hospital, I was given something to relax and sent back to the hotel. Heading straight to the bar, I continued my Ric Flair routine. Then the pain returned. For the second time that night, I was taken to the hospital, and woke up the next morning with Beth sitting at the foot of my bed. The pain was *excruciating*. I think I told her five times, "If I die, tell my kids I love them."

Another night, I was driving home from Orlando when I felt my heart suddenly beating rapidly. I pulled over, went to a pay phone, and called my father. "Dad, I think there's something wrong with me," I said.

"Ric, let me ask you something. When is the last time you had eight hours' sleep?"

"God, I don't even know."

The revelation did not slow me down.

LEX LUGER WAS called "The Total Package" because he was a big, handsome guy with the best body in the business. In 1987, we brought him into the Four Horsemen as an "associate." The story was that Ole needed time off to train his son in amateur wrestling, so Luger would step in from time to time. Of course, we all turned against Ole for putting his family ahead of the Horsemen, and Luger took his spot.

He was an intelligent guy who ate well, trained hard, and had played—under his real name, Larry Pfohl—for the NFL's Green Bay Packers, the Montreal Alouettes of the Canadian Football League, and the Memphis Showboats of the old United States Football League. Because of his background as a pro football player, he had an agent and understood contracts more than anyone else in the dressing room. When he started with Crockett, Luger was smart enough to have a lawyer look over everything—an idea that was absolutely novel to the rest of us. He received an outlandish money deal that made some wrestlers jealous; his educated point of view was refreshing, but challenging.

We called him a locker-room lawyer. If we drew a $200,000 house, he would calculate the percentage due the boys. He'd point out things that were missing in the industry, asking questions like, "Why don't we have health insurance?" Lex brought an awareness to the average wrestler that hadn't existed before.

I thought that he also added a lot to the Horsemen. Arn and Luger had some of the greatest verbal jousts of all time. In the dressing room, Lex would call Arn a "human superball" because of the way he bounced when he took a fall. "At least I can stand there and look good," he'd brag.

"Luger, you're an orthodontist's dream," Arn would retort. "If I had your teeth, I could make two pearl-handled revolvers."

On July 4, 1987, Luger was with us in Atlanta when we participated

The very first *War Games* match was a
brutal, vicious contest . . . which is exactly
how the Four Horsemen wanted it.

**Lex Luger learned just how painful it was
to be kicked out of the Horsemen.**

in the first *War Games*—the confrontation that would later become
known as the "Horsemen's match." The four of us teamed with J. J.
Dillon against Dusty, Nikita Koloff, the Road Warriors, and their manager, Precious Paul Ellering, and fought inside two rings enclosed in a
cage. I *loved* it. There was chemistry between the wrestlers. It was wild.
It was intense. We bled. We gave our all, man.

When Luger turned good and challenged me for the championship,
I had to teach him how to perform *and* draw money. I made all his
power moves look real convincing. As green as he was, I never felt like
I was putting my body on the line. If he lifted me over his head and
press-slammed me, he was always careful.

Naturally, a few of the boys didn't think that a guy so inexperi-
enced merited this kind of treatment from the World Champion. "Hey,
Luger looks like a million bucks, and he's a nice guy," I told them. "I
have nothing against him. He just has to learn how to work."

Even Arn couldn't understand why I would give Lex a suplex and
tell him not to react to it. My reasons were strictly business; I wanted

the people to keep paying their money to see a wrestler who they believed could run away with my title.

With Luger out of the Horsemen, Blackjack Mulligan's son, Barry Windham, became the fourth member of the team. While Luger hung with us, he was almost a virgin in terms of partying when we got him. Barry didn't need any breaking in. Everything about him came naturally. He was a big, handsome blond kid who'd been wrestling since he was a teenager. Barry was also one of the best in-ring performers in the business, and he knew what to do when he had a microphone in front of him. I consider Tully, Arn, Windham, and myself to be wrestling's top "gang" of all time. If everyone was in shape, the four of us could go to WWE today and sell out everywhere.

AS MUCH AS people were spellbound by the Horsemen, most of the attention surrounding Ric Flair still centered on the NWA Championship. In 1987 I lost the title again—not to a physical specimen like Luger, but to a blue-collar hero. Despite the fact that he wore a trucker's cap with an American flag emblem, Rugged Ronnie Garvin was a French Canadian from Montreal, where he became acquainted with local stars Pat Patterson and Terry Garvin. It was Terry who made Ronnie his "brother" in Florida in 1967. Ron's stepson, James Williams, later became the third sibling, Gorgeous Jimmy Garvin.

Ronnie was a good, solid performer. One of his specialties was the "Garvin Stomp"—which consisted of Ronnie simply stomping on your body from head to toe. The people believed that he was tough, and for good reason—those shots were solid!

Garvin beat me for the championship on September 25, 1987, rolling me up in a Cage match at the Joe Louis Arena in Detroit. The fans liked it when he was pursuing me for the title. When he finally won, though, they weren't as impressed. I just don't think he was perceived as a huge star. Let me put it this way: when I wrestled Garvin, we were part of the package. When I wrestled Dusty, we were the main event.

This was another short-term title reign, and plans were made for me to win back the championship at *Starrcade '87*. Every year, *Starrcade* had been held in Greensboro, but this time Crockett decided to move the event to the UIC Pavilion in Chicago. He was trying to make a statement: We're not just a southern company. It was a terrible move, absolute *insanity,* but Jimmy didn't want to hear about it. Greensboro's never going to be Chicago, but don't tell that to the people in Greensboro. These were loyal fans, and we insulted them. They never forgave us.

DAVID CROCKETT: I really disagreed with my brother about the move. *Starrcade* was Greensboro. Jimmy may have wanted a national presence, but guess what? We weren't in the main arena; we were in the *college* arena. To the people in Chicago, we seemed second-rate.

I was in charge of production, and our costs tripled. Nothing against unions, but the South is a right-to-work region, where you don't have to wait for approval from a union boss. Plus, there was the cost of flying all those people up there. It just didn't work.

This was going to be our first Pay-Per-View, and Jimmy was banking the whole company on it. But Vince McMahon decided to create *Survivor Series* to run on the same day. At first, Jimmy didn't think that would be a problem; we'd have *Starrcade* in the afternoon, and when fans watched both Pay-Per-Views back-to-back, they'd see that we had the better product. Then Vince told cable companies that if they wanted *Survivor Series,* they couldn't run any other wrestling Pay-Per-View sixty days before or twenty-one days after. The World Wrestling Federation was a proven commodity, and very few cable companies wanted to take the risk. Of the original two hundred that were interested in *Starrcade,* only five carried it. After expenses, we only took in $80,000.

It was demoralizing. It was a downer. But we should have known something like this would happen. Vince was a businessman.

On November 26, 1987, at *Starrcade '87,* I again stepped into the cage with Garvin. From the beginning, a lot of the fans were booing Ronnie; I remember exchanging chops with him and hearing, "Garvin sucks! Garvin sucks!" See, Garvin was popular in Greensboro and places like that; with my high-living persona, though, Ric Flair was ready-made for a city like Chicago. Ronnie came across as too southern. I know that Dusty Rhodes depicted himself the same way, but Dusty could get away with it because he was a much better interview with a more charismatic personality.

I wouldn't characterize this as a great match, but I definitely enjoyed myself. Ronnie and I pounded the life out of each other. He beat

Starrcade '87 in Chicago was a bad idea.
Rugged Ronnie Garvin and I beat the hell
out of each other in a steel cage.

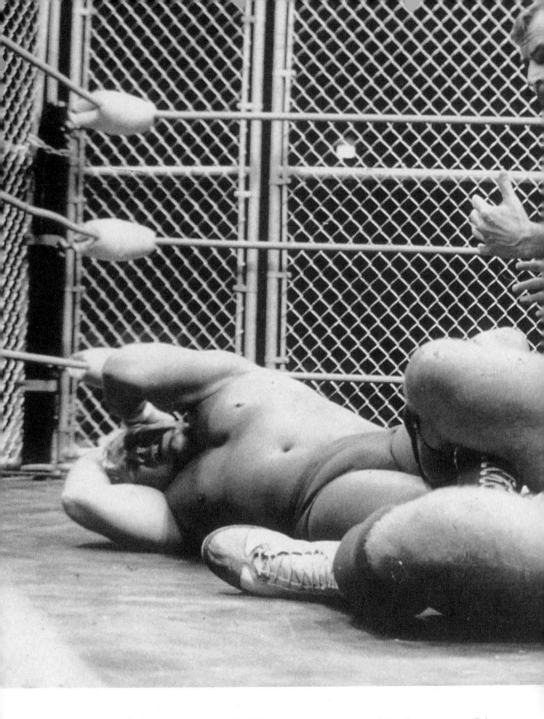

my chest raw. I was rubbing Neosporin into my skin for a year. It's amazing I didn't get a staph infection.

At one point we were standing on the top rope, and Garvin slammed my head twice into the cage. I chopped him, and he stung me

back with a chop so loud that the noise reverberated throughout the building. Then I began walking groggily across the top rope until I slipped and landed on the cable, crotch-first.

The match ended when I whipped Garvin off the ropes and he

came flying back at me. I turned my body and kind of rode him into the cage on the opposite side of the ring. When he hit his head, I clambered on top of him and scored the pin.

Even though I was the villain, the fans exploded, crying, "*Wooooo!*" Jimmy Crockett was standing right outside the cage, where J. J. embraced me and held up five fingers, signifying my fifth title reign.

"From now on," I pledged, hoping to get back some of the crowd's hatred, "I'm gonna be the most obnoxious, overbearing human being on the face of this earth. . . . There's a million wrestlers, past and present, who would have loved to have been there once. I've been there *five times.*"

THERE WERE TWO reasons why the title kept coming back to me: I had proven that I could draw money, and I would do what was right for business. If they wanted me to lose, I did it without sending the company into turmoil. In my mind, I was maintaining my star power by having the best match on the show. There was a touch of sincerity in my words when I expressed the following warning to a future adversary:

"Pal, to walk that aisle—*Wooooo!*—looking as only I can look, night after night, year after year, knowing beyond a shadow of a doubt that I'm the best there is . . . you have to go to bed every night saying to yourself, 'To be the man, you've gotta beat the man.' And, pal, to beat Ric Flair is a whole different world than you know. . . . I just happen to be your master. The ring is my household. I know the squared circle more than any man alive."

Other guys needed to go out there and squash their opponents. I didn't believe in that. I just wanted the match to be exciting, whether I was wrestling Ronnie Garvin or bottom-card guys like George South.

GEORGE SOUTH: I was famous for getting beat up. I'd lose in the World Wrestling Federation on Monday, in Mid-Atlantic on Wednesday, in Alabama the day after that, and in Florida on the weekend. I got beat so much that I could have put advertising on the bottom of my boots.

When I worked for Jim Crockett Promotions, I'd check the booking sheets. If I was working on a TV taping with Ric Flair in the main event, I knew I was making a house payment that week. Ric always treated me right. Once he paid me to drive his robes to Atlanta for an appearance he was doing on *Good Morning America*. I was going down the highway in my $1,000 Nissan, saying to myself, "I've got close to

RIC FLAIR TO BE THE MAN

$100,000 worth of robes in my trunk. Something ain't right about this."

In Atlanta, we'd do our TV tapings at eight or nine in the morning. We're talking a cold studio, freezing, and I didn't want to work, much less the top guys. Flair was always flying out somewhere later in the day, so he'd usually do an interview and not have to dress out. But one Saturday, I got the feeling Dusty wanted to put the screws to Flair. He told him to go out there and work a match. Flair didn't complain. He looked around and said, "Let me at George South." My mouth dropped open. "George," he told me, "today, you're going to be Ricky Steamboat."

We got in the ring, and he called for every spot Steamboat ever did with him. He climbed the ropes, and I reached up and slammed him off the top. I whipped him into the corner, and he did his little flip over the turnbuckles. Then he ran down the apron, and I nailed him. J. J. Dillon jumped up on the apron, and I nailed him, too. Ric tried suplexing me over the ropes, onto the studio floor, but I blocked it and suplexed him into the middle of the ring.

We did a fifteen-minute match. Back then, that was unheard of on TV. What was nerve-racking was that when Flair called something, he didn't want you to go into it right away. He just wanted you to be *ready* for it, so you had to remember.

For the finish, I was going to jump off the top rope, Flair would give me a gut shot, I'd do a flip, and he'd put on the figure-four. Well, I climbed that rope, but I was so blown up [exhausted], I just fell onto the mat. He got me in the figure-four and beat me.

The twenty-five or thirty people in that studio were on their feet the whole time. And I was so goofy that, if I had the chance to get him in a small package, I would have held onto his trunks and become the NWA champion.

On March 27, 1988, Randy "Macho Man" Savage won the World Wrestling Federation Championship in a tournament at *WrestleMania IV*. This time, though, Crockett and Ted Turner came up with a way to stick it to Vince, by simultaneously airing the first *Clash of the Champions* live special on TBS.

Jimmy's expectations were high. "We need you to go forty-five minutes," he said. "We're going head-to-head against *WrestleMania,* so let's tear the joint down."

"That's a very nice position to be in," I told him. "I can't wait."

My opponent had joined the company the year before—along with

Sting at the first *Clash of the Champions*.
Our match helped make him a bona fide star.

Steve "Dr. Death" Williams, Eddie Gilbert, and Rick Steiner—when Jimmy purchased Cowboy Bill Watts's Universal Wrestling Federation (UWF). Steve Borden began wrestling on the California independent circuit, and in 1986 he was part of a tag team called the Blade Runners. Steve was Blade Runner Flash, and his partner, Jim Hellwig, was Blade Runner Rock. Steve went to the UWF, spiked his blond hair, put on a bit of face paint, and became Sting. Hellwig worked for the Von Erichs, then went to the World Wrestling Federation, where he was christened the Ultimate Warrior.

Up until *Clash of the Champions,* I had never wrestled Sting. Because of his youth, it was my responsibility to go out there and lead him through a great match. But I didn't do all the work; Steve definitely held up his end.

Sting got a nice reception coming out, but hardly a superstar's ovation. When the bell rang, we locked fingers and pushed up against each other. I lost the test of strength and howled in torment. Sting gave me a press slam and a flying head scissors. I threw him through the ropes, but he landed on his feet, rolled back into the ring, stood up, and glared at me. I placed Sting in the figure-four, but he pounded on his chest, then reversed the maneuver. He flipped me over the corner turnbuckle, but I staggered across the apron, mounted the opposite turnbuckle, and hit Sting with a flying body press. He clutched onto me and kept rolling, gaining a near-fall. At the forty-four-minute mark, he had me in his finisher, the Scorpion Death Lock, while the public-address announcer counted down the match's final seconds. I screamed and writhed with pain, but the bell rang just before I could submit, and the bout was declared a time-limit draw.

Throughout the match, I could feel the mood of the people, and knew that they were buying Sting as my peer. So was I. Sting had the ability and loved wrestling so much that I knew that he was going to make it. When we got backstage, I was as happy as he was. The show had drawn a record-setting 5.6 rating and lured away millions of viewers who might have watched *WrestleMania IV.* Even more important, both of us realized this was the start of something we would be doing for a very long time.

My match with Sting and the birth of my son Reid were bright spots in what was otherwise a disappointing year. On January 24, 1988, Jim Crockett Promotions tried another Pay-Per-View—*Bunkhouse Stampede,* from the Nassau Coliseum on Long Island. I had a pretty good match with my friend Mike Hegstrand, the late Road Warrior Hawk, but as far as I recall, everything else about the card turned out to be a disaster. Vince countered the show with the first *Royal Rumble*—then called the *Rumble Royale*—on the USA Network, available free of charge to anyone with cable TV. The World Wrestling Federation was at a high point, and eight million viewers watched it.

CHAPTER **12**

THE DUSTY FINISH

Crockett may have thought that he was starting a revolution by promoting in the World Wrestling Federation's backyard, but that wasn't enough to get the fans to like the show. The Nassau Coliseum wasn't even close to full, and why should it have been? As smart as Dusty is, sometimes he was so small-minded. An old-time "bunkhouse stampede"—a battle-royal-style match inspired by the days when farmhands fought it out by the bunkhouse—may have done well in the South at one time. But in *New York*? Italians from the Bronx and Jews from Brooklyn couldn't have cared less about cowbells and bull ropes. Has there ever *been* a bunkhouse in Manhattan? The company just seemed so far behind the times.

DAVID CROCKETT: The best thing for Dusty would have been for him to just book and not wrestle. We probably would have done better. He kept a lot of people down and chased a lot of fans away because he wanted to stay number one. At times, all of Dusty's ideas seemed inspired by one movie, *True Grit*. In our storylines, he had to come back from the dead, just like John Wayne. His creativity got stale.

After the Nassau Coliseum show, the boys ended up in Harry's Bar, at the Helmsley Palace Hotel in Manhattan. Tully was complaining about the direction of the company; he walked right up to Jimmy and confronted him about some of Dusty's decisions. "Dusty should book himself against Dusty," he said.

Jimmy didn't want to hear it, and walked away. Dusty had gotten so close with Jimmy that I couldn't reason with him, either. Jimmy Crockett had been a very important part of my life, but I could see our relationship changing. Here was a person who meant so much to me that I had made him best man at my wedding. I couldn't understand how Dusty could step in and con Jimmy out of that friendship.

Dusty also began telling stories that were too preposterous to believe. During a trip on one of Crockett's private planes, Dusty notified a group of us that we were going to outclass Vince by making these big, Hollywood-style productions. Apparently, the first movie on the company's list was the life story of Terry Allen, aka Magnum T. A., a handsome wrestler who suffered spinal cord damage when he drove his Porsche into a telephone pole one rainy night. We all agreed that Terry had an inspirational story that could make a decent film. Then Dusty added that Sylvester Stallone had agreed to play Magnum T. A., while

Sally Field was committed to portraying his wife, Tamara. The only problem, Dusty said, was that he wasn't sure if Sally Field was really right for the part.

Arn and I looked at each other and rolled our eyes. If Jimmy was dubious, too, he wasn't showing it to us.

Later, when his son Dustin started in the World Wrestling Federation as Goldust, Dusty said that Vince was arranging to put Dustin in a video with Madonna.

ON THE ROAD, fans were getting tired of seeing the same thing, over and over. The referee would get knocked down, and the challenger would toss me over the top rope. A second referee would run in, just in time to see me submit or get pinned. The fans would think that I had lost the championship—until the first ref woke up and announced that throwing your foe over the ropes was a violation of NWA rules. Therefore, the good guy was disqualified.

Among the boys, this ending—with a few variations here and there—was called the "Dusty finish." It worked great in the days of the territories, when the fans in Charlotte knew nothing about the match results in Miami or Oklahoma City. But because of cable and Pay-Per-View, people became so familiar with the Dusty finish they could predict it ahead of time. And that wasn't good for business.

JIM CORNETTE: Ric's goal as the traveling champion had always been to escape by the skin of his teeth and make the local guy look good. But once national cable came in and Crockett emerged as the only major promotion in opposition to Vince, you couldn't have that kind of champ anymore. You had Hulk Hogan winning one-two-three with a leg drop every night for the opposition, while Ric was always getting the shit beat out of him. The NWA champion should have been better protected at that time, and maybe Ric should have stood up to Dusty.

Amazingly, when Dusty and I finally did have it out, the issue wasn't how I was portrayed to the fans, but how two of my friends were being treated by the company. In 1987, Tully and Arn received a terrible paycheck. Dusty knew how hard they worked; he'd been in the ring with them. The Road Warriors' *manager,* Precious Paul Ellering, was getting paid more than these guys. We were at a TV taping, and I demanded that they be compensated better. The conversation went nowhere, however, so when Tully and Arn said they were walking out, I walked out with them.

Dusty called me at home. "As long as I got you," he said, "I don't need anybody else." He was giving me a great compliment, but he was missing the point. I was insulted that he would even consider letting two great performers like Arn and Tully get away.

"It doesn't work like that for me," I argued. "These guys are my friends, and you know how valuable they are. I can't leave my friends behind."

When word got back to Jimmy that I wasn't coming back to work, he personally came over to my home to resolve the stalemate. "If you're fucking around with Arn," I told him, "you're fucking *me* around."

"Don't make the mistake of leaving," he said.

"Well, I'm with them," I emphasized.

I don't remember what was finally worked out, but Tully and Arn did return to the company. Yet they still weren't happy, and it didn't take long for that news to filter to Vince McMahon, who attempted to score a coup by signing the two wrestlers I considered the backbone of the NWA.

ARN ANDERSON: I felt like Tully and I had become invisible because we were no-maintenance employees. We were taking a pounding, teaching the Lugers and the Road Warriors how to work. I'm not saying that we didn't enjoy it—those guys were our all-out friends—but they were strong and green, and we were probably making a third of their money while showing them their craft. It got pretty depressing. At the same time, Jimmy was doing the soft shoe—"I'm selling the company," "I'm not selling the company," "We're going bankrupt" . . . I said, "Yeah, time to get off the ship. It's smoking down there."

We got to the World Wrestling Federation, and it was like night and day. I was a much bigger star being on their TV for three months than I'd been after three years on TBS. No doubt about it, Vince created superstars, not wrestling stars.

In the spring of 1988, Vince McMahon called me with a straightforward question: "What do you think about coming to the World Wrestling Federation?"

He already knew what he wanted to do with me. When the first

SummerSlam debuted on August 29, 1988, I would be in the main event, challenging Randy Savage for his World Wrestling Federation title.

"I'm thrilled that you're giving me the opportunity," I responded, "but I don't know."

I tried to explain that the NWA had been my home since 1974, and parting ways with the organization seemed a little frightening. Even though I was getting the runaround from Jimmy and Dusty, I wasn't politically astute enough to deal with being romanced by this guy who I didn't know.

Despite the strain between Dusty and myself, I approached him and mentioned Vince's offer. But instead of trying to find some sort of common ground, he just countered, "All right. Go to Roanoke today and drop the title to Luger."

In retrospect, I believe Dusty knew that Crockett Promotions was going to be sold, and he wanted to downplay my value to the new owners. I also think that this was the point where our friendship became very strained. It was painful. From the first day we met, I respected Dusty, and I still respect so much about him to this day. But now I was seeing him for what he was—everything had been great between us until the moment I had rivaled him as a top attraction.

I never looked at myself as bigger or better than Dusty. In my mind, he was the lead hero and I was the lead villain, and we were doing this together. Yet I truly felt that he was trying to make me into a second-tier guy. After Crockett purchased the UWF from Bill Watts, Dusty depicted their title-holder, Steve "Dr. Death" Williams, as a world champion whose status paralleled mine. Back in 1985, he had turned Buddy Landel into my mirror image and archrival, "Nature Boy" Buddy Landel. I admit that Landel and I had some good matches, but I didn't see Dusty naming other wrestlers "The American Dream."

Still, I felt an obligation to the NWA. I couldn't walk away from the organization. So I continued working for Crockett while the company crumbled.

Jimmy was bleeding money to pay off the purchase of the UWF. Sure, Bill Watts had more than a hundred syndicated stations, but his promotion was floundering. Once he folded, we could have walked in and plucked off whoever and whatever we wanted. But Crockett was convinced that he needed the UWF to help fight off Vince. Now Jimmy was shackled with all the debts Watts had to the television stations.

What was really shocking, though, was that Jimmy moved into

Watts's office in Dallas, leaving behind the remodeled convenience store that had been headquarters to Mid-Atlantic Wrestling in Charlotte. Once again, Jimmy's goal was to situate himself in a glossy location in the center of the country—even as he hacked himself away from his roots.

DAVID CROCKETT: The office was extravagant, to say the least. It was a castle, all granite and marble. If I'm correct, we took over the whole floor, as well as the lease of the building. I think Dusty wanted to come back home to Texas as the conquering hero.

People let their egos get in the way of good business decisions. When airline costs were pretty hefty, we had a sixteen-passenger Gulfstream. It was like a G-1 Turboprop, and was efficient in a 500-mile radius. Then we bought a jet–a small Falcon 20–and things became illogical. Jimmy bought Dusty a Mercedes, and started paying for these lavish trips for wrestlers, spending with no regard. He was snake-bit.

By now, Crockett Promotions was divided into camps: Dusty and Jimmy on one side, myself and the other Crocketts—David, Jackie, and Frances—and the majority of the office staff on the other. We were still killing 'em east of the Mississippi, but we were dying west of the Mississippi. Whatever we were spending, the return didn't match the output. And the company's money was no longer good in a lot of places. One day, David Crockett looked at me like his best friend had died. "Ric," he said, "I don't believe this. They've run up $100,000 in airfare on my personal Diner's Club card." Things were so bad that the company's accountant must have been having a nervous breakdown.

JIM CORNETTE: If Dusty Rhodes and Jim Crockett had decided, "Let's just keep running Virginia and the Carolinas, and forget about expanding nationally," we could've blown Vince out of there with dynamite. The World Wrestling Federation wasn't drawing in the Carolinas yet; Mid-Atlantic Wrestling was all people wanted to see. We could have still been in business, but the company got in over the small staff's head. That's where the downfall came.

JIM BARNETT, FORMER GEORGIA PROMOTER: Jim Crockett was not doing well. I was very friendly with some people who worked for Ted Turner, and I knew that Turner wanted the company to continue

because they were producing the wrestling that appeared on **TBS** Saturdays and Sundays. Now Ted wanted to buy Jim Crockett Promotions. I asked Crockett if he would be interested, and he said yes. I told him that I would negotiate the deal.

DAVID CROCKETT: I fought it tooth and nail. Governor Jim Martin didn't want the company to move to Atlanta because we were such a big part of the North Carolina economy. He called and said, "What can we do to stop this deal?"

I wanted to go back, regroup, do regional, and make it that way. Ted wanted the whole company and said at one point, "I can stand it longer than you. Even if you are my number one show, I can kick you off." Finally, they pulled what I call the "My Mother Card." My mother, Elizabeth, got a five-year consulting agreement. The rest of us, including Jimmy, were hired by the new wrestling company.

The deal was finalized in November 1988, and the fifty-three-year tradition of Mid-Atlantic Wrestling came to an end.

Someone called me with the news around ten in the morning, so I phoned Jimmy and he confirmed the rumors. Believe it or not, I was surprised. It's not like Jimmy ever confided in me or said, "Hey, this is what's going down." We were barely communicating at that point.

There was a lot of bitterness surrounding the sale. Out of some kind of misguided loyalty, I missed an opportunity to go to the World Wrestling Federation. Crockett also owed everyone money, so the guys were offered ten cents on the dollar. Eventually they received thirty cents on the dollar, which is hardly anything to cheer about.

We were making the jump from being a wrestling company to being a division of a large corporation, and I felt a lot of fear about the unknown. Apparently, those fears were justified—my contract had just expired, so now I had to enter into discussions with Turner Broadcasting about a new agreement. Only later did a TBS executive confide to me that Turner wouldn't have bought the company if I wasn't included in the package. Do you know what that means? It means that instead of the $730,000-per-year contract we settled on, I should have had a multimillion-dollar deal. But neither Jimmy nor Dusty made me aware of that opportunity. I had to learn about everything secondhand—and much too late.

Technically, the new company was called World Championship

Wrestling (WCW)—the official name of the Georgia promotion that had originally been on TBS—but we didn't dub our title the WCW Championship until later on. Turner appointed his vice president of syndication, Jack Petrik, to head WCW. Petrik was in the twilight of his corporate career, so he handed off the day-to-day responsibilities to Jim Herd, who had run KPLR in St. Louis when the station carried Sam Muchnick's wrestling show.

I met with Petrik and informed him that I was ready to be a team player, but I was mad that Jimmy hadn't explained to me about my value to TBS before my contract negotiations. And now, I told Petrik, I would no longer work for Dusty Rhodes.

I celebrated my fortieth birthday at Sabatino's restaurant in Baltimore. Michael Hayes sang some Lynyrd Skynyrd, and someone brought out a cake with trick candles that couldn't be blown out. Kevin Sullivan pulled one off the cake and began heading in the direction of Gary Juster, a lawyer and promoter affiliated with WCW (who had also come into the world in my father's delivery room in Minnesota). Juster's wife at the time was a bit of a prude, so Sullivan slipped the candle in his foreskin and showed it to her. She instinctively put up her hand and shrieked in horror. "Blow it out," Kevin hollered. Once she got over the shock, though, she was laughing with the rest of us.

From the beginning, WCW's policy was to sign up wrestlers who

CHAPTER **13**

TEST
OF
TIME

already had visibility through working for Vince. I naturally recommended Steamboat, who had just had a good run with the World Wrestling Federation, holding the group's Intercontinental Championship and working against guys like Randy Savage, Greg Valentine, and Don Muraco. In the years since our first feud, Steamboat had gotten even better. He cared about his craft so much that he'd watch tapes of boxers being hit so he could stagger the same way and add legitimacy to his matches. I told Petrik and Herd that we had to have him.

On January 6, 1989, Barry Windham, the U.S. champ, and I agreed to wrestle Eddie Gilbert and a "mystery partner" in the TBS studio. We were playing it cool and cocky until Gilbert revealed his teammate to be the "retired" Steamboat. Becoming unhinged, I shouted, "Do you understand something? I'm a multimillionaire, and this doesn't happen to millionaires! Our days are planned, they're scheduled, they're detailed!" I claimed to know the *real* reason Steamboat returned: "You're here for my title, and you're not gonna get it!" My eyes were bugging out of my head like a madman.

Eddie Gilbert barely tagged in during the match; it was all Steamboat. He did all his great maneuvers, usually at my expense. At one stage, after I retreated to ringside, Ricky calmly walked over to the announcers' podium and took the microphone. "If you want to play," he said, "stay in the sandbox."

When I got back in the ring, it was more of the same, with Steamboat scoring the win for his team by pinning me with a flying body press. Jim Ross—who had started announcing on TBS after the UWF sale—screamed excitedly, "The Dragon has returned to the NWA!" Ross was was just as thrilled as I was, believe me.

More than a decade had passed since my first series of matches with Steamboat—and that had been in Mid-Atlantic, before we had anything close to national exposure. Because the clothes-shredding bit had worked so well in 1978, we decided to try it again for a fan base that mostly hadn't seen it. There were a few differences, though. In Charlotte, I'd been threatened by Ricky's good looks and the possibility that he'd dip into my "private stock" of women. Now, Steamboat had apparently matured into an adult who preferred the stability of family life to my chaotic playboy ways.

On February 15, 1989, I had a group of models at my side when I confronted Steamboat in the ring in Cleveland. "Why don't you go home and help the missus with the dishes, pal?" I sneered. "I'm going downtown."

As I turned, opening my arms to display myself to the models, Steamboat grabbed my elbow, spun me around, and slapped me. In between a series of punches and chops, Steamboat began ripping my suit. With one trouser leg missing, I fought back, unloading on Ricky in the corner. He rebounded with a snapmare, pulled my pants off completely, and left me in my jockeys and socks. My on-screen adviser at the time, Hiro Matsuda, inserted himself into the skirmish, grabbing Steamboat from the rear and holding him so I could deliver a flurry of knife-edged chops. Then Ricky burst free, punching out Matsuda, knocking me out of the ring, and throwing me over the security barrier, where he backed me up through the audience with chop after chop.

RICK STEAMBOAT: I wrestled Ric for the title on February 20, 1989, on Pay-Per-View in Chicago. When we got to the building, neither of us knew the finish. I remember asking George Scott, "What's going on?" And he told me, "I haven't made up my mind yet." He ran a couple of things by us—me winning, Ric winning, a draw, a disqualification, a run-in—and they all sounded good. No one knew the outcome until about an hour before the match.

Ricky and I pushed each other physically as hard as we could. Despite how much the business had changed, in the ring, the chemistry was all there.

The tide had shifted a few times when Ricky attempted a flying body press and referee Tommy Young stepped in the way, taking the impact. Steamboat tried another body press, but I moved out of the way. With a second ref, Teddy Long, taking over as a replacement, I tried applying the figure-four. As I leaned down, Ricky reached up, grabbed the back of my head, and pinned me with an inside cradle.

MARK MADDEN, FORMER WCW ANNOUNCER: You could almost feel the audience holding its breath, wondering whether the decision would be reversed. Then, after Teddy Long had counted the pin, Tommy Young went over and raised Steamboat's hand. The crowd went wild. It was a great moment that played off previous mistakes.

Everything was super-smooth in that match. If you watch the tape,

you can see Dave Meltzer, the editor of the *Wrestling Observer* newsletter–a very controversial publication at that time–in the front row, standing and clapping on several occasions. *Not* an easy man to impress. I remember watching them do a neck bridge into a backslide spot, and it looked like ballet. The finishing sequence was relatively complicated, but it was so seamless, it almost defies description.

RICK STEAMBOAT: I wish we had more time to establish our rhythm, so to speak, before the title change. It would have been nice to work with each other all over the country before I pulled it off. But George Scott wanted to capitalize on the shock factor. No one expected me to win the NWA Championship so soon. I had just come back to the NWA, this was our first meeting, and we shocked the hell out of the wrestling world.

In my mind, Rick Steamboat should have been champion years earlier. Unfortunately for him, fan sensibilities had changed by 1989, and a lot of people didn't enjoy the sight of his wife, Bonnie, and young son, Ricky Jr., accompanying him to the ring. They were on all the Pay-Per-Views, with Bonnie wearing long, sequined gowns like Miss Elizabeth, Randy Savage's enchanting wife and manager in the World Wrestling Federation. Bonnie wasn't Elizabeth, though, and fans who should have been screaming for Steamboat were instead making fun of him for being pussy-whipped.

RICK STEAMBOAT: When the fans saw me with my wife and son, they thought I was a goody two-shoes, while Flair was a flamboyant womanizer with girlfriends in every city. I guess some of the people thought he was cooler. It was around this time that I noticed more and more fans starting to like the heels. If a heel entertained them, he was cheered. The babyface didn't get an automatic hooray anymore, and I wasn't used to that.

Once the actual wrestling started, Steamboat won back a lot of the crowd. But—on-camera and off—Bonnie was in the middle of his business, and George Scott was pissed. "Get rid of her," he told me. "She's ruining him."

George was supposed to be the booker, and therefore in charge of those kinds of issues, but he had no desire to handle something so sensitive. "It was your idea to bring him in," he insisted. "We never agreed to use Bonnie. He's your friend. Talk to him."

I didn't want to deal with something like that, either, but George put it on me. So I gingerly broached the subject with Steamboat. "Jesus, Rick," I said, "the people are cheering *me*. That's not how it's supposed to be happening. I mean, Bonnie's a lovely person, but fans aren't into seeing Rick Steamboat, the father and devoted husband. They want to see Rick Steamboat, the sex symbol, the handsome guy that you are, the great body. They want to see the old Ricky Steamboat."

I could see that my words were going in one ear and out the other. Bonnie had so much control over him. Obviously, Ricky was now in an awkward situation and had to tell his wife everything that I said. As a result, Bonnie and I became mortal enemies.

Years later, when both of our boys—Steamboat's kid Richie and my son Reid—began amateur wrestling, a coach came over to me one day with a silly look on his face. "I didn't realize you were the original wild man," he giggled.

I was embarrassed, but played dumb and asked where he'd heard that. "Bonnie Steamboat," was his reply. She'd been telling road stories about me. *To my kid's wrestling coach and God only knows who else!* It didn't matter how much time had passed. She held a grudge for life.

The experience made me realize that everything I did had consequences. I didn't care if other adults heard about my antics on the road. But now my past was invading the safe zone I had created for my children.

AFTER STEAMBOAT'S TITLE win, I began chasing him for the title at "house shows," nontelevised wrestling events. The next big chapter in our rivalry would take place April 2, 1989, on a *Clash of the Champions* special at the New Orleans Superdome. But George Scott didn't want to publicize the match; he was afraid that if fans knew that they could watch us on TV for free, they wouldn't buy tickets to the house shows. As a result, the public was essentially kept in the dark about a free championship bout on TBS, and we drew a disappointing 4.3 rating.

George was fired just before the show, and replaced with a booking committee that consisted of myself, Kevin Sullivan, Jim Barnett, Jim Herd, and Eddie Gilbert. Originally, Steamboat and I were supposed to have a draw, but now I argued for a new ending.

RICK STEAMBOAT: We were going to have a Two-Out-of-Three Falls match. Ric and I had a quick conversation in the dressing room, figured out our finishes, and walked away from each other. Some of the other guys came up to me and said, "Wait, the two of you are going close to an hour . . ."

"Okay."

"And it's two out of three falls . . ."

"Yeah."

"And you've got your finishes. What about the rest of the match?"

I said, "Hell, we're just gonna call it in the ring." We would see how the crowd was going and take it from there. We knew each other so well that sometimes, without talking, we'd go into a spot we both remembered from ten years earlier.

I won the first fall with an inside cradle, the same move Steamboat used to beat me for the title. The second fall ended when he lifted me from behind and hooked my arms behind my back. With my feet dangling over the mat, I shook my head from side to side, refusing to give up, then finally grunted and nodded, submitting to Ricky's double chicken wing. In the third fall, he picked me up again, attempting to apply the same maneuver. But his leg gave out and he fell backward, still hooking my arms behind me. Our shoulders hit the canvas at the same time, but at the count of two, Steamboat raised one shoulder to retain the championship.

Now that I had a hand in the booking, I refused to fall into the same trap that Dusty had. Steamboat was the champion and deserved to win the match. I wasn't consumed with what was right for Ric Flair; it was what was right for *business*.

JIM CORNETTE: It was around this time that people started calling Ric Flair the greatest wrestler of all time. There have probably been better interviews. There have probably been a few people who, for a certain period of time, were better in the ring. There have been people who looked better cosmetically. But nobody has ever been as good at everything for so long.

Clothes *do* make "The Man," thanks to the elaborate ring robes Olivia Walker designed for me.
Courtesy *Pro Wrestling Illustrated*

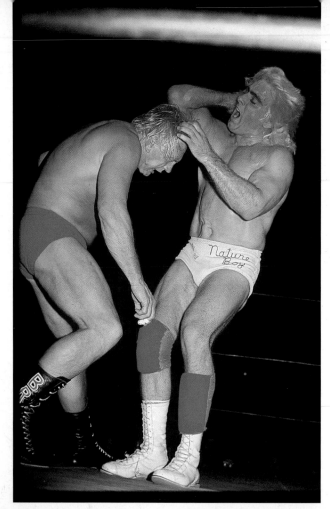

Dropping an elbow on the original "Nature Boy," Buddy Rogers.
Courtesy *Pro Wrestling Illustrated*

Hands down, there was no one tougher in or out of the ring than Harley Race.
Courtesy *Pro Wrestling Illustrated*

It's an indescribable feeling when fans all over the world actually do honor you as the World Heavyweight Champion.

Courtesy *Pro Wrestling Illustrated*

"The *real* World's Champion" tells it like it is after joining the World Wrestling Federation.

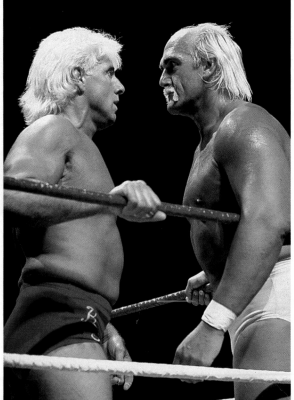

The Nature Boy and the Hulkster. To this day, fans still argue over who the better wrestler is.

Throwing Sid Justice over the top rope at
Royal Rumble 1992 **proved to the world**
once and for all that I was number one.

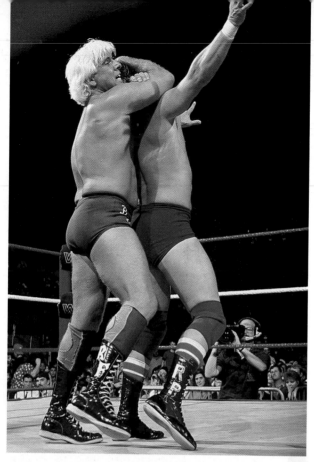

I was glad that my first opponent in a World Wrestling Federation match was my good friend Rowdy Roddy Piper.

Randy Savage took the belt from me at *WrestleMania VIII*, but *I* stole the show and a kiss from his wife, Miss Elizabeth.

Bret Hart was a good wrestler, but I don't consider him a great champion.

Slick Ric, stylin' and profilin'.

Whipping Sting into the corner during one of our matches.
Courtesy *Pro Wrestling Illustrated*

Backstage at WCW with fellow Horseman "The Crippler" Chris Benoit.
Courtesy *Pro Wrestling Illustrated*

One of WCW's greatest mistakes was not hanging on to "Stunning" Steve Austin.

Courtesy Pro Wrestling Illustrated

Problems with Eric Bischoff and WCW fired me up for one of my most memorable interviews with "Mean" Gene Okerlund.

Courtesy Pro Wrestling Illustrated

I love hearing the crowd yell "Woooo!" every time I deliver one of my knife-edge chops.

Courtesy Pro Wrestling Illustrated

Mr. McMahon may have wanted to destroy WWE's "new co-owner" in 2002, but he rebuilt the confidence I'd lost during my final years at WCW.

My boys, Reid and David. I'm so proud of both of them.
Courtesy Ric Flair

After twenty-two years of marriage, Beth is the love of my life.
Courtesy Ric Flair

Celebrating the holidays with my girls, Ashley and Megan.
Courtesy Ric Flair

Battling Undertaker at *WrestleMania X8* was a personal highlight in my career. He's always been one of my favorite wrestlers.

The "People's Elbow" from The Rock at *WrestleMania XX*.

My home away from home: the squared circle, surrounded by you, the fans I love and appreciate.

My feud with "The Dragon" reached new heights in a Two-Out-of-Three Falls classic at *Clash of the Champions VI.*

When I started hearing this type of talk, I took it as a challenge. I still believed in my motto: "To be the man, you've gotta beat the man." If people were going to call me the best, I wanted to *be* the best.

With Pay-Per-View and cable, though, it was harder to have the kinds of great matches I'd used to establish my name. Sometimes you'd be told that—because of entrances and skits and everything else that had to be jammed onto the show—you could only stay in the ring for ten minutes. And I knew that it would take at least thirty minutes to have the kind of match that I wanted. I'd be just building momentum when—*boom!*—it was time to wrap up.

However, when Steamboat and I met for the final match of our televised trilogy—the *Music City Showdown* Pay-Per-View in Nashville on May 7, 1989—we had no such restrictions. Three former NWA champions—Pat O'Connor, Lou Thesz, and Terry Funk—were appointed as ringside "judges," to determine a victor if we went to the time limit. The fans were expecting exactly that, then some controversy over the voting. We had a good, long match, leading everyone in that direction. Then Ricky went for a body slam, and I cradled him to capture my sixth NWA title.

> **MARK MADDEN:** These were two guys whose strengths dovetailed perfectly. They trusted each other implicitly. No one sold for Ric quite like Steamboat, except for maybe Ricky Morton. But Steamboat never oversold and looked silly. This was what wrestling is supposed to be–Ric and Steamboat knew how to get the crowd to where they wanted it to go, like symphony conductors.
>
> Bottom line: the best three-match series ever wrestled in an American ring was Flair and Steamboat in 1989. Anyone who says otherwise is wrong. Unlike many matches from "back in the day," these stand the test of time.

Honestly, I never had a bad match with Rick Steamboat, and we probably wrestled each other two thousand times. In fact, some of our battles in 1978 may have been better than the ones in 1989. But there weren't cameras around for a lot of those early matches, so the memories are confined to the people who happened to be in the arena.

In Nashville, though, my title win was just the start of something else. The crowd was already happy about witnessing a piece of history, and now I raised Steamboat's arm, a sportsmanlike gesture that turned me into a fan favorite. The people wanted to cheer me, anyway. As Ricky left the ring, Jim Ross came in to conduct an interview, and we were soon joined by a tuxedo-clad Terry Funk.

"Hey, Ric," Terry began, "I want to be the first to congratulate you on being the new World's Champion."

I shook Funk's hand, then turned back to J.R. Terry cut in again. "Hey, Ric, I also want to say that if it had gone sixty minutes, that I would've voted for Ric Flair because I think that you're the greatest wrestler in the world today."

"Very nice," replied a slightly exasperated J.R. "Thank you very much, Terry. Thank you very much."

J.R. had turned back toward me when Terry said, "I would also like to go ahead and be the first one to challenge Ric Flair for that new championship."

RICK STEAMBOAT: I looked back in the ring after our match, and they've got another thing going on. No one told me that this was going to happen. I was awestruck. I had just dropped the title to Flair, and thought it would at least warrant one more series of matches to see if I could get it back. I didn't care if I won or not; I never did. I just wanted to work with Ric again. Instead, they went right into another angle.

In the ring, I was telling Terry Funk that although I was flattered by his request, he'd been inactive, so the NWA's top ten challengers would be considered first.

"Wait a minute," Terry said in a quavering voice. "Are you really saying that I'm not a contender? You're saying that I'm not good enough, aren't you, Ric?"

"I'm not saying that at all . . ."

"Yes, you are." He seemed on the verge of tears. "Please, let me say just one more thing. I was just kidding you about going ahead and wanting to challenge you. I didn't really want to challenge you. I was just kidding you. So let's go ahead and . . ."

Terry extended his hand in friendship, and—as the unsuspecting good guy—I shook it. That's when he pulled me forward, and slugged me with his left hand, before hurling me out of the ring and over the guardrail. Terry pulled off his tuxedo jacket and slammed my head into a ringside table. Then, he dragged me onto the table, lifted me upside down, and delivered a piledriver.

He almost killed me. It's pretty hard to protect a guy when you're both crashing through a table. I couldn't turn my head for weeks. But Terry was ahead of his time. People just didn't piledrive their opponents through tables back then.

DAVID FLAIR: My father had called our house and told my mother that he wanted us to get cable, so we could have Pay-Per-View and see what my dad did. He was scared we wouldn't know who our father was. When Terry Funk put him through the table, it was really exciting. My sister Megan didn't enjoy things like that, but I did. I was getting smart to the business.

MARK LAMONICA, AKA BUBBA-RAY DUDLEY: This was one of the most memorable things I'd ever seen on television. You know how now, when I'm wrestling, I scream, "D-Von, get the tables!" Well, it all goes back to the Terry Funk–Ric Flair angle. That's the day the seed was planted in me to use a table as a weapon.

The show went off the air with the image of me seemingly unconscious under the wreck of a table. Terry Funk was still raving, acting paranoid, despondent, and gleeful, all at the same time: "He said that I wasn't good enough, I'm not a contender. Look at him! Look at the horse-toothed, banana-nosed jerk!" I had personified evil for most of my career. Terry Funk may have been the only S.O.B. crazy enough to turn me good.

In the coming weeks, the fans were told that I had a severe neck injury, and I convinced them by wearing a brace around Charlotte while running errands, even while on airplanes. Even though the rigidity over protecting the business was diminishing, the claim was more than plausible. Kurt Angle went into *WrestleMania XIX* with a broken neck. Even after surgery, Stone Cold Steve Austin's neck damage forced him into a nonwrestling role in WWE. Before an episode of *Raw* in 2003, I watched Christian spend the day in the arena wearing a neck collar. He only took it off to wrestle Rob Van Dam—in a ladder match.

For more than a month, I teased a possible retirement, then announced that I wanted to come back for revenge. Terry remained bold as hell, freaking out TBS executives in September 1989 by slipping a plastic bag over my head, tying it shut, and "smothering" me during a broadcast. Terry was forty-five years old at the time and had been getting his brains kicked in for a quarter-century. People who saw him hobbling backstage were astonished that he could actually wrestle, but Terry could deal with pain. Once in Japan, when he was champion, he was scalded with hot water. He gutted it up and wrestled with third-degree burns. He was fearless.

The final chapter in our feud unfolded at a *Clash of the Champions* "I Quit" match on November 15, 1989. The stipulations were that the match could only end via submission, and if Terry Funk lost this effort to win my title, he would have to shake my hand and declare me the better man. We fought all over the arena, dragging along a microphone with a very long cord as we brawled.

On the arena floor, Funk grabbed my head and positioned it between his knees, setting me up for a piledriver. "You remember your neck?" he asked menacingly. "Don't you want to say 'I quit' before I hurt you?"

I refused and was penalized with a piledriver, followed by a leg drop.

"This is a hockey rink," J.R. earnestly told the viewers at home. "There's ice underneath that particle board."

Several minutes later, though, I was back in the match, hitting Terry with chops. His knees trembled, but he wouldn't fall. Instead, he

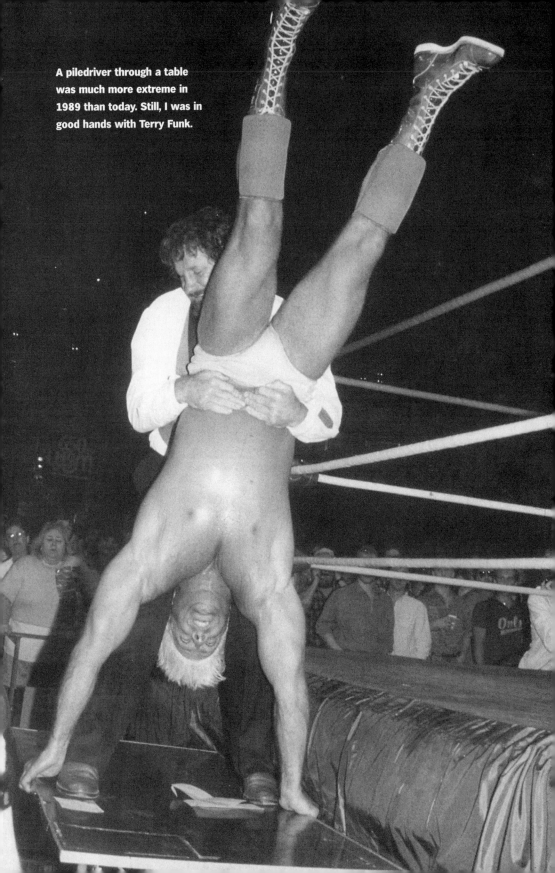

A piledriver through a table was much more extreme in 1989 than today. Still, I was in good hands with Terry Funk.

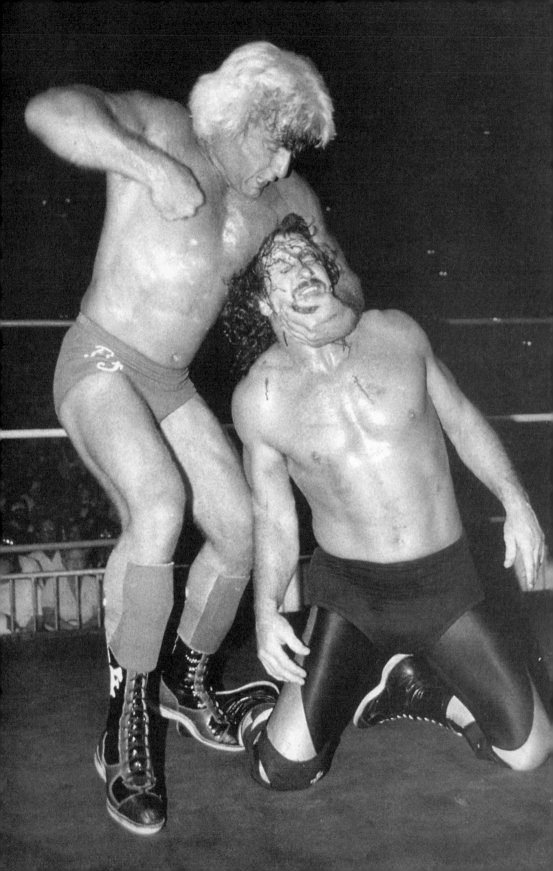

held on to one rope and swung wildly. I ducked under Terry's hay-maker and chopped him again.

The referee was holding the microphone when I locked on the figure-four. As Funk thrashed around, the ref asked if he was ready to quit. "Never!" he screamed.

I propped up my back and appeared to clamp down with even more pressure. Finally, Terry groaned and flapped his arms. "My leg is breaking . . . yes, I quit."

With great agony, Funk boosted himself up on the ropes. "Shake my hand right now!" I demanded. When he hesitated, I shoved him.

Terry shoved me back and blurted, "You're a hell of a man, Ric Flair." I clasped his hand, then threw it down and raised my arm to the crowd.

MEANWHILE, IN THE World Wrestling Federation, Arn and Tully were the Tag Team Champions. I missed working with them and convinced Jim Herd that they would be an asset to WCW. They each negotiated a three-year deal for $250,000 annually, gave notice to Vince, dropped the tag-team straps to Demolition, and agreed to finish out their dates for the World Wrestling Federation. Before they left, though, Tully tested positive for cocaine.

Now everything had changed. Tully was no longer welcome in WCW. Arn could come in, but not for the agreed-upon amount; Herd maintained that he wasn't as vital to the company without Blanchard. I had to be the one to break the news to Arn that Herd would only pay him—almost $100,000 a year less—because his friend was stupid enough to get into trouble.

On December 9, 1989, I was being surrounded by manager Gary Hart's protégés, the Great Muta and the Dragon Master, on TBS. Suddenly, Arn came running to my rescue, and he had Ole with him. The three of us were back together! And yes, it would have been great to reunite all of the original Horsemen, but I don't remember any fans complaining when we joined forces with Sting instead.

On the surface, history seemed to have gone in reverse, to the time before Crockett Promotions caved in. I was the NWA World Heavyweight Champion, and back in the Four Horsemen with the Minnesota Wrecking Crew. Behind the scenes, though, I knew that you couldn't go back—even if going forward was not a welcome prospect.

Even when WCW started heading downhill, I had nothing but admiration for Jim Ross, the very best announcer in the business.

Jim Herd was an idiot. This is not defamation. I'm just telling you history. The man had no right to be anywhere near a wrestling company. Everything you read in this chapter will bear that out.

When Herd was station manager at KPLR in St. Louis, he occasionally got together with Sam Muchnick to talk sports and wrestling. But I think all of Herd's claims about being Sam's close confidant were false. Herd was what he was—a station manager. I can't imagine Muchnick giving him the time of day.

Either way, a station manager is about as qualified to run a wrestling company as I am to work at the Pentagon. After KPLR, Herd worked as an executive for a bank, then for Pizza Hut. Around the boys, Herd—a gruff, white-haired guy—liked to curse

CHAPTER **14**

LIKE
ICE CREAM
TO COW
MANURE

and talk about how tough he'd been during his days as a navy boxer. To us, he was just the "Pizza King," the name the wrestlers called him behind his back.

Because I was on the booking committee, some people have the false impression that I made all the big decisions in WCW at this time. The truth is that Herd ran the committee and we had rotating members, including Jim Ross, Jody Hamilton (referee Nick Patrick's father, and one of the masked Assassins from Georgia in the 1970s), Terry Funk, Jim Barnett, Kevin Sullivan, and Jim Cornette, who Herd hated.

JIM CORNETTE: I cursed Ric for putting me on the booking committee—"Goddamn, Ric, you put me on this booking committee for $300 extra a week, and I gotta work with that fuckin' Jim Herd."

Jim Barnett was also on the committee. He'd run promotions in Australia and Georgia, and worked very closely with Vince and Fred Kohler, who promoted on the national wrestling show on the Dumont Network in the 1950s. Barnett was the acknowledged wrestling expert. Everyone knew he didn't need the money, but he liked to gossip and just keep his hand in the business. With his influence, Jim could have gone over Herd's head, but rather than be confrontational, he sat back and watched.

Herd wanted to copy Vince, but he didn't have the talent or the insight. The one constant thing about WCW was the company's ineptness at the top, and Jim Herd symbolized it. He was unsuited, unprepared, and uneducated about professional wrestling.

When I left the committee, I wanted to give my notice by going into Herd's office, saying, "Herd, I'm done," pulling out a blank gun, and firing about five shots at him. But I thought better of it; I figured anybody as stupid as he was, who had pissed off as many people and screwed with as many careers as he had, probably had a real gun in his desk drawer.

Jim Ross and I have always been friends. I consider him the best play-by-play guy in the history of wrestling, right there with Gordon Solie. Like me, he has adjusted over the years, going from describing the short-arm scissors to the moonsault. We've had a ball together. But when we were on the booking committee, I felt like Herd put us at odds. Look, we both wanted to hang on to our spots; with the territories gone, there were very few places for J.R. to go. And here he was—with all his knowledge—having to go out at night and *pour gins* for that ignorant bastard. It was a matter of self-preservation.

JIM ROSS: There were times when I totally despised Herd's management style, and the lack of product knowledge that fueled his bad decisions. There were other times when I really enjoyed his company. Jim Herd was a tenacious bulldog. He was a stocky, combative, gin-drinking, blue-language guy. He'd led an interesting life, and could be very engaging over a half-dozen drinks.

But Herd often made decisions based on the last person he talked to. People who weren't even working for us would call him. He talked to Sam Muchnick. He talked to Lou Thesz; hell, Lou would have us go back to wool tights. We would think that we had something established, a long-term direction, and then Herd would change it.

The problem for guys like Ric Flair and Jim Cornette was that they were on the road, doing their bookings and fulfilling their obligations. They would come back and see that Herd had changed his mind about something, and people like me—who worked in the office in Atlanta—got painted with the same brush. We were implicated. It was guilt by association.

Ric and I didn't always agree on direction, but we always agreed on philosophy. We knew what a heel was, what a babyface was, and what elements had to be in place to be successful. We both agreed that we liked ice cream, but he liked chocolate and I liked vanilla. Every now and then, we'd both like the same thing.

We have had our challenging times, but I don't think either guy has ever lost respect for the other. Over time, we both realized that it was the divide-and-conquer thing.

This was the first time in my career when I had to think about survival all day long. The only time I could concentrate on the thing I loved was when I was actually in the ring, doing it.

Herd's gimmicks are legendary. Matt Borne—a guy who'd later convincingly give life to the character of Doink the Clown in the World Wrestling Federation—was Big Josh, a lumberjack who hung around with dancing bears. And Arn—who once tag-teamed and shared rooms on the road with Borne—had to lose to him! Then there were the Ding Dongs, a masked tag team with *bells* hanging from their costumes; whenever they made a tag, they rang a big bell in their corner. Had he

not been stopped, Herd would have also brought in the Hunchbacks, a team that was unbeatable because their shoulders couldn't touch the canvas.

During one meeting, Kevin Sullivan started kidding Herd about the Hunchbacks concept. "I know what we can do," he said. "We'll throw them outside the ring, get a shovel, dig a hole, put the hump in it, and cover—one-two-three."

"Great idea," Herd replied. The asshole was serious, too.

KEVIN SULLIVAN: I've had some pretty fair ideas in my day, but I don't think that was one of them. Because Ric had been around for so long, Herd thought that his image needed updating–from the Nature Boy to a Roman gladiator. He said, "Let's cut Ric's hair, put an earring in his ear, and give him a shield. We'll call him Spartacus." He actually wanted to change Ric Flair's name! I said, "While we're doing this, why don't we go to Yankee Stadium and change Babe Ruth's number?" Herd just didn't realize who Ric Flair was, or what he meant to wrestling fans.

The dancing bears knew better than to be seen here with poor "Big Josh" (Matt Borne), one of Jim Herd's "big plans" for WCW.

In Herd's mind, he could transform me into a character that could compete with Vince's characters. When I talk about it now, people laugh. At the time, though, it was very upsetting. My robe was outdated, he said, and I needed a new look. I never became Spartacus and refused to wear the earring, but I let Herd talk me into cutting my hair, and I hated myself for it. I don't think the fans liked it, either. I didn't look like Ric Flair. I'd spent all these years putting up with shit, sacrificing my body, and never seeing my oldest kids, to find myself manipulated by the whims of a moron, a fuckin' pizza company executive with his finger on the trigger.

This is the kind of shit that I was putting up with—despite the fact that I was on the booking committee. That's why it pissed me off when Mick Foley blamed me for not recognizing his full potential during that period. In his book, *Have a Nice Day,* Foley wrote, "Ric Flair was every bit as bad on the booking side of things as he was great on the wrestling side of it."

First of all, I'll never call myself a great booker, because wrestling always came first. But Foley took a shot at me. Here's his receipt—I'm taking a shot at him.

When I first started on the booking committee, Foley was working as Cactus Jack and doing an angle where he was living in a homeless shelter. I admit it—I didn't know what to do with a three hundred-pound guy living in a homeless shelter. It took P.T. Barnum, in the form of Vince McMahon, to take a guy whose claim to fame was his willingness to get thrown off a cage, turn him into Mankind, and make him into a champion.

Foley has a cult following because of his contribution to hardcore wrestling. But hardcore is such a small part of the history of this business. When I was training, falling off a ladder was not a prerequisite to making it as a professional wrestler. Being fundamentally sound was. Occasionally seeing the inside of a gym was. When I trained under Verne Gagne, we started with 500 free squats, 250 push-ups, 250 sit-ups and a two-mile run over farm terrain in zero-degree weather. Then we came back to the barn to be wrestled into submission, cross-faced into submission, stretched into submission—and if Verne didn't like the way things were going, we'd start all over. He would have looked at Mick Foley on day one—after Mick failed to do even one thing Verne required—and said, "Mick, I don't think so."

I don't care how many thumbtacks Mick Foley has fallen on, how many ladders he's fallen off, how many continents he's supposedly bled on, he'll always be known as a glorified stuntman.

Verne Gagne didn't fall off a ladder. Dory Funk, Jr., didn't fall off a ladder. Neither did Wahoo, Steamboat or Steve Austin. Terry Funk was a great worker before he started doing that. Kurt Angle, Shawn

Michaels, and Chris Jericho can do it and maintain their reputations because they're *already* respected as athletes. And what about people who never did anything else, like the Sandman? He's no wrestler. Hardcore became a niche for a lot of guys who couldn't do fuck-all in the ring.

I'm not saying that Mick Foley wasn't a star, that he wasn't a great attraction. But in my estimation, Mick Foley was not a great worker. He couldn't punch. He couldn't kick. In the World Wrestling Federation, he'd spend half the day before television broadcasts sucking up to the writers—because he's such a fan of himself.

There's a difference between being a great performer and being a guy—like Brutus Beefcake or the Ultimate Warrior—who became famous because he happened to be working for Vince. It's the same with Foley. When he hasn't been working for Vince, there's been no demand for him whatsover. He's just another guy.

Mick Foley doesn't understand what it was like to be on that booking committee. Jim Herd humiliated me and made me cut my hair—after I'd won the NWA championship six times. How much power did I have? When I was going through all that, how should I have been able to look at Mick Foley, push everything else aside, and mold him into a superstar?

STING, ON THE other hand, was worthy of becoming the champion.

We started laying the groundwork for the title switch at *Starrcade '89,* when Sting won an Iron Man tournament, going through Lex Luger and the Great Muta, then pinning me in the final round. By winning, he was granted a title shot against me. Since the Four Horsemen were getting so many cheers, this was designed to turn the rest of us bad as the people rallied behind Sting.

On February 6, 1990, in Corpus Christi, Texas, we officially kicked Sting out of the group at *Clash of the Champions,* with Ole cutting a great interview on him that really earned us the crowd's hatred. In the main event that night, Arn, Ole, and I were in a cage against Muta, the Dragon Master, and Buzz Sawyer when Sting came out to attack us. Then the unexpected happened—as Sting climbed the cage, he blew out his knee and had to take time off. "Don't worry," I reassured him. "I'll be waiting for you, with the championship belt, when you come back."

Jim Herd was mad at Sting for getting hurt and wanted me to

drop the title to Luger instead. I objected. This had nothing to do with Luger; I spoke to him about it and explained everything. I was keeping my word to Sting. Since the first *Clash of the Champions* in 1988, we'd been portraying him as the future of the company. My job initially had been teaching him how to work, but it was like training a prime racehorse. He picked up his craft inside the ring and, on the run, was learning how to be a character and draw money. He'd passed every test. His knee would heal soon, I told Herd, and it was stupid to change course now.

For refusing to lose to Lex, I was kicked off the booking committee. But I wouldn't waver on my promise to Sting. At *The Great American Bash*—now an annual Pay-Per-View show—in the Baltimore Arena on July 7, 1990, he cradled me as I attempted a figure-four, and became the NWA Champion. Sting was well aware of the battles I'd been waging backstage, so he stepped out of character when the title was awarded to him. "Listen to what I have to say," he told the crowd. "Ric Flair is the greatest champion of all time. As for me, I am a champion . . . only because I have some big shoes to fill."

The speech was confusing to fans. According to the storyline, the Horsemen and I were out to destroy the new champion. But Sting was being gracious. He was being a gentleman. And it reaffirmed my belief that I'd been fighting for the right guy.

WHEN YOU SWITCH the title, it's crucial to have the right opponents lined up for the new champion. Otherwise, he flounders the way I did in 1981, when I defended the title in Florida against Charlie Cook. Once Sting became champion, he was out there by himself—without me to take his press slams and suplexes, or to feign being terrified while he stood in the middle of the ring, beating his chest. With a limited range of adversaries, Sting wasn't drawing money—something that probably tickled the other good guys who thought they were more deserving of the championship. In our business, people like when a guy does well— but not *too* well. They'll pat someone like Sting on the back, then get in the car, go on the road, and bitch that he can't draw.

Someone came up with the idea of the Black Scorpion, a mysterious masked man who'd stalk Sting while he was in the ring. We played Ole Anderson's distorted voice over the public-address system, claiming to be a figure from Sting's murky past. Some fans assumed that it was the Ultimate Warrior, but since he happened to be holding the World Wrestling Federation Championship at the time it seemed unlikely that Vince would allow him to participate on our show.

The original Black Scorpion was Al Perez, a muscular guy who worked for a small promotion in Texas. But when he discovered that he'd have to get beaten at the end of the storyline, he backed out—even though no one knew who he was to begin with. The plot went haywire. A bunch of other guys played the Scorpion at different shows and, at *Starrcade '90,* the company had Sting meet his hooded nemesis in a cage and reveal his identity.

To salvage the story, the Scorpion would be exposed as a plot by the Horsemen to play with Sting's mind. Barry Windham would have been great for the part, but he and Arn had a "street fight" against Butch Reed and Ron Simmons that night. So out of every wrestler in the locker room, I was picked to wear the mask, lose, and have my face revealed. The match was ludicrous, and included such timeless moments as other guys in Black Scorpion costumes fighting it out with Sting and special referee Dick the Bruiser—the Crusher's tag-team partner during my childhood—after the bell. It looked as ridiculous as it sounds.

I have no doubt that Jim Herd knew exactly what he was doing by putting me in this situation, and I was distraught over it. How ironic that the incident took place in the Kiel Auditorium in St. Louis, where some of the greatest NWA title matches were held, back when men who wore the championship belt were treated with deference.

Sting was more incensed than I was. He believed the Black Scorpion angle had ruined his reign. He was right. We still weren't drawing, and on January 11, 1991, Herd made a change. Just like every other time WCW needed a designated hitter to go to the plate and drive home a run, they came to me.

MARK MADDEN: Ric won back the title at the Meadowlands during a snowstorm, with about 5,000 fans in the building. The New Jersey crowd rooted vociferously for Ric, probably a 70/30 split. They heckled Sting to the point that Sting was heckling back from the ring, which was out of character for him. When Ric would get an advantage in a match, he'd taunt the crowd, "Now we go to school!" Well, he did that in the Meadowlands, and the fans popped like nuts. A few seconds later, when Sting reversed the advantage, grabbing Ric's leg as if to put

him in the Scorpion Death Lock, he shouted real sarcastically to the fans in a singsong baby voice, "Now we go to school!"

The title change did nothing for business. Our rematch in Chicago drew just 1,300 fans, and the TBS executives switched the blame from Sting to me. Now the word was going around that, at forty-two, I was too old to maintain my position.

Once my program with Sting ended, I was matched up with Jorge Gonzales—"El Gigante," who at seven-foot-six was perhaps the tallest wrestler ever. Gonzales had played basketball in Argentina and been drafted by the Atlanta Hawks, but wasn't skilled enough to play in the NBA. Since Ted Turner owned both the Hawks and WCW, Gonzales was told, "Guess what? You're now a wrestler." He wasn't skilled enough to do that, either.

Jorge didn't understand anything about wrestling. They dressed him up as a gladiator, and he looked completely awkward out there. I tried as hard as I could with him—bouncing off the ropes, colliding with his body, doing anything that made him look like a legitimate threat. I'd go to the top rope, and he'd come under me and give me a slam from twelve feet in the air. It was spectacular, but no one cared.

It was around this time that the announcers started referring to the WCW Championship rather than the NWA title. It was still the same championship. But the people running WCW were getting tired of dealing with the remaining members of the NWA board—Don Owen in Oregon, Steve Rickard in New Zealand, and others. These guys wouldn't give up the NWA name, so WCW refused to use its talent to support their cards.

American wrestling fans have always had a tendency to forget history. The NWA title was starting to lose meaning in the United States, but in Japan, it was still a huge deal. On March 21, 1991, WCW did a combined show with the New Japan wrestling promotion, pulling in 64,500 fans and nearly $3.2 million at the Tokyo Dome. In the main event, I defended the title against Tatsumi Fujinami. Japanese fans were unfamiliar with the Dusty finish, so the company used it—but with a new twist.

In the middle of the match, I was running off the ropes, toward Fujinami, when he stepped out of the way and I hit referee Bill Alfonso. Fujinami pinned me with a backslide, but Alfonso was in no position to count it. We both stood up as a Japanese ref, Masao "Tiger" Hattori, came into the ring. I charged Fujinami, but he bent over and flipped me over the top rope. When I got back on the apron, he reached over the cables, suplexed me into the ring, trapped me in an abdominal stretch, and rolled me onto the canvas, where Hattori slapped the mat three times.

American fans—watching this as a tape-delayed Pay-Per-View—had been through all of this before, and took it for granted that Fujinami was disqualified for tossing me over the ropes. In a postmatch press conference they saw, I stormed over to Fujinami, swiped the championship belt out of his hands, and seemingly took off for the airport. The Japanese were told some convoluted story about how Fujinami was the new NWA champion, but because of American rules, I was still the WCW champ—the first time the titles were acknowledged as separate entities.

We were scheduled to meet again May 19 on a Pay-Per-View in St. Petersburg, Florida. While American stars are a big deal in Japan, Japanese guys are just Japanese guys in the United States, so there wasn't a lot of interest. WCW also did nothing to further its own cause, neither acknowledging the title controversy nor showing clips of Fujinami beating well-known Americans in Japan. In the rematch, Hattori was the referee who went down. Alfonso came in, and I scored the win with a rolling reverse cradle—and a handful of trunks. In Japan, the media reported that the two titles had been unified. In the U.S., the few fans who bothered tuning in were largely happy. It was 1991, and they liked bad guys like me. If I cheated to get the win, so what? Plus, they never knew anything about Fujinami in the first place.

UNDER JIM HERD'S leadership, there was no semblance of discipline in WCW. Contracts were doled out, and some wrestlers—secure they were going to be paid, anyway—began finding reasons not to go to work. I can list a lot of big names—Ricky Steamboat, Triple H, Wahoo, Steve Austin, Kurt Angle, Shawn Michaels, Arn Anderson, Harley Race, Terry Funk, Undertaker—who, contract or no contract, in any era, would walk through fire to get to the arena. Unfortunately, a lot of other guys saw the disorganization at the top and concluded that they weren't going to do any more than they had to. One night in Greensboro, one of the greatest wrestling cities of all time, *sixteen* out of the twenty-four wrestlers on the card didn't bother showing up.

I never did anything but produce, and yet, when it came time to renew my contract, the company tried to cut my salary. Their plan was to phase me out of main events and scale back the number of my dates. Instead of the $730,000 I'd been receiving, I was offered a deal where I'd make $350,000 for two consecutive years, then $250,000 for the last year of the agreement. That's $900,000 over three years, as opposed to $1.2 million a year for Sid Eudy, a useless muscle-head who—under the names Sid Vicious, Sid Justice, and Sycho Sid—would bounce back and forth between WCW and the World Wrestling Federation, contributing zero to either company. Sid exemplifies the worst of this business; he got rich despite never learning his craft or drawing a dime.

Herd could justify reducing my salary because—as I've already mentioned—if business was down, it had to be *my* fault. I was thinking about this recently while watching a show about Dan Marino on ESPN Classic. Okay, so he never won a Super Bowl, but how could you ever blame him for anything? Did he fumble the ball sometimes? Yeah. Did he make some bad decisions? Of course. But the guy threw 420 touchdown passes, 4,967 pass completions, and 30 or more touchdowns in three consecutive seasons. How do you *not* hold the Holy Grail over his head for consistency? I never missed work, lost when they told me to lose . . . and I got picked apart for all the wrong reasons.

It's hard to say you've been dicked around when you're making big money, but I just couldn't handle the confrontations day to day. It was the first time that I ever had to deal with not being wanted. I lost my confidence and started having terrible anxieties. There were times when I thought I couldn't feel my hands. I imagined that my jaw was stuck and I couldn't move it. I remember being thrown across the ring and getting scared that I wouldn't be able to raise my arms before I hit the turnbuckles. I started pinching myself during my matches. I'd roll onto the floor, bite my fingers, and pinch my forearms and biceps. It definitely affected my performance, and I couldn't tell anyone because I didn't understand what was going on. I still melt down just thinking about it.

KEVIN SULLIVAN: Jim Herd made Ric feel that he wasn't even worthy to wrestle, never mind being in the main event. Herd made him feel like he was a beginner—and a very poor one—not a guy who'd held the NWA World Championship seven times.

One night in Detroit, Ric went back to his room and was visibly shaking. The next morning, he called me and said, "You have to come down to my room."

When I went in, he was huddled like a jellyfish. He could hardly talk. He'd start to sit up, then fall back down on the bed. He was emotional and crying, saying, "I can't go on, I can't go on. You have to take me home."

I said, "Okay, Ric, let's get on a plane and go."

"I can't do that."

"Why can't you do that? It's very easy. You just go to the airport, and you get on a plane."

He told me, "I can't leave this room without your help."

I had to pack his bag for him, pick it up, put my arm around him, and walk him to the elevator–the way you would an invalid or a baby. I changed my own flight so I could go with him to Charlotte. I helped him on the plane and packed him into a seat like he was a vegetable. When fans came over, I warded them off, saying, "Ric's got the flu. He's not feeling good."

In Charlotte, I took him off the plane, drove him home, and actually had to walk him into his house. Anyone who knew anything about Ric Flair would never believe that this was the same man.

Before the publication of this book, no one knew about my inner torment except for Kevin Sullivan, Arn Anderson, my wife, and the McMahons. On the road, I'd hide it as best I could. At home, when I wasn't drinking, I'd sit up all night, touching my face and pinching my arms. Beth just kept saying, "Ric, we need to go to a doctor."

I couldn't even drink away my misery. It was absolutely terrible.

Eventually, I followed her advice. I had a CAT scan, an MRI, everything. When all the tests were done, the doctor told me, "What you're going through is all up here." He pointed at his head.

It may not sound very macho to go to a shrink, but—plain and simple—I needed help. So I started seeing a sports psychologist.

In the meantime, I refused to accept the contract renewal terms WCW had offered, so now I was working without any kind of binding agreement. Herd initially wanted me to lose the championship to Lex Luger at *The Great American Bash* on July 4, 1991. But he must have gotten frightened that I would refuse, because he asked me to lose to Barry

Windham three days earlier at a TV taping in Macon, Georgia. Then, the company reasoned, Luger could beat Barry at the *Bash* and become WCW's Hulk Hogan—who, coincidentally, had recently won back the World Wrestling Federation Championship at *WrestleMania VII*.

I was ready to leave for Macon and drop the title when a termination notice was faxed to my attorney. As I was walking out the door, Herd called me and said, "Fuck it. You're fired."

"What's that?"

"You'll have your release. You're fired now."

Herd offered to have WCW's head of security, Doug Dellinger, come over to my house and pick up the championship belt. I said, "Well, tell Doug to bring my check, and he'll have it." Herd knew damn well that the NWA champion always put down a $25,000 deposit when he won the title, then received his money back when the reign ended. Because I kept winning the title again and again, I had never bothered collecting. But if my relationship with the company was over, I wanted the deposit—plus interest. (And that interest was pretty significant; when I finally did receive a check later on, the amount was $38,000.)

"You guys owe me my money," I said, "and I don't trust you." We were at that level of communication. "Call Barnett. He knows all about it."

"Fuck Barnett. And fuck you."

"You are an incompetent, overbearing, fuckin' asshole," I replied. "And I promise you that after I leave, you'll be fired within three months. I'll come back, and you'll be gone."

I sent the championship belt to Vince McMahon the next day.

AS SOON AS Vince found out that I didn't have a contract, he was interested. He didn't kiss my ass, and I didn't kiss his; the mutual respect was already there. Vince's main concern was that in 1988, I had cried wolf, then chose to stay with Crockett. Was the same thing going to happen now?

The most gratifying part of the ordeal was the way the fans responded. At *The Great American Bash*—before, during, and *after* Lex Luger defeated Barry Windham for the vacant WCW title—the people chanted "We want Flair!" so loudly that the viewers could hear it at home. Mainstream sports commentators in the Charlotte area called for a WCW boycott. The NWA issued a statement emphasizing that its members still recognized the Nature Boy as its champion. Now Herd was under fire, and he needed to get back at me.

My lawyer told me to lie low, and that's what I did, staying inside my house for close to thirty days. Herd called, but I didn't answer the phone. WCW tried having Jimmy Crockett, who still worked for the company, make contact. I wouldn't take his call, either.

I went up to the World Wrestling Federation's office in Stamford, Connecticut, to meet Vince one-on-one. We talked money, and I told him what I'd been earning in WCW. "I don't give contracts," Vince said, "but I'll shake your hand and tell you that you'll make the same with me, or more." He had another guarantee: if I was ever used as anything *but* a headliner, I would be free to seek employment elsewhere—even WCW.

There was one obstacle in the way, and I told Vince about it. Herd had finally broken through to me, and WCW wanted a final meeting. I felt that I owed it to myself to at least hear their offer. Then I'd get right back to Vince.

We shook hands, and Vince looked me in the eye. "Is your word good?"

"Yes, it is."

"When I shake your hand, Ric, I'm taking you at your word, and you're taking me at mine." Finally, a professional, I thought.

As soon as I got downstairs, I called Arn. "I think I'm gonna go with Vince."

"Aw, fuck," he groaned, not because he wasn't happy for me, but because we'd be in different companies again. It had taken a lot of maneuvering on my part to reunite with Arn. Then he got flim-flammed out of his money, and WCW cracked me. Now I'd be up North and he'd be down South—best friends separated by this bullshit.

ON AUGUST 10, 1991, Bobby "The Brain" Heenan appeared on World Wrestling Federation television, standing alongside cohost Gorilla Monsoon and holding the championship belt I had shipped to Vince. "How about *this,* Gorilla?" Heenan bragged.

"What's that?"

"This happens to be the *real* championship belt."

"That's not Hogan's belt, Brain. I know the champ's belt when I see it."

"You're right. Comparing this belt to Hulk Hogan's belt would be like comparing ice cream to horse manure. . . . You see, the man that owns this belt is now under contract to another organization. In the very near future, he might be coming to the World Wrestling Federation. The man is also a very long, dear, personal friend of mine."

"Does the guy have a name?"

"Yes, he has a name. This man has challenged Hogan on numerous occasions. *Unanswered,* I may add. If you want to compare them, fine. Then let's compare Hulk Hogan . . . to *Ric Flair.*"

WCW HAD BEEN publicly disgraced, and they couldn't do a thing. I hadn't received a check for the championship belt (at that point) and was under contract to no one. When I flew down to Atlanta to have my final conversation with Herd and Jack Petrik, the power was in my hands.

Suddenly, everybody couldn't be nicer to me. Herd and Petrik offered to put a clause in my contract assuring that I'd be depicted as the Babe Ruth of professional wrestling. In addition, they wanted to increase my salary to $800,000—or $2.4 million over three years—even though I'd never broached the subject of a pay raise. And they were just getting started; in their desperate state, I could have earned $3 million if I was interested.

But I wasn't. In the end, I chose a handshake with Vince and an uncertain salary over $2.4 million. And I never regretted it once.

Unlike other wrestlers who'd earned fame in rival promotions, Vince didn't try to reinvent me. I was still "Nature Boy" Ric Flair, not "Million Dollar Man" Ric Flair, like Ted DiBiase, or "King" Ric Flair, like Harley Race. (Nor was I put in polka dots and made to look foolish, like Dusty Rhodes.) Those things worked for them, but they wouldn't have worked for me. I was just allowed to be myself, which was the greatest compliment Vince could have given me.

I also felt like I was taken seriously when I approached Vince about issues in my nonwrestling life. During a tour of Japan with Beth, I called him about a critical tax problem—I owed $200,000 to the IRS. When I arrived home, the money was there—despite the fact that I was working on only a handshake. Simply, Vince came through for a guy he believed in. No notes signed, no guarantees asked.

It's no shock that as soon as I entered the World Wrestling Federation, my crippling anxieties evaporated. And, as I predicted, Jim Herd got canned in the fallout from the incident. I'll have a large pie with pepperoni, please.

Bobby Heenan introduces the World Wrestling Federation to "the real World's Champion." I'm here with my NWA title.

Vince loved the idea of me flaunting the WCW title on television, just to rub it in the organization's face. WCW sued and attempted to obtain a temporary restraining order that would prevent me from wearing the title. Since I was still the NWA champion, the company lost. But the judge—probably realizing that the championship belt would eventually be returned to WCW—expressed some concern over our treatment of the title. To minimize any future damages, I began wearing a World Wrestling Federation tag-team title, which was then digitized for the viewers at home. Either way, the message was the same: Ric Flair had walked out of his old company as the "real" world's champ.

My first regular opponent in the World Wrestling Federation

CHAPTER **15**

THE *REAL* WORLD'S CHAMP

was Roddy Piper, but the match-up most people wanted to see was Hulk Hogan versus Ric Flair. It was forbidden fruit, the impossible dream, the battle no one thought would ever happen. When I was in the NWA, Hogan and I stayed in the same hotel on a few occasions. It would become a mob scene in the lobby; fans would practically hang from the chandeliers to get a picture of the two of us together.

We got along fabulously. Yeah, we had completely different styles, but we respected each other's accomplishments. Hogan once said, "The man who makes the most money is the best worker." I knew what he meant, and we both laughed.

The one thing about Hogan that I thought was awesome was the way he'd spend time with the terminally ill children in the Make-a-Wish program. I'll never forget watching him block out everything else—an upcoming big match, a TV interview, celebrities who wanted to hang out with him—and make these kids feel important. I remember saying to myself, "This is the biggest star in the business, and he has his priorities in order." In my mind, he was a quality human being.

If things were done properly, my first match with Hogan would have been hyped for months, and on Pay-Per-View. But when we finally wrestled on October 25, 1991, in Oakland, no one outside the local market was even aware that the event was taking place. The same was true with our other matches in Los Angeles, Phoenix, Boston, and Madison Square Garden. Yeah, Oakland, L.A., and Boston were sold out, and we came close at the Garden, but people had been craving this match since 1984, and it should have been the biggest thing ever.

I've done steroids, like a lot of other wrestlers, and guys in the NFL, the NBA, and Major League Baseball. I did them in 1972, 1978, 1983, 1989, and a little bit in 1990, but always for short periods of time. I did them to enhance my appearance, but never my performance. It was my own choice. Just before my first stint in the World Wrestling Federation, I was concerned I didn't have "the look." But when I asked Vince if my appearance was good enough, he said, "Absolutely. You're Ric Flair."

THE WORLD WRESTLING Federation was a much different place than WCW, in both good ways and bad. I remember getting frustrated with Vince and the booker Pat Patterson, because back then, matches usually didn't go longer than ten or fifteen minutes. Well, that might have worked for Hogan—no one wanted to see him wrestle thirty min-

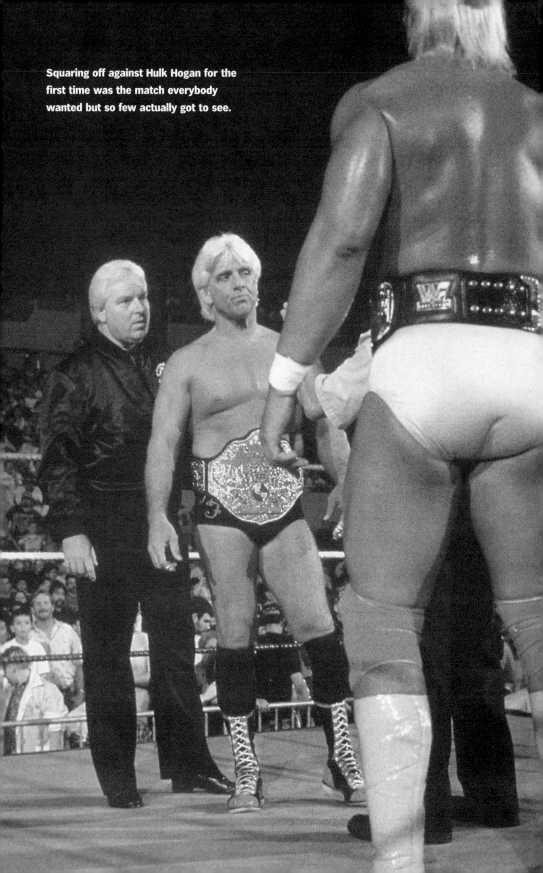

Squaring off against Hulk Hogan for the first time was the match everybody wanted but so few actually got to see.

utes, anyway; it would have been rotten—but why impose *his* standards on *everyone?* The company had a lot of talented smaller guys who could really go. When people like Shawn Michaels, Randy Savage, and Owen Hart wrestled a longer match, the fans loved it.

After the shows, a lot of the guys amused themselves by pulling jokes on each other. The Nasty Boys, Brian Knobs and Jerry Sags, were

two of the most fun-loving guys in the history of our business, but if they could get under somebody's skin, they rode him into the ground. I remember one time in London when I took off my alligator shoes, put them on the bar, and said, "Knobs, these shoes cost more than your house." He then proceeded to fill them with beer and throw them behind the bar.

At the China Club in Manhattan one night, the Nasty Boys decided to torture my friend Robby Kanoff, a representative for one of the top toy companies in the world. Robby was drunk and joking around, cutting a wrestling-style promo and calling himself "Jewish Lightning"—the term guys use in New York's garment district when they torch their own businesses. Knobs and Sags responded by pulling off Robby's sunglasses and stomping on them, ripping his suit.

That was too much. I said to Knobs, "Hey, leave the poor son of a bitch alone." Knobs just twisted his face like a dope and squealed, "Fuck you, Flair."

I slapped Knobs across the face. He tried to fight back, but I had it under control. (Arn once said, "Knobs is a human jellyfish. Sags is actually pretty tough.")

Sags was hanging out with Vince and a couple of other guys by this point. But when he saw what was happening, he dove at me from about ten feet away—just like in the movies. He hit me with a pretty good shot in the eye, and the two of us started brawling. When it was over, the China Club threw *me* out of the bar and put the damage on my credit card. What's wrong with this picture? The *Nasty Boys* stay in, and *Ric Flair* goes out? I don't get it.

PAUL LEVESQUE, AKA TRIPLE H: Ric Flair was the be-all and end-all for me. I hadn't been in the business long, and heard that he'd be staying at the same hotel as me in Columbus, Georgia. I'm nervous, wondering if I'll see him when I check in. I'm standing at the desk when I hear it—"Woooo!" I turn to look, and here he comes, strutting down the hallway.

BOBBY "THE BRAIN" HEENAN: Vince asked me to go on the road with Flair for six months. I was mainly announcing then, but Vince thought that having me manage Flair would have more entertainment value. So did Hogan. I needed neck surgery and was really aching, but we stayed up every night and drank and drank and drank and drank. My neck was hurting; I told Vince, "Why don't you just put me on death row or something?"

We were on a plane coming back from Phoenix, and I just couldn't take it. We were drunk and Flair was laughing and I said, "Tomorrow, when we get to Madison Square Garden, I'm telling Vince to take me off the road." Flair kept laughing, and I said, "You're killing me. You hear that? You're killing me. I can't keep track of time. I hope all your hair falls out and comes back red. I hate you."

EARL HEBNER: I'd known Ric since I was refereeing in Charlotte. When Heenan was taken off the road, Vince put *me* with Flair, to keep him straight. I think the experience took five years off my life. If we got three or four hours of sleep every night, we were lucky. I like to party and can handle some of that, but every day for months took a toll. I was missing flights. I was late getting to the arena. Flair was just *draining* me.

There were a lot of things in the world I didn't know about till I met Ric Flair. One time, the two of us were in Japan and he took me for a hot oil bath. Flair had it all set up. He's standing there, smiling, and I'm going, "Ric, what the hell is this girl doing?" And he goes, "Relax, Hebner, relax. Have a good time." And when she started going underneath my belly button with that hot oil, I tell you, it was a thrill I never thought I'd have.

Ric also started taking me to this massage parlor in Richmond, Virginia, where I live. After the show was over, I'd get home at five or six in the morning. My wife would watch me pull up in the driveway and say, "Why does it take you so long to get home when we're only thirty minutes away from the building? It don't make no sense." I can't blame Ric completely for that divorce, but he definitely played a role in it.

Jake "The Snake" Roberts was the one who told me that I was going to win the World Wrestling Federation Championship. He'd been hanging out in the dressing room, I guess, and heard some rumors. The company's figurehead president, Jack Tunney, had declared the title vacant on television after two controversial matches involving Hogan and Undertaker. The new champion, the fans were told, would be the winner of the *Royal Rumble 1992.*

When I got to the Knickerbocker Arena in Albany, New York, on January 19, 1992, I discovered that Jake's gossip had been accurate. Whatever mistakes Vince had made with the Hogan series were being nullified. Not only was Vince having me win the title, I was going to defeat twenty-nine other wrestlers.

In a royal rumble, the wrestlers are supposed to draw lots. The men who pick numbers one and two start the match. Every two minutes, a buzzer goes off and someone else joins the fray. It ends up becoming a giant battle royal, with one guy after another getting eliminated over the top rope until one survivor stands alone.

I was wrestler number three in the rumble. That gave me the entire match to show my stuff to World Wrestling Federation fans who had never watched WCW, and to WCW fans thinking of transferring their allegiance. It was easy. The Knickerbocker Arena was alive and sold out. And just about everyone else in the ring—including Piper, Shawn Michaels, "British Bulldog" Davey Boy Smith, Hacksaw Jim Duggan, Savage, Hogan, Kerry Von Erich—was a star, a phenomenon that I feel doesn't exist today.

I took everybody's big moves and kept going. The British Bulldog held me over his head, then pressed me up and down four times before slamming me onto the mat. Shawn hit me with his Sweet Chin Music side kick. Hogan gave me a suplex. I was alone in the ring at one point, having dispatched my other opponents, when the buzzer sounded and Piper rushed down the aisle. I squeezed my eyes shut, opened my mouth, and tilted my head back as if to cry, "Oh, no!"

Piper delivered a backdrop and dropkick. I rolled under the ropes—elimination entailed going *over* the top rope—and Piper followed me to ringside, chopping me against the guardrail. Then he rolled me back into the ring, where he whipped up the crowd by giving me an airplane spin.

BOBBY "THE BRAIN" HEENAN: Ric would barely survive–*barely* survive–then, at the last second, avoid elimination. He knew how to do it so well. You had the drama of the perennial NWA champion trying to prove that he was really the greatest, going against everyone in the World Wrestling Federation. It was the best match I ever announced, the only time I ever felt that a match I was calling was one hundred percent real.

The final four wrestlers in the rumble were myself, Hogan, Sid Justice, and Randy Savage. I kneed Sid from behind while he dangled Randy over the ropes, and the Macho Man fell to the floor. Hogan then started battering me all over the ring. As he stomped me in the corner, Sid sneaked up from the rear and flipped Hogan over the top. Hogan protested from the arena floor, clutching onto Sid's hand when he took a swipe at him. That allowed me to creep up on Sid and shove him out of the ring.

Now it was only me standing in the squared circle. The fans were leaping up and down, basking in the historic significance of the moment. "Nature Boy" Ric Flair had become the World Wrestling Federation champion.

"I want to jump, I want to party," I told announcer "Mean" Gene Okerlund during my postmatch interview. "For the Hulk Hogans and the Macho Mans and the Pipers and the Sids, now it's Ric Flair, and you *all* pay homage to the man! *Wooooo!*"

I had one other point to make, specifically to Jim Crockett, Jim Herd, Dusty Rhodes, and everyone else who diluted the NWA Championship until it wasn't worth a damn: "This is the *only* title in the wrestling world that makes you number one!"

THE MORE FAMOUS I became, the more my social circle widened. In Charlotte, I found myself getting invited to political events and speaking about issues that were important to me. It's ridiculous that teachers in North Carolina are underpaid when the bureaucrats in the system are earning twice as much; our poor test scores reflect the fact that money's being dumped in the wrong places. I think that we should raise funds by putting toll booths at the top and bottom of the state— nowhere else—and collecting from all those cars going to and from Florida. And as my parents aged, I became sensitive about elderly health care.

Some Republican factions in North Carolina even asked me to run for governor. Obviously, my sordid past would preclude me from doing that. But I have appeared at fund-raisers for people like Senator Jesse Helms, former Charlotte mayor Sue Myrick, and President George W. Bush.

Sue was sitting with me at an event in 1992 when the forty-first president, George Herbert Walker Bush, got up to speak. People were paying $10,000 to have their pictures taken with him, but Beth and I had been escorted to the head of the line. I already knew Bush from riding on the Spirit of America train with him during his campaign against Bill Clinton. He'd been friendly with promoter Paul Boesch in Houston and, believe it or not, had been Wahoo's Little League baseball coach. For about five hours, the two of us sat together, talking about politics and sports.

"I want to introduce the most famous North Carolinian of all," he said, and everyone looked over at Jesse Helms. "*Ric Flair.*"

To Elizabeth and Ric Flair
with best wishes, Guy Bush

AFTER THE *ROYAL RUMBLE,* the plan had been for me to wrestle Hogan in the setting the match deserved: *WrestleMania VIII,* on April 5, 1992, at the Hoosier Dome in Indianapolis. The original storyline would involve me losing to Hogan and giving him the title back. But Vince's relationship with Hogan had deteriorated by then, and Hogan was aspiring to become a full-time actor, so the *WrestleMania VIII* lineup was switched around. Hogan would wrestle Sid, then take a long sabbatical. I was booked against Randy "Macho Man" Savage.

Vince's strategy at this point was to leave the title on me, but Randy whined and moaned until the decision was changed. I had no qualms either way; having known Randy from when we worked together in Charlotte in the 1970s, I admired his intensity in the ring, and I had wanted to wrestle him since his first championship run in 1988.

What I didn't know was that Randy was a very insecure guy. He wanted me to come to his home in Florida and *practice* the match. "Mr. Perfect" Curt Hennig was also there because he was going to interfere on my behalf. I'd never done anything like this in my life. I found out that the same thing had happened in 1987, when Randy defended the Intercontinental Championship against Ricky Steamboat at *WrestleMania III.* Randy drove Ricky insane, going over each move again and again. When people praised the match as the greatest in

World Wrestling Federation history, Steamboat would kind of shrug. He shared my belief that the best matches are called in the ring and on the fly, not laid out on paper.

Make no mistake about it—I respect Randy Savage for his skills and accomplishments. But because of his unwillingness to just get in the ring and improvise, I won't call him a great worker.

In Florida, I realized that there was real tension between Randy and his manager, Elizabeth. Elizabeth and Randy were married in real life, and for reasons I'll never understand. The only good thing about the situation was that it also became part of their act. Randy came off as a nervous, somewhat crazy guy who, even in the middle of a match, seemed to be keeping an eye on Elizabeth.

Unlike other female managers and valets, Elizabeth always seemed a little vulnerable when she was at ringside, so it made sense that officials would "ban" her to the dressing room at *WrestleMania VIII* out of fear for her safety. With Elizabeth unable to object, my "executive consultant" Mr. Perfect and I could double-team Randy with impunity in the early part of the match. When Randy made his comeback, he wanted emotion, and asked if I could bleed. I agreed—even though, at the time, Vince was still marketing his company as family entertainment and had forbidden any bleeding.

To counter my predicament, Hennig tossed me a foreign object, prompting Elizabeth to scurry out of the dressing room while a bunch of anonymous suits—including a very young Shane McMahon—beseeched her to leave. Inside the ring, I worked over Savage's leg, taunting Elizabeth with, "It's for you, baby," before inflicting more damage. As I snatched his limb and prepared to pummel it again, Savage blocked the move, delivered a punch, rolled me over, held my trunks, and won the title.

Nonetheless, Randy appeared barely able to walk, facilitating a situation where I could terrorize Elizabeth. With blood staining my blond mane, I trudged over to her and whispered, "Liz, come here." Then I grabbed her and kissed her on the lips. "Now slap me," I said. She pulled back and, with a look of revulsion on her face, hauled off on me. Pained by his inability to protect the woman he loved, Randy leaped on me, and we rolled around on the mat, throwing punches while officials tried to wedge between us.

Despite Randy's legitimate jealousy—and my reputation as a womanizer—he was okay with the kiss. He knew me well enough to understand that I'd never hone in on his woman. When I got backstage, though, Vince was pissed about the blood. "Just as you get this close to greatness," he scolded, "you do something stupid like this and take two steps backward."

RANDY AND I were going to continue our program after *WrestleMania VIII.* We had already started implying that Elizabeth had been my lover before she was with Randy. I was going to produce doctored nude photos and mock him by saying, "Before she was yours, she was mine."

Sadly, their real-life marriage was falling apart. Behind Randy's back, Elizabeth was hanging out with Hulk Hogan's wife, Linda. While Randy was on the road, Linda took Liz to the Jockey Club in Miami, and Liz never came back. I was with Savage in Vancouver when he was on the phone and couldn't find his wife; he was out of his mind.

This isn't kind to say, but fans didn't care about Randy as much once Elizabeth was no longer part of the package. The company tried reversing this; they gave Randy the "Macho Midget," and made Randy a color commentator like Bobby Heenan and Jesse "The Body" Ventura. But the departure of Elizabeth had taken away some of his edge as a performer. It's another reason why I don't consider Savage great; he just couldn't carry it on his own.

I think Randy grew so miserable that he didn't care if he had the championship or not. As a result, Vince had him drop the belt to me at a TV taping in Hershey, Pennsylvania, on September 1, 1992. The backstory was that Hennig and I had attacked Randy's leg at *SummerSlam,* so he was going into our contest in a susceptible state.

The match itself was terrible; Randy's heart wasn't in it at all. Scott Hall, then playing a swaggering Cuban called Razor Ramon, was supposed to interfere. Savage didn't like Scott personally, so that made it even worse. In fact, things got so bad that in the middle of the match, Bobby Heenan came out of the dressing room, whistled to get our attention, and made the cut sign across his throat. Vince didn't like what he was seeing on the monitor, so he was calling a conference in the back. With the fans looking at one another in confusion, the two of us just stopped dead in the ring and bailed.

Vince was standing on the other side of the curtain, not looking very happy. "This isn't what I laid out," he told us. We went over the

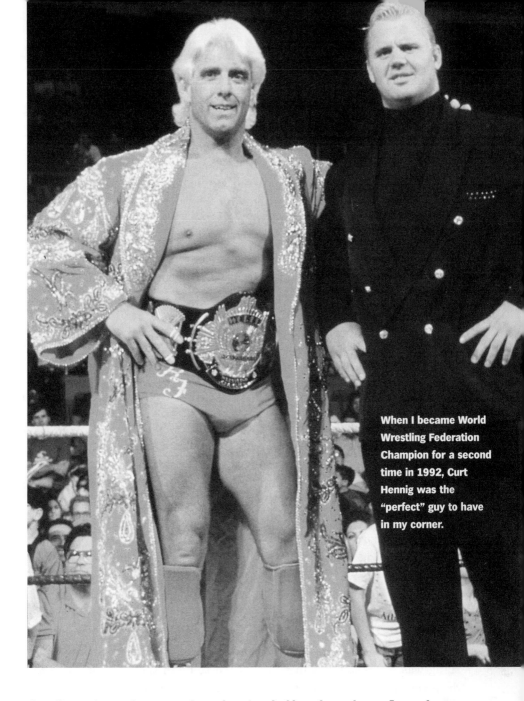

When I became World Wrestling Federation Champion for a second time in 1992, Curt Hennig was the "perfect" guy to have in my corner.

details again, and returned to the ring half an hour later. It made no difference. Hershey can be a wise-ass crowd, like the Nassau Coliseum on Long Island. Sometimes, for no reason whatsoever, the fans will decide to boo all the good guys, and chant, "Boring," even when you're working hard.

There wasn't a fall I could take that could get the crowd into it. Randy looked like he was overselling his bad leg, and the people weren't buying it. Mr. Perfect tried getting involved, and when Randy went after him, I came up from the rear and kneed Savage through the ropes. At ringside, Razor Ramon stomped on the leg and rolled Savage into the ring, where I applied the figure-four. Randy attempted to fight his way out of the hold, but apparently didn't have the strength. Still, he refused to submit, and eventually he "blacked out."

When Stone Cold Steve Austin played the same role five years later at *WrestleMania XIII*, "collapsing" from Bret "Hitman" Hart's Sharpshooter, the Texas Rattlesnake was transformed into a courageous hero who never quit. In Hershey, we were just going through the motions.

I WAS JUST a go-between champion. Vince's intention was to put the title on Bret Hart and crown him the leader of the World Wrestling Federation's "New Generation." The fans liked it when Bret was pursuing me for the title even in a down period for the company—when Vince was preoccupied with his legal problems—we drew good houses in Ottawa, Boston, and L.A.

In Phoenix, the Ultimate Warrior gave me a suplex and messed it up. I landed on my head, dislodging a chip in my inner ear and upsetting my sense of balance. But I didn't realize that anything was wrong at first. Charles Barkley, the basketball star, was sitting in the front row and I wanted to show off for him, so I told the Warrior to throw me into the corner for an upside-down flip. That's when everything started spinning wildly. I completely missed the turnbuckle and flew out onto the floor. I stood up, and fell down again. Fortunately, before the Warrior could put his hands on me, Earl Hebner stopped the match.

I couldn't figure out what happened, and I wondered if I'd had a stroke. I was okay if I was standing or tying up with my opponent, but once I was on my back for an extended period, I became dizzy. One thing was obvious: I was in no condition to be in the ring. So I had to drop the title to Bret right away. I flew to Saskatoon, Saskatchewan, and lost the championship on October 12, 1992, in a match that was never televised. It was awful.

From Saskatoon, I went to the Mayo Clinic in Minneapolis with my dad, and the mystery was solved pretty quickly: I had something called benign paroxysmal position vertigo. The doctors explained that when I leaned upward, the chip that had broken in my inner ear went backward through a canal of fluid, unsettling my equilibrium. If I sat upright, the chip would float back in the opposite direction and, after about thirty seconds, drop into place.

After seeing three specialists—at the Mayo Clinic and Duke University, as well as in Charlotte—I applied for the benefits of an existing Lloyd's of London policy. It would have paid me $30,000 a month for three years, with a balloon payment of a half-million dollars. The day before I went to file my claim, I woke up in the morning and had no sensation of dizziness. I couldn't believe it; I even banged my head against the wall a couple of times. As a result, my Lloyd's of London policy stayed in place, and I went back to work. I have no regrets. I wouldn't trade good health for any amount of money.

When I returned, the fans weren't interested in watching me chase Bret for his championship, and our rematches drew poorly. Personally, I never saw dollar signs on Bret Hart. He was a good, sound, physical wrestler, but with limited charisma and interview skills. He also could have been president of his own fan club. Bret truly thought that he was the best technical wrestler who ever lived, and he was stuck in a routine that he refused to break. When he'd make his comeback, he'd rely on the same sequence of moves—an atomic drop, a clothesline, a gut punch, a Russian leg sweep, a backbreaker, a fist drop from the second rope, and finally his finisher, the Sharpshooter—night after night, with no variation! Every well-known wrestler has patented things that he does in his matches, but you can still entertain your fans by putting those things in different spots or doing them in different ways. If I tried adding things to Bret's comeback—like hitting him with a chop—he couldn't stand it. It had to be in rotation.

Don't get me wrong—Bret could have a tremendous match when it really counted. But, day to day, I found him to be inflexible. And in 1997, when Bret punched out Vince McMahon over a finish in Montreal, I was appalled. At the time, Hart had just signed with WCW. Since he happened to be the World Wrestling Federation champion, he needed to drop the title. Vince wanted Bret to do it at *Survivor Series,* but Hart wouldn't. As a so-called Canadian hero—and I really don't think Bret has anything on Wayne Gretzky—Bret refused to lose in Canada. That would be the equivalent of me saying that I'd never let anyone beat me in North Carolina. Give me a break!

Obviously, Vince could see that Hart thought that he was bigger than the World Wrestling Federation, and Vince did what was necessary to protect his company. When Shawn Michaels put the Hitman in a Sharpshooter, McMahon ordered the timekeeper to ring the bell. The match was over, Vince said, and Shawn was the new champion. When people argued that Vince had screwed Bret, McMahon accurately replied, "Bret screwed Bret."

The facts are this: Hogan, for all he did, right and wrong, drew a lot of money. Savage, for all he did, right and wrong, drew a lot of money. Roddy Piper, Dusty Rhodes, and Ric Flair drew big money. Bret Hart did not. Vince had other distractions at the time, but when Bret beat me for the title, the company went to hell for a while.

WE WERE IN Madison, Wisconsin, when Vince pulled me aside and told me, "We're going to start going with the younger guys. I want you to wrestle Razor Ramon. Do the favor for him, and then I'm not sure where we're going to go from there."

There was nothing ambiguous about what he was saying. After holding the championship twice, I was about to embark on a reduced role in the World Wrestling Federation. My friend Robby—"Jewish Lightning"—offered me a job with his toy company, using my notoriety to travel around the world and schmooze clients. He was ready to give me a three-year deal with a $175,000 base salary, plus a percentage. It was a nice gesture from a loyal friend, but I wasn't ready to say goodbye to wrestling.

Down in Atlanta, Bill Shaw was now running WCW and had hired Cowboy Bill Watts as booker. Watts was a big star—even challenging Bruno Sammartino for the title in the WWWF—had run the UWF, and was a disciple of Eddie Graham, credited with perfecting the best-conceived match finishes in the history of the business. He also had a huge set of balls. So when he contemplated my situation, Watts picked up the phone, called Vince personally, and told him, "I'd like to talk to Flair about coming back to WCW."

Before I started with the World Wrestling Federation, Vince had pledged that if I ever wasn't satisfied with my spot, I was free to go elsewhere. And he stuck to his word. His only request was that I put over Mr. Perfect in a "loser leaves town" match on *Raw*. I made Hennig look "Perfect," shook Vince's hand, and managed to walk away from a wrestling company without burning a bridge.

Cowboy Bill Watts was gone almost as soon as I arrived. I knew that something was wrong when I walked into the Turner offices and saw how he was conducting himself. Everybody in the North Tower was wearing a suit. And then there was Bill Watts, in tennis shoes, a T-shirt, and Zubaz workout pants, putting Bill Shaw in an armlock. "Hey, Ric," Watts wisecracked, "Shaw thinks he's pretty tough. He used to wrestle in high school. Let's see if he knows how to shoot."

I just thought, Oh, my God. Watts was a smart guy and could have impressed the executives with his intelligence. Instead, he was giving them this old-school attitude—"I don't give a shit. I may work with all you suits, but I'm fuckin' Bill Watts." I knew that shit wasn't going to fly.

CHAPTER 16

THIS GUY'S GOT A VISION

Within days, Watts had gotten himself in trouble for an interview he did with the *Pro Wrestling Torch* newsletter. Things were going relatively well until the topic got to race. Personally, I do not believe that Watts was a racist. As WCW booker, it was his idea to make Ron Simmons the first African-American champion of any major promotion. In Bill's territory in Oklahoma and Louisiana, the Junkyard Dog had been his pride and joy. Not only did Watts push Ernie "The Cat" Ladd to the moon, but the two were good friends outside the arena. Once, when Watts was driving Ernie and his wife around, Ladd joked, "I always wanted a big, fat honky chauffeur."

For the interview, however, Watts decided he had to prove that he did things *his* way and nobody else's. "If you own a business, why shouldn't you be able to discriminate?" he lectured. "I mean, why should I have to hire a fag if I don't like fags? If I don't want to sell fried chicken to blacks, I shouldn't have to. It's my restaurant."

A copy of the interview ended up in baseball immortal Hank Aaron's hands, and he wasn't too happy. Aaron was an institution in Atlanta, and a TBS executive. Ted Turner's been known to run his mouth himself, but this wasn't cool at all. When Bill Shaw saw the quotes, he confronted Watts, who had no choice but to quit.

ALL THE EXECUTIVES wanted to know about Vince's operation. "He's got his own Disney World up in Stamford," I told them. "A state-of-the-art television facility. They have a light grid that must cost a half-million dollars, and they haul it around from one TV taping to another. Our production values down here are so far off the mark."

Then they asked what WCW could do to catch up. I replied that *I'd* go out and hire Bobby "The Brain" Heenan and "Mean" Gene Okerlund. Before we bothered stealing away wrestlers, we needed two announcers who could help make them popular with the fans. At that time, Bobby and Gene were the hottest announcers in the business.

Remarkably, the company followed my advice, aggressively recruiting Bobby and Gene until they both came on board.

With Watts gone, Shaw wanted to know if I was interested in overseeing the day-to-day wrestling operations for WCW. The answer was a resounding no. I had no desire to leave Charlotte and move to Atlanta, nor did I consider myself responsible enough to have that type of position. At that stage of my life, I really just wanted to be a wrestler.

If I'd been interested in an office position, I could have stayed with the World Wrestling Federation; I'm sure that Vince could have found lots of things for me to do there.

In the interim, my friend Bob Dhue was put in charge. Bob was a sharp, slick, wonderfully nice guy who had run the Omni arena in Atlanta. He knew infinitely more about wrestling than Jim Herd, but understood that there was a difference between managing a building and managing the boys. "I just don't feel right in the chair," he confessed to me.

Bob asked if I could make myself readily available to help him, and I had to tell him the truth. "Look, Bob," I said, "I can't be an executive and a wrestler. I don't want to spread myself that thin."

He then followed up with a question that would live in infamy: "What do you think of Eric Bischoff?"

Bischoff was a wrestling announcer who seemed to have a lot of knowledge about the entertainment business and was constantly pitching ideas. "I like Bischoff," I replied. "I think he's aggressive and smart."

I had the same discussion with Bill Shaw. He was torn between Bischoff and Ole Anderson. I know that this is going to hurt some feelings, but I honestly wasn't impressed with Ole at this point. Yes, he had the history, booking the old Georgia territory and working at the Omni, but he was a gruff, rough-and-tough guy. His mind was rooted in the past. When he booked WCW for a while, it was a disaster. Eric seemed much more contemporary.

At first, Bischoff and Bob Dhue were a team, but almost immediately, Eric started maneuvering to get rid of Bob. Something I still feel guilty about is that I unwittingly helped Bischoff with his scheme.

"How's Bob doing?" Shaw asked one day.

"He's struggling," I admitted.

"Does Bischoff seem like the kind of guy who can make decisions?"

"Definitely."

In reality, I did Bob a favor. He still had his job with Turner's corporation, so he just went back over to the Omni. And when WCW started falling apart, Bob Dhue was nowhere in sight.

ARN ANDERSON: Ric liked Eric, and so did I. I thought he had a lot of ideas, and he was ambitious. He was young and driven, and it was good to see that. The main thing was that he was a wrestling person. He'd started out announcing in the AWA, and now worked on our show,

so he had experience in the business. At that point, that was a hell of a lot better than what we were used to.

Meanwhile, Dusty Rhodes became the booker again. One of his first acts was regrouping the Four Horsemen—with myself and Arn and Ole and Paul Roma. Basically, Paul had been a very lower-tier guy in the World Wrestling Federation who'd gotten a moderate push there, first as a member of the Young Stallions tag team with Jimmy Powers, then in the Power & Glory tag team with Hercules Hernandez. In my opinion, he also had a shitty work ethic, once leaving an opponent waiting in the ring so he could finish up a game of cards. As soon as Roma's name was announced in Atlanta, the Omni went silent. "It never ends," I thought. "Here's Dusty screwing with me again."

There was still a lot of confusion over the WCW and NWA titles. On July 18, 1993, I beat Barry Windham for the NWA title with a figure-four in Biloxi, Mississippi. Officially, I was a ten-time champion, but the fans didn't react like they were witnessing anything momentous. That's because Vader—a menacing guy who wrestled under his real name, Leon White, in the AWA, and as Big Van Vader in Japan—was the WCW champion at the time, and that title was portrayed as more important. In September, the company finally withdrew from the NWA, and the title was vacated.

On December 27, 1993, Vader was supposed to lose his WCW Championship to Sid at *Starrcade*. As I mentioned previously, aside from his imposing physique, Sid offered nothing to the business. He didn't want to learn how to perform or build up to execute an exciting match. On more than one occasion, he claimed to be injured or sick, but managed to play in his softball league. Still, promoters kept throwing money at him because of his monster look. During a booking meeting in the Jim Herd days, Jim Cornette raised a reasonable objection to placing Sid in a prominent role on an upcoming show: "We have to go back to that town someday."

The title change was supposed to take place at the tenth anniversary of *Starrcade*. The show was in my hometown of Charlotte. At this point Sid was no longer with WCW and I was booked in the main event. You wouldn't believe how much animosity there was over this. Ravishing Rick Rude, Paul Orndorff, and some of the other guys thought that they deserved to be champion, and here was Ric Flair getting the title again. But—despite our problems at other times—Dusty

Barry Windham discovers firsthand why I'm considered "the master of the figure-four."

and Eric really did a great job of building up the match. As I've alluded to before, Dusty could be a genius. There were periods when he had a vision that was second to none. He clearly had the creative aptitude to compete with Vince. Unfortunately, his inability to separate himself from his personal feelings often threw those talents off-track.

The show began with a montage of photos of me from childhood onward, newspaper clippings from my plane crash, and clips of me in other *Starrcade* main events. Then they switched to footage of Vader working out in the ring at the empty Independence Arena hours earlier. Then I was seen at home, kissing my wife and four children goodbye. "Mean" Gene Okerlund and I stepped into a limo, and as we rode to the building, I spoke about retiring for good if I couldn't win the title one more time. It was a real cool deal.

Harley Race was Vader's manager. With all our history, it was kind of special to have Harley there. And for the first time, my parents watched me wrestle, alongside Megan, David, Ashley, Reid, and Beth. All around them, the people were clapping their hands together and chanting, "Flair! Flair! Flair!"

I know that the other guys were kidding Leon backstage for having to lose the title to me, so when we got in the ring, we practically fought for real during parts of the match. When Leon suplexed me from the top rope, he protected me. When he jumped on me from the turnbuckles, he was ten times easier on my body than a lot of other guys. But when he punched me, it was *legit*. My ear was cauliflowered. My nose was swollen. He came at me with two fists at once, busting open my mouth.

We went to the floor, and Leon said, "I'm going to beat the fuck out of you if you don't fight back." I told him, "You want it, buddy? You got it." And I just started tagging him. I'd been in fights like that before, but I never expected to have one at nearly forty-five years of age.

HARLEY RACE: Leon was being an asshole. He was hitting Flair with potatoes [direct shots to the head] the whole time. There was no need for it at all. Then Flair whaled back at him. Both of Leon's eyes were swollen, and he started to loosen up after that.

I was biting Vader, and the fans loved it. As I covered him for a near-fall, Harley climbed the ropes, then came careening down with one of his flying headbutts. I rolled out of the way, and Vader took the hit. We got up, and I began chopping Vader. He knocked me down, then turned toward the crowd. That's when I grabbed his ankle, tripped him, and rolled on top for the pin.

It was one of my finest moments in the ring. The people were so happy. Even when I went backstage, the fans were still screaming, "*Woooo!*"

I never really had the feeling that my parents liked wrestling. They told me all the time that they were proud of me, but I know they had no passion for the business. I was glad that they could be there with my kids that night, and see how much I meant to people.

MEGAN FLIEHR KETZNER: We watched the match, and then we were brought backstage. I was used to my father bleeding in the ring, but he was usually showered by the time we met up afterward. This was the worst I'd ever seen him face-to-face, up close. There was blood everywhere. It was disgusting.

MIKE MOONEYHAM: Ric Flair embodies many traits, but perhaps his two most admirable are charm and class, qualities that he learned from his father. His unparalleled professional career has epitomized a mental and physical toughness that come with surviving several thousand professional wrestling matches. Years earlier, Ric told me he had asked his dad for permission to become a pro wrestler. Many parents might have panicked, and some would have laughed it off. But Dick Fliehr handled his son's life-changing question with the same measure of grace, compassion, and common sense that punctuated his life. "Go ahead, do it. Just make sure you're the best."

In the dressing room, I cut an interview with Beth and all of my kids present. Reid started to wander out of camera range, and—with blood all over me—I steered him back into the shot. I had tears in my eyes as I lisped through a bloody mouth, "I've been a very, very fortunate man." I couldn't help it; the business was real to me. I'd given everything I could in that match for myself, for the fans who'd grown up watching me, and for my family.

I was finally beginning to mature, and realizing how important it was to make my marriage work. My old system wasn't cutting it anymore. If I went to Japan, I brought back pearls for Beth. If I went to Hawaii, it was sapphires and diamonds. I bought her four wedding rings over the years, but at the end of the day, it didn't make me a good husband. I needed to make more of a commitment, to both her and our family.

It was also crucial to me to clear up whatever misunderstandings there were with my older kids. I tried using material things to offset my selfishness. In Japan, I'd buy Megan and David $2,000 worth of gifts—in particular, toys that you couldn't find in the United States—and then the Road Warriors would carry them back to Minneapolis and deliver them personally. I thought that money could buy damage control. Then I learned that you get much further by talking about what's wrong.

> **MEGAN FLIEHR KETZNER: I was jealous of my little brother and sister for a while. They had what I wanted. When my dad was home, Ashley and Reid got to be around him.**
>
> **I went through a period when I was angry at my dad. Sometimes I'd remove myself from him emotionally, and he would ask what was wrong. Other times, we would have it out over the phone. "I need someone here," I'd yell at him. "I want a father." I'd cry, and usually he'd cry, too. And I could tell that he really loved me.**

The morning after I defeated Vader, my phone rang. It was Hulk Hogan. He was busy taking his kid to school, but he had one thing to tell me: "You made me cry last night, you old bastard."

The next time I saw Eric Bischoff, I told him about the conversation. "You get along with Hogan?" he asked.

"Yeah, I get along with him very well."

"You think he'd consider coming here?"

"I don't know. I'll talk to him."

So I called Hogan and started to sell Eric to him. "This guy's got a vision," I said. "He's got some good ideas. And they have the money here to make things happen."

Hogan was busy making a TV show called *Thunder in Paradise.* "I don't know, brother," he answered. "I'm kind of doing this other thing."

"Well, why don't you just talk to him?"

Eric and I began a campaign to lure Hogan to WCW. "We'll do this together," Eric said.

My goal was to get Bischoff in front of the Hulkster. The two of us flew to Orlando and drove to the *Thunder in Paradise* set. We sat in the trailer for three and a half hours before Hogan had time to talk with us. Then we came back the next week, and the week after that. Pretty soon, he was ready to make a deal.

Bischoff wasn't in a position to offer big-money contracts, so a meeting was set up between Hogan and Ted Turner. They reportedly agreed on a phenomenal contract, one that guaranteed Hogan twenty-five percent of all Pay-Per-View revenue. Under that arrangement, for every Pay-Per-View Hogan worked, he'd earn between $600,000 and $1.5 million. By contrast, I was only making $500,000 a year.

I didn't hear about the numbers until much later, but I always assumed that the company would pay Hogan more than me; he had the bigger name. In my mind, twice as much would have been okay—but not more than twice my yearly salary for a single Pay-Per-View! Still, I believed that having Hulk Hogan in WCW was a good idea.

A bigger problem was that Hogan was given creative control, which allowed him not only to refuse to lose, but to veto storylines he didn't find satisfactory. Later, when he'd exercise this option, a lot of people would bad-mouth Hogan for screwing up the company. Honestly, I don't blame him. I blame Eric for allowing a situation like that to occur in the first place.

IN ORDER TO accommodate Hogan, I turned myself bad once again. Sting had what was then known as the WCW International title, and he was supposed to defeat me to unify the titles. Now those plans were scratched. I beat Sting and prepared to lose the championship to Hogan. Sting was mad, and with good reason. He'd been completely cut out of the picture.

We conceptualized a three-match series, with the title bouncing back and forth and the fans never certain about who would come out on top. Hogan would win the championship at the *Bash at the Beach* Pay-Per-View on July 17, 1994. Then I'd beat him at *Clash of the Champions* on August 24. We'd meet one last time at *Halloween Havoc* on October 23, and he'd capture the title again.

I volunteered to do all this; who else was Hogan going to feud with? Vader and Ravishing Rick Rude flat-out refused to work with him and vice versa. Leon saw himself as a legitimate ass-kicker who went out and beat the hell out of people. To him, Hogan was the poster boy of the phony World Wrestling Federation, a guy who hit people with feeble punches. Rude hated Hogan for not giving him a title run when they were both in the World Wrestling Federation.

For his first few months in WCW, Hogan was booed everywhere. He'd been on Vince's TV, and we had to reeducate our fans to accept him as a good guy. It was so bad that on TV, the company had to dub in a sound track of cheers for Hogan. At *Bash at the Beach* in Orlando, we did our best to make sure that dubbing wouldn't be necessary. While I was accompanied by my manager, "Sensuous" Sherri Martel, Hogan brought along Jimmy "The Mouth of the South" Hart, Mr. T, and Shaquille O'Neal in his Orlando Magic jersey.

Everyone busted their ass to make the match exciting. Hogan hit me with his legdrop and was about to finish me off when Sherri pulled referee Randy Anderson out of the ring and smashed his head into the barricade. Then she climbed the ropes, splashed onto Hogan, and choked him with her nylon stocking. Hogan rebounded, of course, giving Sherri and me a double clothesline. She tossed me a pair of brass knuckles, but even after I slugged Hogan and covered him for the pin, he kicked out at two. As Mr. T carried Sherri back to the dressing room, Hogan "Hulked up," shaking off my punches and unloading a few of his own, then whipping me off the ropes, into a big boot, and pinning me after another legdrop.

The Pay-Per-View ended with Shaq and Jimmy Hart holding up Hogan's arms just before the new champion went into his posing routine.

ARN HAD A great angle planned for the *Clash of the Champions* in Cedar Rapids, Iowa. He was going to put on a mask and attack Hogan's leg with a club backstage, like he was a henchman for Tonya Harding. We originally intended to do this to Sting, but he was out of the title picture, and there was no point in wasting a good idea—especially one that would give Hogan a face-saving excuse when he dropped the title.

The problem was, Hogan decided that he wanted to keep the title. "I'm not ready to lose it," he explained. "The people aren't ready for me to lose it, and it would hurt merchandise sales." So, after setting up this whole Tonya Harding bit, I got a half-assed countout victory. We caved in Hogan's knee with a club, but I still couldn't make him quit with the figure-four. Since the title could only change hands via pin or submission, Hogan was still the champ.

This presented a problem going into *Halloween Havoc* in Detroit. It was supposed to be our rubber match. After Hogan won the championship and I took it back, we'd settle our differences in a steel cage with Mr. T as the referee. But since Hogan hadn't lost the title, was there really any point in even having a third match?

At a television taping in Atlanta, Bischoff and Hogan called me aside to give me some "stunning" news: Zane Bresloff, the promoter in charge of booking arenas for WCW, had reported that *Halloween Havoc* tickets weren't moving.

"What did you expect?" I told them. Yet somehow, they couldn't understand why people weren't lining up to watch Hogan beat me again. Hoping to electrify the buying public, they proposed a new idea: I would put up my career against Hogan's—and lose.

I went home and thought about this stipulation. Then I contacted Eric. "Here's the deal," I said. "I'm willing to lose, but I'm not ready to retire."

"You won't," he promised. "You'll be out for at least a year, just to make it look legit, but you'll work in the office. Then we'll bring you back."

I was a little worried. I'd been with the company for about a year, and my contract hadn't been extended. Everyone told me that it would happen very soon, but I didn't have anything on paper. And I knew why—Dr. Harvey Schiller was about to come in and take over Turner Sports. Eric didn't want to incur any major expenses and make himself a target for his new boss. All well and good, but what about me? With all the turbulence behind the scenes, what if Bischoff got fired, and no one remembered that I was supposed to return?

Later on, I was accused of holding the company up because I refused to lose the retirement match until I had a contract. But I needed to know that I still had a job, so I stood my ground to the very end, until Bill Shaw arrived at *Halloween Havoc* with my contract in his hand. I looked it over, signed my name, went out, and lost to Hogan in the cage.

The one-year deal made me uncomfortable, but I kept telling myself that I had nothing to be concerned about. Think about it—I helped Eric Bischoff get his job, recruited Hulk Hogan, allowed him to win the championship, then lost a retirement match. I just assumed that Eric would take care of someone like that. He *had* to, I reassured myself. There was *no way* that he would screw me.

I was always aware that I needed to rely on more than wrestling, and I had begun investing in other businesses. Personally, I don't think it's healthy for anyone in any field to *not* have outside interests, for you invariably end up burdening your family with problems that shouldn't be their concern. And the wrestling lifestyle is even worse, because you're already living by a different set of rules than the rest of society, and when you reach a certain age, you can no longer do the thing you love. I think that's part of the reason we've seen a number of ex-wrestlers disintegrate—losing themselves to drugs and getting into legal trouble—after they were out of the limelight.

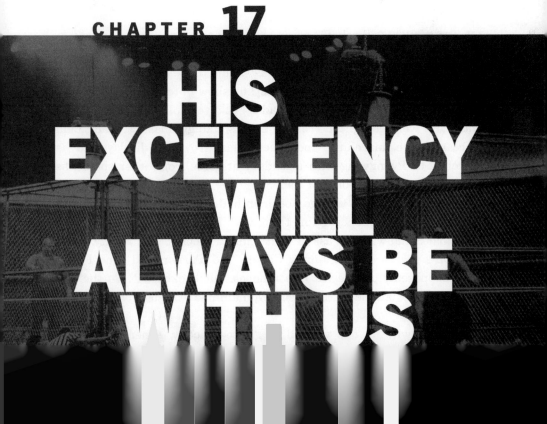

CHAPTER 17

HIS EXCELLENCY WILL ALWAYS BE WITH US

I have to thank Scott Storick and Pete Wirth for taking me under their wing and teaching me about the real estate business. Because of them, I was exposed to opportunities I never would have known about. At one point, I owned eleven Gold's gyms. My goal was building a chain of Ric Flair's Gold's Gyms all over the Caribbean. I already had one in St. Maarten, and we were doing great; I was a king down there. Unfortunately, I couldn't control the weather. One night, after doing a guest appearance on *Baywatch,* I walked into my room at the Marina Del Rey Hyatt in California and turned on the Weather Channel. For the next few hours, I went through three bottles of wine as I watched a hurricane destroy the island of St. Martin.

In the aftermath, the whole country went bankrupt. The government put a phony tax lien on my business, took a half-million dollars out of my bank account, and put about $230,000 of my gym equipment up for auction. My insurance company in St. Martin went bankrupt. My banks—which had been uncomfortable about doing offshore investments in the first place—called back their loans.

It was a painful lesson in diversifying outside of wrestling. In the United States, at least, the majority of my gyms did well. But as of right now, I only own two facilities. It's just more manageable.

IN 1995, ERIC Bischoff took me to lunch to talk about a special festival that WCW and the New Japan wrestling promotion were holding in Pyongyang, North Korea. It was going to be held at May Day Stadium and outrank any other wrestling show in terms of attendance. The government of North Korea had spent a year planning the festival, and there were going to be related events, like gymnastics, traditional Korean dance, marching, and spectacular fireworks displays. I'd be traveling to Pyongyang with legendary athletes from other sports, as well as business and political leaders.

Eric told me that George Foreman had been approached first, but wanted too much money. Same thing with Hulk Hogan. I later discovered that Sting was also asked to attend, but declined. In reality, I was Bischoff's fourth choice. Jimmy Carter, Ted Turner, and Jane Fonda were supposedly on the list of attendees, but backed out. So the two biggest names at the festival were Muhammad Ali and "Nature Boy" Ric Flair.

Here's why no one wanted to go: technically, Americans aren't even allowed in North Korea. The country is a sworn enemy of the United States and has continuously defied international treaties on the development of nuclear weapons. The dictator, Kim Jong II, has kept his people completely isolated and impoverished. Children are literally starving to death there, but virtually nobody knows about it; news usually can't get in or travel out.

Personally, I didn't need North Korea on my résumé to say I had a good life. Nor was there any monetary incentive. I went because it was an opportunity to associate myself with someone like Muhammad Ali as an international sports dignitary, and represent professional wrestling to a huge population who had never seen it. Bischoff told me, "I promise you I will make you bigger than Lawrence Taylor," the football player who was participating in *WrestleMania XI* that year and monopolizing headlines around the United States.

There were other wrestlers I knew on the show, including Chris Benoit, Dean Malenko, Rick Steiner, Road Warrior Hawk, Too Cold Scorpio, and Scott Norton. On the second night of the festival, I was going to lose to Antonio Inoki, a Japanese icon who helped organize the festival (and had fought Ali in Tokyo nineteen years earlier). But I was assured that the match wouldn't be publicized in the United States. No one bothered to tell me that WCW was actually planning to broadcast the encounter on Pay-Per-View.

The second that we arrived in Pyongyang, our passports were confiscated. Then each of us was assigned a "cultural attaché" to follow us everywhere; these guys even sat in the dressing room while we went over our matches. In the dining room where the wrestlers ate, there was a camera in each corner, monitoring every movement. When Scott Norton called his wife and said, "This place sucks," his phone line suddenly went dead.

Muhammad Ali and I were taken everywhere in separate vehicles, while the rest of the guys were on a bus surrounded by government cars. They split us up at the hotel—the way they did suspected traitors they wanted to segregate and brainwash. I didn't see anybody until our handlers decided that the time was right.

The event itself was unlike anything I'd ever witnessed. A total of 380,000 spectators attended over two nights. As we approached May Day Stadium, I looked out the window and saw a sea of people huddled together, all on foot, converging on the venue from every direction. During the show, you could look up and never see where the people ended. The fans held up different colored placards to create incredible mosaic images. It was beautiful, but also creepy. The first couple of sections were occupied exclusively by guys in military uniforms. The spectators cheered on cue. I almost got the feeling that they had been *ordered* to attend.

The first night, I was seated with the head of the North Korean sports ministry. I forget which match was in the ring, but he suddenly asked me, "How come that wrestler was able to knock down his opponent so easily? That doesn't look real."

"You never know until you're out there," I answered. "Those guys are pretty strong."

"How can he pick up his opponent like that and hold him over his head? Doesn't the other wrestler fight back? I don't understand."

"Well, when I wrestle tomorrow night, no one's gonna do that to *me.*"

He and the other bureaucrats were only figuring out right then that it was all predetermined. I don't know what line of shit Inoki had given them, but the North Koreans obviously thought that they had the Olympics coming.

The tour was supposed to last two days. WCW had paid for Beth and Reid to stay at a hotel in Japan as an incentive for my participation, and they were waiting for me there. For reasons that were never explained, we ended up staying five days, and Ali and I found ourselves being dragged from place to place to meet with different Communist officials.

At one point, my minder asked me how much my watch cost. When I told him, he marveled, "Can anybody really have that kind of money? That's more than I make in five years." I asked him his salary. It was the equivalent of about seven American dollars a week. Had I realized that, I never would have worn that watch in front of him.

Because of the ravages of Parkinson's disease, it was difficult to understand Muhammad Ali when he spoke. But at one function, we were sitting at a big, round table with a group of North Korean luminaries when one of the guys started rambling on about the moral superiority of North Korea, and how they could take out the United States or Japan any time they wanted. Suddenly, Ali piped up, clear as a bell, "No wonder we hate these motherfuckers."

My hair practically stood up on my head. "Oh, shit," I whispered, "don't start talking *now.*"

Before we left North Korea, our handlers requested that I make a speech at the airport. They even had specific points that they expected me to articulate—things like North Korea being a worker's paradise, and that America sucked. I looked at Bischoff and told him, "I can't say this." The last thing I wanted was to be quoted in the American press making statements that I didn't mean. So I just spouted out some generic comments and thanked everyone for their hospitality.

This is how I was quoted by the official North Korean press agency: "Before I leave this beautiful and peaceful country, I would like to make a tribute to the great leader, Mr. Kim II Sung (the late father of the current dictator), who had devoted his life to the Korean people's happiness, prosperity and Korean unification. His Excellency, Kim II Sung, will always be with us."

As soon as our plane landed in Japan, I bent down and literally kissed the ground. I was so glad to be back on friendly soil.

UNFORTUNATELY, MAYBE I shouldn't have been. The moment I returned from Japan, I discovered that Hogan had started changing storylines around. He'd been manipulating things since a secret meeting I'd been at just before our first match in WCW. It was held at the Grand Floridian in Disney World, and Eric was there along with Kevin Sullivan and Jimmy Hart. Hogan said that he had some suggestions about improving the company, then handed out a list of people he wanted hired: Ed Leslie, or "Brutus Beefcake"; "Earthquake" John Tenta; Fred Ottman, who'd been Tugboat and Typhoon in the World Wrestling Federation; Wayne Ferris, aka the Honky Tonk Man, and "Hacksaw" Jim Duggan. Beefcake was Hogan's best friend, and Tenta and Ottman were big guys who Hogan enjoyed wrestling—and beating. The others were also guys who Hogan liked having around. I liked Ottman and Tenta, too, but what Hogan was trying to do was infiltrate the company with his buddies, so he'd have a comfort zone around him.

Hogan also had some thoughts about people he thought should leave WCW—in particular my closest friend, Arn Anderson. I guess Hogan considered me a threat to his power, and wanted to eliminate anyone he perceived as my political ally. "You're out of your fuckin' mind," I told Hogan, and he let the matter drop.

Anyone who accuses me of playing favorites with Arn should compare him to Brutus Beefcake. Arn was a great wrestler and a phenomenal interview. Today he works behind the scenes in WWE as a road agent, using his extensive experience to coach the tag teams and help them lay out their matches. When you see a great match pitting, say, Charlie Haas and Shelton Benjamin against Chris Benoit and John Cena, a lot of the credit belongs to Arn.

Brutus Beefcake, on the other hand, is an idiot who'd insert himself into situations where he didn't belong because of his association with Hogan. In Monroe, Louisiana, one night, Eddie Guerrero and I tore the joint down. Eddie was the good guy, I was the bad guy. But I was in a program with Hogan at the time, so Beefcake was worried. You see, Eddie's only five-foot-eight, and Beefcake was afraid that if I took too much of his offense, the fans wouldn't buy me as a viable opponent for the Hulkster.

As soon as the match was over, Beefcake walked up to me. "Hey, let me tell you something here," he said, like he was going to give me a hit of cocaine. "I don't think the big man's gonna like the way you were selling for Guerrero. You're giving him too much."

I looked at him with disbelief. Eddie's one of the best in-ring performers in the world; if anyone deserves to be made to look good, it's him.

"Come on, Ric," Beefcake continued, "think about the big picture."

As I look back on the conversation now, I'm astonished at how stupid Beefcake really was, thinking that he could tell me anything about wrestling.

RICK WILSON WAS a male stripper with a good body who Hogan brought in as "The Renegade." Wilson painted his face and dressed up like the Ultimate Warrior. A lot of fans believed that he *was* the Warrior, but using a different name.

Not long after entering WCW, the Renegade wrestled Arn for his TV title. Hogan and Bischoff wanted the Renegade to win in thirty seconds, just like the Warrior did against many of his opponents, almost reducing Arn to enhancement status. The match took about fifteen minutes, and sucked; the Renegade didn't know how to wrestle. Afterward Bischoff complained, "We should have done it in fifteen seconds."

"No," I said, "we shouldn't have done it *at all*. If the guy can't work longer than fifteen seconds, he doesn't belong in a position where he's defending a championship."

Around that time, Kevin Sullivan and I were eating lunch with Hogan, and I asked him about it. "What do you see in this guy?" I asked.

"I see a guy who wrestles like the Ultimate Warrior."

I thought he was kidding me at first, but he wasn't. Hogan was still mad about having to lose the World Wrestling Federation Championship to the Ultimate Warrior at *WrestleMania VI* in 1990. He was actually grooming the Renegade as an Ultimate Warrior clone that Hogan could beat, somehow getting back the win. How many WCW fans do you think cared about a match that had taken place in another promotion *five years* earlier? But it sure seemed like Hogan was still losing sleep over that loss.

In 1999, four months after being released from WCW, the Renegade shot himself to death in his kitchen in Marietta, Georgia. The guy obviously had other problems, so I'd never blame Hogan for the suicide. But I *do* blame both Hogan and Bischoff for inflating the kid's ego and giving him the impression that he was capable of being a star.

UNLIKE THE RENEGADE, there were so many guys I saw in WCW who were loaded with talent, among them Guerrero, Benoit, Chris Jericho, and Steve Austin. He and Brian Pillman were a tag team called the Hollywood Blonds. I had worked against Steve a few times, as did Steamboat and Arn, and we all agreed that he was a great performer. He had a positive attitude and went out of his way to make other people look good. Once, before a match, he approached me with a few ideas—almost all of them involving him making me look good. I appreciated his generosity, but had to stop him: "Steve, we're all in this together. You don't have to bounce around for an hour tonight. We'll both bounce around. We're equals."

I saw a ton of potential in Steve Austin, and believed that he could be a singles star. But the people running WCW claimed that he was injury-prone and bland, and resented his habit of speaking his mind. So when Steve was home recuperating from a triceps injury, the company fired him.

ONCE AGAIN, I was on the WCW creative committee—for a while, I was even considered the primary booker—but it was the same as last

time. The members rotated; Kevin Sullivan, Mike Graham, Greg Gagne, and "Superstar" Bill Dundee were all on the committee during various periods. And regardless of my position, I didn't have enough stroke to keep a guy like Austin on our roster.

Hogan always maintained creative control of his character, and often had us fly down to Tampa to have booking meetings at his *house.* Not that it made any difference—we'd spend weeks putting a TV show together, but on the night of the event, he would come in and change things around. It's hard to be the booker when your primary job responsibility is making sure that one guy is happy.

I gained some interesting insight into Hogan during this period. He was fixated with Dave Meltzer's *Wrestling Observer* newsletter, the so-called "dirt sheet" that a lot of the guys condemn—even though they regularly pass it around and read all the gossip. Like Bret Hart and Mick Foley, Hogan thought the *Wrestling Observer* was the Bible. I swear, he spent more time talking about Meltzer than Sting, Ted Turner, or Vince McMahon. I once asked him, "Why would a guy with fifty million in the bank care so much about Dave Meltzer?"

"Twenty million," he corrected me.

MY ENTIRE MOTIVATION for being on the booking committee was finding a way to survive. I wasn't paid an extra dime. But the strategy frequently worked against me. I caught a lot of heat for my relationship with Arn. I pushed for him to join the committee, and make no apologies about it. Arn's the perfect guy for that position; he has people skills, the knowledge and authority, and—perhaps most important—he's respected by his peers. Not everyone shared my opinion, and the friendship drove a wedge between Bischoff and myself. Once, when I suggested that Arn win the TV championship, Eric sneered, "You could roll Arn Anderson in shit and he wouldn't draw a fly."

Let me explain just how offensive this was to me. Despite the fact that our matches are predetermined, wrestlers are forced to be competitive with each other. We're independent contractors, so we have to find our own way in the business. It's almost like we're not allowed to be friends. Even when wrestlers are nice to each other, they're still walking around lonely. Yet Arn and I had become as close as brothers, and everyone knew it. For Bischoff to make a comment like that in front of a group of people was like slapping me in the face.

I could practically hear Hogan's voice coming out of Eric's mouth as he elaborated, "Arn's not colorful. He doesn't move merchandise." Well, how many wrestlers *did* once they left the World Wrestling Federation marketing machine for WCW?

One guy who I was certain could sell a few T-shirts was Randy "Macho Man" Savage. He'd been relegated to an announcer's job in the World Wrestling Federation and could have been doing more, so Eric and I used the same strategy we employed to recruit Hogan. First, I called Randy up, then Eric and I flew to Florida and took him out to dinner, selling him on the company.

Later, when the discussions turned to dollars and cents, Bill Shaw asked me, "Is Randy Savage worth half a million?"

"I think he is," I replied. "Name recognition. We're trying to build a company. He's another piece of the puzzle. He's still got a lot left in him."

I was happy when Randy joined WCW—we'd been friends for most of my career—but almost immediately, Hogan had a pretty big influence on him. I felt that Hogan had convinced Savage that they were bigger than the company. Soon it wasn't just Hogan messing around with finishes; he and Savage would go out in the afternoon, drink beer, show up at the building, and start changing things—with Eric's approval. After a while, Eric was drinking with them himself!

The company was anxious for me to do something with Savage, but as you may recall, they had "retired" me. Kevin Sullivan and I came up with an inventive way to get around this dilemma—on March 19, 1995, at the *WCW Uncensored* Pay-Per-View, I stormed the ring dressed as a woman and jumped Savage in the middle of his match.

Now that I was back, I could also interfere in Hogan's strap match with Vader later in the night. Because Leon wouldn't lose to Hogan (and vice versa), I did the honors. Hogan dragged me to all four corners of the ring to get the win. It was a mind-boggling finish—how could an intruder come in and lose the match? Well, because the company was really fucked up.

In the storyline, I now "purchased time" on WCW programs and pitched "top ten" reasons for my reinstatement. Both Hogan and Savage also petitioned the "WCW Board of Directors" to end my retirement, and just like that, I was back in the ring, teaming with Vader against Hogan and Randy at the *Slamboree* Pay-Per-View on

May 21, 1995. Of course, I lost again, but after the bell, I beat up Savage's father, retired wrestler Angelo Poffo.

On Father's Day, Randy was supposed to get his revenge at *The Great American Bash;* not only that, but now I was expected to make *Angelo* look good, too! Enough was enough. I'd brought Hogan and Savage into WCW, dropped the title, retired, come back in drag, lost Vader's strap match for him, and had gotten pinned at *Slamboree.* Call me paranoid, but I was starting to feel a little manipulated.

"This time," I told Randy, "I'm winning. Take it or leave it."

Savage agreed, and I won the match after stealing Angelo's cane and bashing the Macho Man with it. The fact that I finally put my foot down was shocking. The fact that I was instantly kicked off the booking committee was not.

The "Monday Night Wars" officially began on September 4, 1995, when *Monday Nitro* debuted on Ted Turner's TNT network. Eric's plan was for the show to run every week opposite *Raw*. On the first program, broadcast from the Mall of America in Minnesota, I got beaten again, this time losing to Sting. But the big news was the surprise appearance of Lex Luger, who had toured with the World Wrestling Federation just the weekend before. Suddenly Lex was in WCW, demanding a title shot at Hulk Hogan. I don't remember where Vince McMahon was that night, but he had to be saddened. Eric Bischoff had kicked him squarely in the nuts. And it was only the beginning.

CHAPTER **18**

HUMILIATION

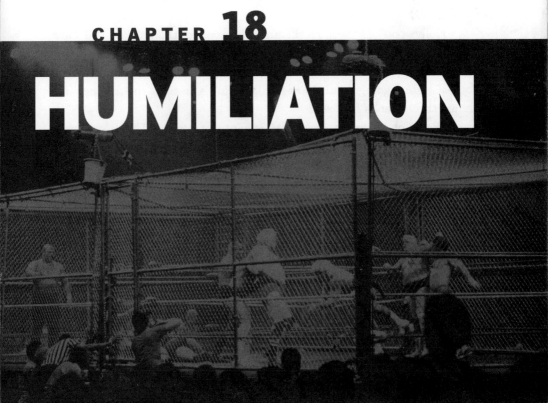

On March 27, 1996, Scott Hall—who was known in the World Wrestling Federation as Razor Ramon—came out of the crowd at *Nitro* and disrupted the program. Scott was famous for having a classic ladder match with Shawn Michaels in 1994 at *WrestleMania X,* and on a given night, he could be a very good performer. But when people called him "great," they lowered the bar ten feet. At *WrestleMania X,* Shawn had that match with the *ladder;* Scott Hall just happened to be in the vicinity. Because of that match, Scott got the rub from Michaels—who really *is* great—and a huge career push.

The following week on *Nitro,* Hall was joined by Kevin Nash. Nash, as Diesel, had held the World Wrestling Federation Championship for a year, spanning 1994 to 1995. The announcers called the pair the Outsiders, and the implication was that they didn't even work for WCW. Instead, fans were led to believe that they were World Wrestling Federation guys who had raided our show. The next week, they shocked the fans by grabbing one of the announcers—Bischoff—and literally slamming him through the stage.

In July 1996, at *Bash at the Beach,* the Outsiders unveiled a third ex–World Wrestling Federation renegade—Hogan. WCW fans had wanted to boo him for years, and now they had their chance. They bombarded the ring with garbage as he mocked his loyal Hulkamaniacs, telling them that while they had believed in him, "I did it for the money." Which was true.

"Hollywood" Hogan, Nash, and Hall called themselves the New World Order—nWo—and continued acting like a pack of outlaws who weren't really affiliated with the company. For a while, it was the hottest thing going, and *Nitro* kicked *Raw*'s ass in the ratings for eighty-three weeks in a row.

Like a lot of people in WCW, I wanted to feed off nWo's energy. The moment Nash arrived from the World Wrestling Federation, he told me how much he hoped that we could work together, but I felt like Bischoff was trying to keep us apart. I'd figured out that he wanted everyone to be at odds—Hogan and Savage on one side, Luger and Sting on another, Hall and Nash on another, Arn and myself on another. Because if we all got together, do you know what would have happened? We would have said, "This guy's a shit-disturbing motherfucker, and we don't need him anymore."

No matter what Bischoff claims, he used *me* to get Hogan and Savage. After that, I was a bit player to him. And I heard that he blamed me for decisions I didn't even make. When I was on the booking committee, Arn was asked to cancel a planned vacation and tour Japan. Why? Because, Eric told Arn, "Flair wants you to." Ron Simmons—later known to WWE fans as Faarooq—was led to believe that I didn't perceive him as a championship-caliber performer. Bullshit! It was *Hogan* who didn't want to work with Simmons.

The differences between Eric Bischoff and Vince McMahon were striking. Vince wants his wrestlers to respect each other. Bischoff didn't care because I don't think he respected anyone else. It got to the point that when I saw Eric backstage or in the airport, we barely even made small talk. I knew what he was—an asshole—and there was nothing for us to talk about. Eric knew if he had used me as a top guy, nobody could get over me. Hogan knew it, too.

DAVID CROCKETT: When I was working for WCW, I noticed some of the same patterns that I saw at the end of Crockett Promotions. I think Eric and Ric got along for a period of time, but then Eric's ego seemed to get in the way. He was a creative person, but he put himself on television—he made himself the boss of the nWo after a while—and wasn't able to step back and keep things at arm's length. It was just like Dusty. And Hogan was Eric's guy, so Ric was left as the weak sister.

CHRIS JERICHO: For whatever reason, Eric seemed to have a vendetta against Ric. Maybe it was because Ric Flair was the one big star that he couldn't take credit for creating or buying from the World Wrestling Federation. I don't know. But there was definitely some heat there.

ARN ANDERSON: At different times, the people who had control over WCW wouldn't nurture Ric and use him as an asset. They felt that no one else would be able to get over unless they killed him—unless they just shoved him so far down that someone might pass him by.

I noticed that I was constantly losing in the Carolinas and Virginia, the places where I really had history with the fans. There was no logic behind it at all. Even when the people booed me, they didn't want to see me being humbled over and over again, and a lot of them started to lose interest.

Just before *Halloween Havoc* in 1995, I left to have surgery on my cataracts—a condition I developed from lying in tanning beds for too many years. Sting and I were teaming on the card, so we taped an interview together. Then I flew home for the operation. When Bischoff found out about it, he called me up, screaming that he had never given me permission to take any time off. Besides, he claimed, the interview sucked and had to be done over. So I had my surgery on a Tuesday morning, then—against doctor's orders—rushed to the airport to get back to Atlanta and reshoot the interview. To this day, the vision in my right eye is so bad that it's going to require surgery again.

Eric also seemed to take pleasure in demeaning me in front of the boys. Before a match with Bret "Hitman" Hart, Bischoff walked up to me in front of a group of people and said, "In your match with Bret tonight, I want the Sharpshooter. Get it done in twenty minutes." Then he walked away. The prick acted like he was talking to a guy at the bottom of the card. Once, when I questioned why he was having me lose to Konnan, he shouted at me in a dressing room hallway, "Why are you always complaining about something? Just fuckin' do what we write down. This is a team. This isn't about you anymore, Ric."

CHRIS JERICHO: Before one show, we had a big meeting backstage, and Eric was giving us this speech about how he was going to put Vince out of business in six months, guaranteed. And he knew how to do it. The rest of the guys didn't because, Eric said, nobody in the room had ever drawn a dime except for Hogan, Savage, and Piper. Ric Flair—one of the greatest draws of all time—was sitting right there, and everybody's kind of looking at him, and he just had to take it. It was a very bad atmosphere.

It was degrading. Eric looked right past me when he made that remark, and I never knew it was coming. I was humiliated. My only choice would have been to stand up and walk out the door. And I thought about it. I thought about it every day.

Yet I knew that the guys looked up to me, and I wanted to help the organization succeed. It didn't matter what Eric said—the company always fell back on me. And when it did, I always went all-out.

"MEAN" GENE OKERLUND: You could make a pretty valid argument about why Ric should have left the business. He's got a great family, he lived in an upscale home, he liked boating, and he had a lot of things

that could occupy his time in terms of leisure. But when guys like Flair get into it, they bleed wrestling. That *is* their life.

At *Starrcade '95,* on December 27 in Nashville, I won my twelfth world title from Randy Savage. Randy wanted blood and cut me without telling—the only time another wrestler has ever done that in my career. Brian Pillman and Chris Benoit interfered on my behalf, and as Randy fought them off, Arn Anderson belted him with a pair of brass knuckles, and I got the pin. When three men have to help, *they* win the match, not you. That's not like beating Harley Race one-on-one for the championship. That's absurd. I remember going into the back, where guys like Diamond Dallas Page and Johnny B. Badd congratulated me: "You're back! You're back!" And I was thinking to myself, Guys, I'm so over this. It was such bullshit.

Savage recaptured the title at *Nitro* in Vegas on January 22, 1996, when Arn went to hit Randy with a foreign object and smashed me

I didn't always agree with Randy Savage at WCW, but I did respect him.

instead. Then, at *SuperBrawl VI*, on February 17 in St. Petersburg, Florida, we had a rematch in a cage. And I had fun that night.

Woman—who'd managed me in the eighties—was back in my corner. And despite their divorce, Elizabeth had reunited with Randy in wrestling storylines and accompanied him to ringside. At the end, Woman hurled a handful of powder at Randy, but he ducked out of the way. Then came the swerve: Elizabeth turned on Randy and handed me her shoe. I used it to crack Savage over the head and win the title. It wasn't a traditional championship victory, but Randy and I had worked well together, and the Nature Boy ended up with both girls. I enjoyed it.

In fact, I was starting to feel like Randy and I had a good feud going. For whatever reason, Hogan wasn't in Savage's ear during this period, and—in the ring—Randy was the performer I had respected in the past. The fans were interested. I was actually looking forward to dropping the title to him one more time. Before that could happen, though, I was ordered to lose the championship to the Giant—Paul Wight, later known as the Big Show in WWE. I was happy to do the favor for Paul because he's a nice guy, but it was stupid to prematurely end my series with Savage.

What happened was that I had missed a show in Little Rock, Arkansas, because I'd taken my son, Reid, to compete in an amateur wrestling tournament in Columbus, Ohio. When I got to the airport, the only flight to Little Rock was canceled. This was probably the second show I'd missed in twenty-five years. Still, the company had to punish me. So on April 26, 1996, the Giant became the WCW champion at *Nitro* in Albany, Georgia.

MY SHOULDER WAS already troubling me when, on September 23, 1996, Kensuke Sasaki fell on me in a ring in Japan, completely tearing my rotator cuff. When other wrestlers have surgery for such a severe injury, they're gone for at least six months. I wasn't afforded the same luxury. Within two weeks, I was back in the dressing room—in case I was needed for an interview, or some other task Bischoff could come up with.

That said, at least I was able to return. When Arn Anderson had four vertebrae removed from his neck in 1997, he was left with a hand too weak to hold a glass or fasten a button. At that point, the Horsemen had been expanded to a group of five, including us, Chris Benoit, Dean

The symbol of excellence: me with fellow Horsemen Chris Benoit, Dean Malenko, and the Enforcer, Arn Anderson.

Malenko, and ex–Chicago Bears star Steve "Mongo" McMichael. Personally, I thought we blew away the nWo. Arn could talk better than those guys. Benoit and Malenko were great in the ring. Mongo was a marginal performer, but he had a million-dollar look to go along with his Super Bowl ring. To the fans, we all were tough, believable guys. The only problem was that Arn could no longer continue as an active wrestler.

On August 27, 1997, Arn relinquished his Horsemen spot to Curt Hennig, and delivered his retirement speech on *Nitro*. After relating a heart-wrenching true story about the pain that shot through his body when somebody in the gym had innocently slapped him on the back, he told the crowd, "For all you people out there that ever bought a ticket to see Arn Anderson wrestle, whether you loved me or hated me, you know that when the bell rang, you got all I had that night. Whether I won or whether I lost, I gave you everything I had. And you knew that. And when you did this to me"—he turned his palm toward his body and displayed four fingers to the crowd—"that was your acknowledgment."

It was awesome television. I know that it was real to me, and real to Arn. Sting had tears in his eyes. It hurt me to know that Arn was really saying good-bye to something that meant so much to him.

The next week, without informing us, the nWo came out and did a spoof of the entire speech. Sean Waltman—who'd now joined the group and worked as Syxx in WCW (and had been the 1-2-3 Kid and X-Pac in the World Wrestling Federation)—was dressed as me, in a blond wig and false nose, bouncing off the ropes and strutting. Kevin Nash was Arn, with a bald wig, fake beer gut, neck brace, and Styrofoam cooler. They wore T-shirts depicting the Horsemen as the Four Jackasses. "Arn" described himself as having "average size, average speed, average quickness, average looks, average intelligence, average carpentry skills," and despaired that his left arm could no longer open a beer can. Whenever he came to town, he told the crowd, he left an unpaid beer tab behind.

What was suspicious was that no one scheduled us to run into the ring and get revenge by beating up these guys. Arn's kids watched the show and didn't get the joke; they just saw their father being portrayed as some pathetic drunk. With all the political mistrust in WCW, Arn believed that the parody was part of a plot to undermine him, and he knocked on Kevin Nash's door later that night. Arn's neck might have been damaged, but it wouldn't have made a difference. He was ready to fight.

> **ARN ANDERSON:** **Kevin had no idea that any feelings were hurt. He didn't see it as a personal attack; he just looked at it as a piece of business. It was television, and he was trying to be entertaining. After talking a while, I got the impression that he was telling the truth, and I calmed down.**

Later on, we found out that the whole thing was thought up not by Nash or Bischoff or Hogan, but by Terry Taylor, one of Arn's good friends. Terry was on the booking committee and just wanted to be humorous. There was no ulterior motive.

As for Kevin, he was just doing what he'd been told. Later, when Arn wrote a book that mentioned the incident and the distress it caused his family, Nash contacted him and apologized a second time. I thought that was very classy.

CURT HENNIG DIDN'T last long as Arn's replacement. In a War Games match, at the *Fall Brawl* Pay-Per-View on September 14, 1997, he and I teamed up with Mongo and Benoit against an nWo team of Nash, Syxx, Konnan, and Buff Bagwell. Less than a month after the emotional night when Arn handed over his spot, Hennig turned on the Horsemen, slamming my head in the cage door and joining the nWo. The match took place in the heart of Horsemen territory—Winston Salem, North Carolina—and basically killed the city for WCW. For the second year in a row, the Horsemen lost War Games in their own back-yard. In terms of storyline, the turn and result didn't make sense. The only motive seemed to be burying me.

The plot continued, with Hennig stealing my robe, tearing off the sleeves, and awarding it to Hogan. Forget the fact that I had paid $5,500 for the robe and wasn't reimbursed. When it was handed to Hogan, the fan outrage transferred over to him. In other words, it wasn't Curt's storyline anymore. Hogan stole it.

Vince McMahon wasn't the type of guy to sit back and let another company run over him. So in 1998, in the middle of the wrestling war, he reached into his pockets and got Mike Tyson to take part in the main event at *WrestleMania XIV*—as the "special enforcer" in a match between Stone Cold Steve Austin and World Wrestling Federation Champion Shawn Michaels.

I'd always admired Michaels's in-ring ability, but I began watching him extra closely when I came home one day and my son Reid asked, "Can you do a moonsault like Shawn Michaels?"

"Why do you want to know that?" I asked.

"Well, Shawn Michaels can do a moonsault. Can't you?"

CHAPTER 19

FIRE ME! I'M ALREADY FIRED!

My older son, David, already idolized Shawn, and now Reid was pointing out something that Michaels could do and I couldn't. That's when I realized that the Heartbreak Kid was starting to eclipse me.

In the weeks leading up to *WrestleMania XIV,* World Wrestling Federation television viewers were led to believe that Tyson would side with Shawn in the main event. Thousands of people who weren't wrestling fans purchased the Pay-Per-View out of curiosity, and watched the surprise ending of Tyson decking Shawn after Stone Cold Steve Austin beat him for the title. With Austin, Undertaker, Triple H, Mick Foley, The Rock, and others leading the way, the World Wrestling Federation embarked on its most successful era.

During that time, I ran into Austin in Gold's Gym in Venice, California, and gave him a big hug. He'd always been one of my favorites, and I was so happy for him. Every week, I had to listen to Eric talk about how the World Wrestling Federation was dying; he was *obsessed* with beating them. And I was elated that a guy who he'd fired had become such a big star.

Even in a nonwrestling role, Stone Cold Steve Austin has the second-best gimmick—after Undertaker—in the history of the business. As a wrestler, he tore the joint down. His interview skills and charisma are almost unparalleled. After the *Raw* cameras turn off, I've watched Steve get in the ring, do his beer-drinking routine for the fans, and not leave until they're ready to go home. That's what makes him great—he cares about his trade, and he cares about the fans.

STEVE WILLIAMS, AKA STONE COLD STEVE AUSTIN: As far as Ric Flair's place in the business, in my opinion he's the greatest professional wrestler in history. If I had to name a guy from the entire WWE that is the best worker in the business right now, who could have the best match with anybody on any given night, working heel or babyface, Ric Flair would be my choice. Right now, at fifty-five. He's just that good, and it's just that simple.

I never wanted to put Vince McMahon out of business, nor did I want to see a group of wrestlers lose their jobs. I knew Triple H from when he was Jean-Paul Levesque in WCW, and the "Road Dogg" Jesse James through his father, "Bullet" Bob Armstrong. My daughter Megan had played with Rocky Johnson's son, Dwayne, when they were

Steve Austin's "Stone Cold" attitude took him to the top of WWE.

children. I tracked him through college football at Miami and his early wrestling days. Then, suddenly, he was calling himself "the most electrifying man in sports entertainment." And he wasn't lying.

The Rock reminded me very much of myself in his interviews, creating a lot off his own energy. The entertainment value in his performance is so great that it's made him a movie star. In the ring, he's always given 120 percent, and even though his time in the business has been relatively short, I would have to categorize him as "great."

In WCW, Bill Goldberg became the company's only homegrown superstar. Bill had played football for the University of Georgia, the Los Angeles Rams, and the Atlanta Falcons before meeting a bunch of the boys at the Gold Club, an Atlanta strip joint, and being steered into the Power Plant, WCW's training facility. With his shaved head, goatee, commanding physique, and incredible intensity, Goldberg fired up the crowd by going out there and just *squashing* foes—spear, jackhammer, pin. The company invented a winning streak for him—170–0—and on July 7, 1998, Goldberg even got to beat Hogan on *Nitro,* winning the WCW title in front of 35,000 fans at the Georgia Dome.

Not long afterward, Bill and I drew a big house in Minneapolis—not far from where I roomed with his brother at the University of Minnesota. Goldberg won the match, and that was fine. As big as he'd gotten in the business, he never forgot who Ric Flair was, or my connection to his family.

BILL GOLDBERG: I told Ric that it was a pleasure to get in the ring with him because I kind of felt like I was beating up my brother. We were in the Target Center, and I speared him, then picked him up for the jackhammer, when Ric pinched me and whispered, "Kid, remember two things: I love you, and I'm fifty years old."

When Bill Goldberg wanted a salary increase, he got it. So did a lot of other guys in WCW. I heard that eighteen wrestlers were earning more than me, including Nash, Hall, Luger, Sting, Scott Norton, Booker T, and even his brother, Stevie Ray. Rick Steiner allegedly cut a good deal with Eric during a hunting trip—Rick supposedly called a WCW lawyer to give her the contract details upon his return—and Diamond Dallas Page was a millionaire simply because he was Bischoff's neighbor. When Bret Hart joined the company, Eric paid a fortune to a guy Vince didn't even want anymore.

Bret never regained the fame he'd had in the World Wrestling Federation. Part of it had to do with terrible booking, the other part with Bret's own deficiencies. What unnerved me most was the way he used his brother's death (Owen Hart slipped out of his harness and fell from the ceiling of Kansas City's Kemper Arena during a World Wrestling Federation Pay-Per-View in 1999). Through his column in the *Calgary Sun,* Bret relentlessly bashed Vince McMahon. I sympathize with the emotion—and even the anger—he felt over losing a brother, but I lost respect for him when he made the case into a public spectacle. Why didn't he take up the matter privately with Vince? It seemed to me that Bret cared more about getting "screwed" in Montreal than he did about Owen's death, and he used his brother's tragedy to grind his ax with Vince.

As for me, I was struggling with anxiety issues again, only this was a little different than in 1991. Now I was beginning to lose my self-respect. I was questioning my own value as a performer. After a match I'd walk up to a friend like Mark Madden, the announcer, and ask, "Was that okay? Did you think it was good?" I'd never acted like that before. Mark thought I was crazy. "You're Ric Flair!" he'd say. "It's always good!"

When you're miserable at work, you bring the misery home. I'd sit around in my house and try to drink away the reality. Beth wanted to help, but there was only so much that she could do. I was in a state of depression.

MEGAN FLIEHR KETZNER: He just told me that things weren't good, but my dad never talked about trouble at work. Not with me. It was something that he felt I didn't need to worry about. He would say, "One day, you're going to have a husband, and then his problems will be your problems."

ARN ANDERSON: Ric was having anxiety attacks. He'd hyperventilate and think that he was having a heart attack. He couldn't stand being alone. I would literally have to go down several times a night to his hotel room to check on him. He was a wreck, and it was because he had been rendered to the point where he was second-guessing himself. He was thinking, "They must be right. Shit, I must be over the hill. Passé."

I never wanted to be the highest-paid guy in WCW; I just wanted my salary to be competitive. Bischoff was begrudgingly giving me five hundred grand while other guys who did so much less for the company were getting paid a million or more. It still makes me so angry just thinking about it.

My contract with WCW expired on February 16, 1998. For much of the previous two years, I'd been attempting to negotiate a new agreement: a three-year deal, reasonable involvement in storylines, fair treatment, and legitimate consideration of my experience and status as a multiple-time world champion. I'd been told that all those requests would be met, and—just as Jim Herd and Jack Petrik had pledged several years earlier—I was assured that WCW would portray me with respect.

In November 1997, I received a "letter of agreement" that expressed the basic terms that would be listed in the contract. Among other things missing were the provisions promising my involvement in storylines and requiring that I be treated in a "civil and respectful" manner. WCW also wanted the right to eliminate me from their programs as long as I was getting paid. That wouldn't work: if I wasn't on TV, what value would I have later on if I tried to shop myself somewhere else?

I was at an impasse with the company. Jim Cornette, who was working for the World Wrestling Federation by then, called and told me that he was sure Vince would love to have me again. When I ran this by my agents—Barry "Don't Tell Anybody I Told You This" Bloom and Michael "Don't Even Tell Barry I Told You This" Braverman—they urged me to stay put. "We can do a big deal with WCW," they assured me. "Guaranteed money. We can help you."

These were the same guys who had promised me a book deal—including a $360,000 advance—with Crown Publishing. Then the project was put on hold when Bill Goldberg started writing a book for the same company. When that book bombed, mine was completely forgotten about. Over the course of my entire relationship with Bloom and Braverman, they never got me one outside project, not even an autograph signing.

Bloom and Braverman told me they'd make sure that my salary would be in correlation to that of every other WCW star except for Hogan, Nash, Hall, and Sting. I knew those guys had better deals than

I did, and I didn't have a problem with it. My agents represented other wrestlers in WCW, so they knew what the talent was making. But I don't believe that they really went to bat for me and demanded that my salary at least be equitable. I always wondered whether it was because they also happened to represent Eric Bischoff. I can never prove that there was a conflict of interest, but it sure seemed like I wasn't a priority. And the whole experience led me to feel even more isolated, like the people I trusted weren't on my side.

In April 1998, my son Reid qualified for the AAU national wrestling tournament in the 110-pound weight class. He was only ten, and our family was really looking forward to it. I let the company know that I was going there with him. Eric was in Japan, but called to say that I couldn't go to the tournament; they suddenly needed me in Tallahassee for *WCW Thunder,* the second-rate show that the company aired on TBS Thursday nights. I hadn't been on *Thunder* for a month, but now they offered to charter a plane to fly me to Tallahassee from the tournament in Detroit—on the condition that I paid half the airfare. If Hogan needed a plane, would they make *him* pay half the airfare? Fuck that! So I told the company no.

Eric fired me from Japan, then sued me for breach of contract. Except I didn't *have* a contract; there was only that letter of intent that I had rejected. The company said that my absence on a single edition of *Thunder* had cost them about two million dollars—a pretty interesting number, since I was getting paid just a quarter of that to work a full year.

I spoke to my lawyers—Bill Diehl in Charlotte, and John Taylor and Otto Feil in Atlanta—and countersued. We said that the company had underutilized me, and that, according to our claim, Bischoff "seems to think he has dictatorial authority over Flair. Bischoff's language towards Flair is rude, crude and socially unacceptable, even in the world of professional wrestling." By tying me up in litigation over a contract that didn't exist, we added, WCW was scaring away potential employers, like the World Wrestling Federation.

At the April 13 *Nitro,* Eric gathered the wrestlers backstage. I later read that this is what he told them: "Look, Ric Flair is a liar, and everyone lets him get away with it because he's Ric Flair. Let him *be* Ric Flair. I'm gonna sue him and his family into bankruptcy." A major executive of a major corporation actually said that about an employee in front of other employees.

Not only is Bischoff a prick, but they don't come any dumber.

CHRIS JERICHO: Basically, the tone of the meeting was that Ric Flair had fucked up bad. Now he was going to get blackballed out of the company, and Eric said he was going to make sure that Ric and his family starved.

In the arena, the fans were chanting, "We want Flair! We want Flair!" Because of the Internet, everyone knew precisely what was going on. I'm not sure how much of a coincidence it was that this was the same night when *Nitro*'s eighty-three-week ratings win streak over *Raw* came to an end. Nonetheless, something I'm still bitter about is that Reid won his tournament—a *national* AAU tournament—and I couldn't enjoy it the way a father should.

I had to sit out for five months without a paycheck while all this bullshit got cleared up. At one point, Bloom and Braverman orchestrated a meeting between Bischoff and myself at an Atlanta hotel. Like a fool, I met with them.

Eric wanted to give me an ultimatum, and implied that I could never possibly win my countersuit. "What the hell is a divorce attorney going to do for you?" he sneered in reference to Bill Diehl, my lawyer in Charlotte. Bill, one of the most respected attorneys in the United States, has always been known to kick ass and take names later, and John Taylor is equally tough when he has to be. They were both brilliant lawyers. I know they would have eaten Turner's legal team for lunch. However, we all knew that if we took the case to trial, the time I would have to spend in court would have ended my wrestling career. So we agreed to make a deal with them. If I followed their advice to the end, I'd probably own a percentage of Time Warner right now—and Bischoff was trying to make it sound like he was a small-timer specializing in domestic law.

"Fuck you," I told Bischoff. He stood up and started to yell, but I didn't even bother listening. I just left the room.

When the World Wrestling Federation came to Greensboro, I actually considered going there with Reid and sitting in the front row. Jim Ross could come over to us with his microphone and tell the television audience, "Today we're going to be speaking to one of the great champions of wrestling." Then, instead of talking to me, he'd interview Reid, who'd say, "I'm here with my dad because WCW is suing him, so he's got time off."

The only thing that prevented me from doing anything like that was knowing that I still had friends at WCW. Benoit, Malenko, and Mongo were still calling themselves the Horsemen, with Arn playing a speaking role. I would have felt like I had let them down.

Every day, Arn would call me up: "Come on, Ric. We need you here." Ultimately, that had an impact. When I finally came back to work, I simply agreed to extend my old contract for four more years. I just couldn't hold out for $1.5 million when Arn was trying to keep the Horsemen together.

On September 14, 1998, I made my return to WCW in Greenville, South Carolina. The Horsemen were in the ring with J. J. Dillon, all dressed in tuxedos. When Arn introduced me and my theme music played, the fans screamed so loudly that the floors shook. As I walked down the entrance ramp, my eyes scanned over a multitude of people howling up at me with four fingers stuck in the air. One guy held up a sign that read IMPEACH CLINTON. VOTE FLAIR. My eyes started to well up with tears, but I stiffened my face, spun around in my tux, and shouted, "Woooooo!"

When I got in the ring, I hugged Arn, then spoke to the fans from my heart: "Thank you very much. I'm almost embarrassed by the response. But when I see this, I know that the twenty-five years that I've spent trying to make you happy every night of my life was worth every damn minute of it."

Previously backstage, Bischoff and I had been very businesslike with each other. I knew that he was going to come out and interrupt me at some point, and he knew that I was going to fire back at him. Beyond that, everything else was ad-libbed. "This is *real*," I hollered to the crowd. "This is a *real-life situation!*"

From there, I remembered Eric once telling me how the Horsemen were outdated, and now I decided to talk to the crowd about it. Looking over at Arn, I shouted, "This guy, my best friend, is one of the greatest performers who ever lived. And *you*"—I gestured toward the dressing room curtain—"you squashed him. You get on the phone and tell me, 'Disband the Horsemen. They're dead. Disband the Horsemen.' *Me?* You know what? I looked myself in the mirror the next day, and I saw a pathetic figure that gave up and quit! And for that, I owe you, the wrestling fans, and I owe these guys an apology. Because it won't happen again."

Now Bischoff came out of the dressing room, flapping his arms

I ad-libbed what I was saying to Eric Bischoff on *WCW Monday Nitro*, but the feelings were all too real.

around like he was legitimately trying to end the segment. Just the sight of him pissed me off, so I let the words keep flowing: "Bischoff, whatever you think, you're an overbearing asshole! That's right! You're an obnoxious, overbearing ass! Abuse of power! You! Abuse of power! Cut me off! Come on! It's called abuse of power! You suck! You! I hate your guts! You are a liar! You're a cheat! You're a scam! You are a no-good son-of-a-bitch! Fire me! I'm already fired! Fire me! I'm already fired!"

The fans were jumping up and down, pointing and cursing at Bischoff, screaming like they were no longer watching sports enter-tainment, but something that had previously been confined to the dressing room. And they were right. It was all out in the open. And it *was* real. Absolutely 100 percent real.

Once I was back in WCW, it was yet again more of the same—the most disorganized clusterfuck of all time. Scott Steiner would finish his match and barge through the curtain, screaming at road agents, knocking down tables, and throwing around television monitors. Kevin Nash and Scott Hall, meanwhile, no-showed important dates.

At least Eric Bischoff was willing to play off our real-life friction. Maybe he was trying to con me, or perhaps he was trying to pacify the situation. It was kind of sad because he came up with some really good television. Sometimes I'd be charmed into thinking that there was something decent about him. But there wasn't.

CHAPTER 20

THIS IS HOW I TRAVEL, YOU JACKASS!

In one segment we shot, I was supposed to be out of town. Knowing this, Bischoff went to the ring and dared me to wrestle him, then called me a coward when I didn't come out. Suddenly, Arn appeared and declared, "Flair is here." Eric acted surprised, and then the camera panned to the entrance ramp, where my son Reid emerged, wearing his singlet and AAU championship medal. He got in the ring and let out a long "*Wooooo!*"

"I want him out of here," Eric yelled at Arn. "I can't fire this punk, but I sure can fire you. I want him *gone.*" But as Bischoff turned to the crowd, Reid took him down from behind. Obviously, Eric had to cooperate to make this seem believable, but it came off well. Eric leaped up and faced Reid, who took him down again with a single leg. Arn then stood in front of Reid, who dramatically tossed back his head, Ric Flair–style.

"You just got took down *twice* by a ten-year-old kid," Arn gloated. "Do you know sign language? Give it to him, Reid."

Reid raised four fingers, exhilarating all those Horsemen fans in Columbia, South Carolina.

MEGAN FLIEHR KETZNER: I thought it was hilarious. At the time, I didn't have the greatest taste in my mouth for Eric Bischoff, so I really enjoyed it.

Some of the decisions that the company made were so arbitrary. When Atlanta Falcons coach Dan Reeves suffered a heart attack, Eric and Diamond Dallas Page had a brainstorm on an airplane. When they got to the arena, I was told, "You're going to have a heart attack in the ring tonight. Don't tell *anyone*—not the boys, not your family."

Well, I had to call Beth; there was no way that I was going to let her watch something like that on TV and think it was real. But just about everybody else was kept in the dark. When the time came, I got in the ring and started doing an interview, sweating and jumping around and screaming myself hoarse . . . then held my heart and fell backward. People were calling my house for a week.

We brought my family into this angle, too. While I was allegedly convalescing, Eric made a big production out of apologizing to Beth, David, and Reid inside the ring. Then my boys were suddenly attacked by Barry Windham and Kevin Nash, while Bischoff grabbed my wife and kissed her. Despite my history with Eric, I wasn't upset by the move, and neither was Beth. It was just business.

The whole point of this was to set up a match between Bischoff and myself at *Starrcade '98.* Eric liked to portray himself as a martial-arts specialist. Even so, the idea of him fighting a guy my size, with my experience, was kind of stupid. But so were a lot of things about WCW at that time.

The two of us were backstage at the MCI Center in Washington, D.C., when Bischoff asked, "What do you think about me going over tonight? Tomorrow at *Nitro,* we'll work again, and you'll go over."

"Fine."

"How do you feel about getting juice?"

I didn't object to that, either. I never mind bleeding if it serves a purpose.

In the ring, I ripped off Eric's shirt and chopped him across the chest, then lifted him up and brought him down to the mat with a vertical suplex. Regardless of my personal feelings, I never went into business for myself and hit him with a legit punch, or failed to protect him when he gave me his body. I'm a *professional* wrestler, and that's the most unprofessional thing I could have done. You never take advantage of a person who's put his trust in you that way. Even if he is an asshole who deserves to get hurt.

After referee Charles Robinson was knocked down, I put Bischoff in the figure-four. Curt Hennig came down to the ring and slipped brass knuckles onto Eric's fingers. Just before Charles came to, Bischoff hit me with the knucks and covered me for the pin.

The next night, on *Nitro* in Baltimore, I did one of the best interviews of my life, daring Bischoff to come out and wrestle me. Dragging my luggage into the ring, I confronted announcer "Mean" Gene Okerlund. "Mean Gene, who made this coat?" I demanded. "Hugo Boss? Armani?" I pulled it off and threw it down, then stripped off my sweater. "Who made this? Perry Ellis?"

Next I went into my suitcase, now addressing my comments to Bischoff, who was presumably watching my tirade backstage. "This is how I travel, you jackass! I'm custom-made from head to toe. Have been and always will be, you jackass." I dumped my clothes in the ring. "That's me! I've lived the life of a king because the people have allowed me to! *Woooo!*" I removed my belt and watch. "Two-thousand-dollar

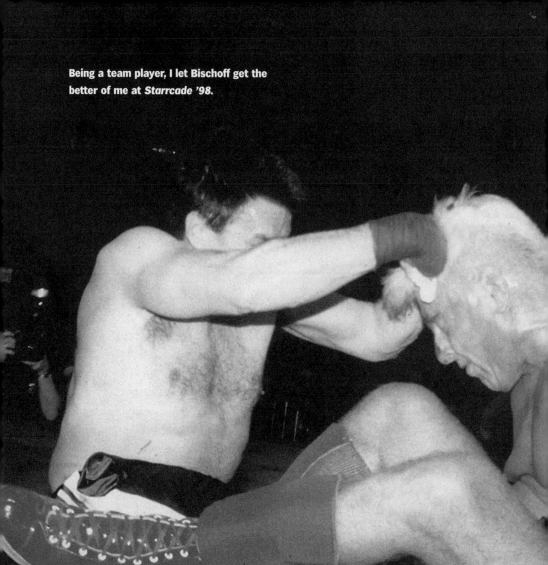

alligator—it's *yours!* Thirty-thousand-dollar gold Rolex—it's *yours!*" I
started ripping up money, shouting, "*Yours, yours, yours!*"

Then I pulled off my shoes and tossed them into the crowd.
"Bischoff, I ain't leaving"—I took off my pants, did a little dance, and
dropped an elbow on the canvas—"till you get something straight! I'm
telling you, Bischoff, I will leave the wrestling world *forever!* I will sign
my house, my cars, whatever money I have, I'll sign it over to you! I *will*
give you the satisfaction of saying you *raped* the Nature Boy, if you have
the you-know-what to walk the aisle here tonight, one more time! *But,*

the one stipulation that I'm begging you—God, I'm *begging* you, Bischoff, be a man—if I—grace the good Lord, *woooo!*—beat you, I get to run WCW for ninety days!"

From that point, I started to talk reality. "And the first thing I'm gonna do is take your head out of Hogan's ass! *Woooo!* You have had Turner blindfolded. You're a scammer. You're a schemer. You've got the brain of a pissant, and you run an empire. You're not smart." Finally, I handcuffed myself to the top rope: "Bischoff, I ain't goin' home until you get your ass out here!"

Okerlund cautiously interrupted me to say that it was time for a commercial, but I warned, "Bischoff! You turn the camera off, and I'll be naked when you come back!"

After the commercial, Eric came down to ringside, taunting me. "Beating up your kid, kissing your old lady, ruining your career, has all been great," he began, "but nothing is better than literally taking all of your money." As he scooped up the dollars off the canvas, he said, "You're a nut, and you're a man who's going to die of a heart attack if you don't settle down."

"When I die of a heart attack," I fired back, "it'll be on *your girlfriend,* pal!"

Eventually, Bischoff had to be carted to the ring—with Mongo slinging him over his shoulder, and Benoit and Malenko each grabbing a leg. The match ended up with the entire nWo—which had now expanded to include about a quarter of the population of DeKalb County—brawling with the Horsemen, while I suplexed Bischoff and forced him to submit to the figure-four.

FOR SEVERAL MONTHS, my oldest son David had been monitoring the developments in WCW from very close range. He'd lived with us in the ninth grade, then returned to Minnesota to stay with his mother and graduate from Hopkins High School. Now he'd moved into our home in Charlotte, worked at one of my gyms, and attended Central Piedmont Junior College. His goal was to eventually become a North Carolina state trooper.

> **DAVID FLAIR:** WCW asked if I wanted to be part of an angle that would start a program between Barry Windham and my father. I'd be sitting in the front row at a *Thunder* taping at the Independence Arena, and Barry would beat me up. I thought it would be cool. A few days before, I went to Atlanta and Barry took me through it. That night, at the Independence Arena, he pulled me out of the crowd, slapped me, slammed me, and gave me a suplex.

Windham's attack on David led to a special match on January 17, 1999, at the *Souled Out* Pay-Per-View in Charleston, West Virginia—and an incident that I've never put behind me.

David and I teamed up against Curt Hennig and Barry Windham. David, obviously, had no idea about how to wrestle, but Barry and Curt—being great guys and great workers, with no agenda other than having a good match—really made David look like a million dollars. Every spot they'd practiced came off like clockwork. We were doing everything that we worked out beforehand. Arn Anderson ran in with a tire iron and took it to Hennig, and David shocked the fans by getting the pin.

That's when Hogan and the nWo hit the ring.

> **DAVID FLAIR:** It was Hogan, Hennig, and Windham with Buff Bagwell and Scott Norton. They grabbed my dad and handcuffed him to the ropes. Then they held my arms and legs while Hogan whipped me with a belt. He told me he was going to hit me three or four times, and I was like, "Okay." But he must have hit me fifteen, maybe twenty times. He just whipped the shit out of me. The belt would go around my back and slash me in the stomach. I was black and blue.
>
> I'll never forget how Scott Norton, this big strong guy who used to be an arm-wrestling champion, kind of squeezed my hand as he held my arm down and asked, "Are you okay, kid?" I never expected that from him. But then, I also never expected to get whipped like that. That shit hurts.

I'm not surprised about Norton. He was the toughest one there and had nothing to prove. What no one had told me was that Hogan would try to be cute and whip David over and over again. It wasn't fair to make my son go through that—he wasn't even really a wrestler yet—but there was nothing that I could do. I was handcuffed to the ropes. I couldn't jump up and say, "Hey, don't do this to my kid." I wanted to, though. I felt like running over and holding David in my arms, and just stopping that stupid angle right there. He wasn't ready.

David didn't say a word. He took it like a man. You had Curt Hennig and Barry Windham, two of the best performers during their primes, and they bounced around for every one of David's moves. My son couldn't do anything, and they made him look like a star. And then there was Hogan—with all his experience, and all his celebrity—trying to be cute. He whipped David like a dog. It was sickening, and I'll never forgive him for it.

We continued the storyline on *Nitro* the following night. On television, I accused Bischoff of orchestrating the whole episode, and we set up a contest: David against Eric. If my son won, Bischoff would have to shave his head. If David lost, I'd shave mine and relinquish the presidency of WCW. In the match, David hit Bischoff with a roll of quarters and scored the pin, and the Horsemen cut Eric's hair.

DAVID NEVER SPOKE about becoming a wrestler when he was growing up. Not once. I'd always felt that he was a little shell-shocked from not having a father in his day-to-day life, and I worried about him. Now I wasn't sure if he was going in the right direction; he was almost too nice a person for this insensitive business. I spoke to him about forgetting wrestling and going back and taking the state trooper's exam, but he was so happy it was hard to say no.

The company soon booked David to turn against me. On February 21, 1999, I was in the ring with Hogan—challenging him for the WCW Championship at the *SuperBrawl* Pay-Per-View—when Torrie Wilson made her first wrestling appearance, strutting out of the dressing room in a sexy dress. The announcers played it like no one knew who she was or whose side she was on. Then she slapped me across the face. After that, a guy in a mask marched down to the ring and zapped me with a Taser, then pulled off his hood. It was David, and he had on an nWo

T-shirt. As the fans looked on in bewilderment, he and Torrie started making out on camera.

> **DAVID FLAIR:** The story was supposed to be that Hogan and the nWo had this pretty girl seduce me so that I would side with them against my father. I then shot another angle where I got in the ring and told my dad something like, "You've never been a role model in my life. When I needed a role model, I looked to Hulk Hogan."
>
> I was just twenty years old. I didn't know what the hell I was doing. Torrie didn't have a clue, either. I mean, you can't pick up all this stuff in one day. They were going to send me to training school, but that never happened. It was, "Here you are. Go out and wrestle tonight. You're Ric Flair's kid. You'll figure it out."

To counter David, the company gave me Charles Robinson—"Little Naitch"—the bleached-blond referee and lifetime Ric Flair fanatic. Robinson was the ref when I challenged Hogan for his title on March 14, 1999, inside a cage in Louisville, Kentucky. Hogan had me pinned at one point, but Charles deliberately counted slow. Then David and Torrie came down to ringside to interfere. Arn rushed to my defense, going after my son. Torrie jumped on Arn's back, but he threw her off and slipped a tire iron through the cage. I belted Hogan with it, then put him in the figure-four. As soon as Hogan's shoulders touched the mat, Robinson fast-counted and awarded me the title. According to the plot, the victory also enabled me to become WCW "President for Life."

IN 1994 MY parents started to have major health issues, with one illness after another. The following year, I moved them to a retirement home, close to me in Charlotte. My mother developed a form of Parkinson's disease that knotted up her body and prevented her from speaking. I think that she was occasionally aware of what was going on around her, but only for short periods. She died in 2003, while I was writing this book.

My father had broken his neck in a 1975 car crash and, even after his recovery, ended up with a tremor in his hand. He still saw patients, but he could no longer perform surgery. In 1979, he decided to shut down his practice. While undergoing a routine physical in 1994, doctors discovered an aortic aneurysm—a widening or bulge of his aorta, the artery that carries and distributes all the blood pumped out of the

heart. During an operation to correct this, his colon was damaged. From there, his kidneys went, and he was forced to have five hours of dialysis three days a week.

While I was growing up, I never thought of my father as a "tough" guy; he was so articulate and well read. As bad as I was, he never resorted to violence to punish or restrain me. And here, because he was a doctor, he knew exactly what he was up against. Still, he wouldn't quit. Despite all the pain, he never complained. He was so strong.

I remember driving my father to the hospital for his final operation in 1999. The kidney doctor had already informed me that he didn't think my dad would survive. We went in for the pre-op, and I was just cracking. I asked him, "Dad, you okay?"

"Yeah, Ric, I'm fine," he answered, without a tear in his eye.

That's my last memory of Dr. Richard Reid Fliehr, the man who took me into his home as a baby, loved me despite all I had put him through, and tried his best to teach me how to be a man. He'd been sick for five years, and he had become the bravest person I have ever known.

His death hit me harder than I expected. I probably drank more than I ever did in my life. It wasn't until he died that I realized how close we really were. From the day I buried him, I must have promised myself a hundred times that I would become a better father, and a better person.

WHILE MY FATHER'S death had changed me drastically, life in WCW continued in the same haphazard way. I'd always been astonished by the crazy fans who ended up in the dressing room; either they knew one of the boys, or they knew an athletic commissioner, or they were friends with one of the security guys. Some of these fanatics became "runners"—fetching things for the wrestlers during the show— or ring attendants, or wrestling writers. A couple even wound up becoming wrestlers themselves. It's embarrassing.

Diamond Dallas Page was willing to do anything to get into the business. He worked as a manager and color commentator in the then-dying AWA, drove his custom car to *WrestleMania VI* in Toronto, and let Greg "The Hammer" Valentine and the Honky Tonk Man bring it to the ring with them for their match. There's a story that after WCW had shut down, Page was in an airport and happened to run into Vince McMahon. Suddenly, Dallas snatched him in an embrace and—as Vince squirmed with a perplexed look on his face—exclaimed, "*Finally,* we're together!" (This is the same guy, don't forget, who stood by Bischoff as he was knocking McMahon week after week on TV.)

Page was a nice guy who I think respected me, but his climb to the top will go down in history as one of the biggest jokes ever perpetrated on our industry. The guy was an average wrestler and an average talker with a bunch of tattoos that did nothing to win over fans. He was always very respectful to me in the dressing room, but so nervous. He reminded me of a high-school kid lying awake at night, trying to come up with a big play for Friday's football game.

Nonetheless, Dallas was Bischoff's boy, and Eric demanded that the WCW production crew shoot one vignette after another of DDP, forcing the guy down the fans' throats. Eric even let him win the title on April 11, 1999, in a Four Corners match in Tacoma, Washington, that also involved myself, Hogan, and Sting. Almost as soon as the bell rang, the crowd wasn't buying any of it, but Page didn't have the capacity to start improvising to get people back into the action. He just followed the plan that had been worked out beforehand—step A, then step B, then step C. Remember, I came up when a champion had to be a "ring general," taking command of the crowd and the ring while leading his opponent through the match. When Page finally got the title after hitting me with his Diamond Cutter, it was an insult to everything I'd learned from men like Verne Gagne and Wahoo McDaniel.

Quite literally, I went from being the WCW World Champion to being a mental patient on television. This idea came from Kevin Nash, one of the company's many revolving bookers. In the storyline, my son David—with prodding from Roddy Piper—committed me into an insane asylum. Still, I have to admit, some of the stuff we did *was* really funny. I just told myself, "If this is what they give me, I will entertain the people to the point where the angle gets over."

On the April 26, 1999, edition of *Nitro,* there I was, in the Central Florida Mental Hospital—except I was wearing one of my robes instead of a hospital gown. Since I was supposed to be the president of WCW, I was shown throughout the program on a split screen with my new vice president—"Little Naitch," Charles Robinson—delivering specific instructions on how I expected him to handle the issues of the day.

CHARLES ROBINSON: I had mixed feelings about this; I thought it was degrading to Ric. On the other hand, it was pretty entertaining. And I was involved in it, so I liked that. For a minute there, I thought I really *was* second-in-command. And believe me, there were a *lot* of people in WCW I wanted to fire.

The last time that I got off the phone with Robinson on the show, the camera stayed on me while I taught the inmates how to strut and dance like the Nature Boy. Suddenly, the shot widened to reveal a grim-looking Scott Hall—in a hospital gown. In the coming weeks, the two of us would break out of the nuthouse, and I'd reconcile with David, eventually awarding him the U.S. Championship.

DAVID FLAIR: My father, Arn, and Asya–this bodybuilder who'd played a nurse when my dad was in the mental hospital–would interfere in all my matches. When I wrestled Buff Bagwell in Atlanta, they dropped all these red, white, and blue balloons from the ceiling, like I was the greatest champion who ever lived. And then Charles Robinson refereed the match and got an "arm cramp" while Bagwell was pinning me. I also wrestled Dean Malenko, and lost the U.S. title to Chris Benoit. Benoit and Malenko are great technical wrestlers, and they probably hated having to get in there and tell me what to do. But they were both really nice. They knew that I didn't know anything, and they couldn't get mad at me.

MEGAN FLIEHR KETZNER: I have a picture from that period of my brother and my dad walking out to the ring together; it was probably on *Nitro* because there was pyro going off behind them. My dad had on a red robe. David was wearing red and black tights, and he'd also dyed his hair blond. The first time I looked at it, it scared me how much they looked alike. I thought, Oh, my God, he's really following in my dad's footsteps. Then, all of a sudden, there David is on TV, walking out and yelling at people. I'm like, "That's my brother, the shy kid who I used to have to watch all the time. Where did he learn do that?" It was freaky. I wondered, Is this going to be his life? Are we going to have two in the family? One's enough.

There were so many preposterous ideas being conceived and dropped all the time in WCW that, looking back, I honestly cannot remember half the shit I did. Bischoff was lost, promoting a WCW movie and tie-ins with KISS and rapper Master P and his No Limit Soldiers. Every year, we'd do the *Road Wild* Pay-Per-View from the biker rally in Sturgis, South Dakota. Admission was free, so we weren't making much money live; it just seemed like a vanity project for Eric because he liked motorcycles. When I went out and blew money, at least it was mine. That idiot was doing it with Ted Turner's cash.

A lot of people had started calling Bischoff "ATM Eric." For all his sizzle, there wasn't any profit. Eventually, Bischoff wore out his welcome with the company's accountants. It just takes information a long time to float to the top in a large corporation. When all his overspending finally came to the attention of Dr. Harvey Schiller, the president of Turner Sports, Bischoff was gone.

On September 10, 1999, Bill Busch, an accountant, was named executive vice president of WCW. Eric's "president" title was eliminated. The same day, I had a very honest discussion with Schiller about the future of the company. "You made another mistake," I said. "It won't work."

"What do you mean, 'It won't work'?"

"You can't have an accountant running a wrestling company. You need a wrestling person."

"Who do you have in mind?" Schiller asked.

"Off the top of my head, I can't tell you." And I couldn't.

Vince Russo was a tall, cocky guy with a New York accent who'd been fascinated with wrestling his entire life. He called himself "Vicious Vinny" and did a wrestling radio show on Long Island. Then he became the editor of the World Wrestling Federation's magazines. Russo had a lot of ideas, and the balls to barge past Vince McMahon's inner circle and pitch things personally to the boss. Soon, Russo wasn't writing *about* wrestling anymore—he was actually helping McMahon come up with storylines and plot twists.

Just after Bischoff left WCW, Russo flew down to Atlanta while McMahon was at a show in the United Kingdom. When McMahon came home, Russo called him with the news: he and his writing partner, Ed Ferrara, were leaving the World Wrestling Federation. They were going to Atlanta to save WCW.

Even before Vince Russo walked into the arena in Biloxi, Mississippi, the boys were buzzing. This was supposed to be the guy who created the World Wrestling Federation's ballsy "Attitude." "Attitude" that allowed Stone Cold Steve Austin to beat the hell out of his boss, Vince McMahon; enabled Chyna to get in the ring and wrestle guys; drove The Rock to tell opponents to stick it up their "candy ass"; and encouraged the New-Age Outlaws to do the crotch chop and tell fans to scream, "Suck it!"

When Russo finally arrived, I watched all the guys walk up to him, one by one. He never said a word to me, and I certainly wasn't going to get in line to kiss his ass.

CHAPTER 21

IS ZSA ZSA GABOR SICK THIS WEEK?

The first time we really spoke at length was after *Halloween Havoc '99,* at the MGM Grand Garden Arena in Las Vegas. Bill Banks, an assistant writer who Russo had brought with him from the World Wrestling Federation, approached me during the show. He told me that Russo wanted to drive out to the desert later that night and have the "Filthy Animals"—Rey Mysterio, Billy Kidman, Eddie Guerrero, and Konnan—literally *bury* me in the sand. I would have much rather wrestled someone like Mysterio or Kidman, but if that's what Russo wanted, then that's what we were going to do.

After the show, I got in a car with Russo, Banks, and Ed Ferrara, and started to leave town. We were making general small talk when Russo suddenly asked, "So, you must really hate my guts, huh?"

"I don't know you well enough to hate you. Why are you saying that?"

"Well, your friend Jim Cornette hates me," he said; apparently, the two had some conflict in the World Wrestling Federation. "I just figured that you hated me, too."

"And what makes you think that you're important enough for Cornette to even *mention* your name to me?" I told him. "Cornette's a busy guy. We talk about a lot of other things. And anyway, this business is full of stories, full of rumors. After more than twenty-five years, I've learned to treat people the way they treat you, not treat them the way you *heard* they treated someone else."

That seemed to end that conversation. We rode a little while longer before Russo said, "So, are you gonna ask me why we're doing this to you?"

"You mean burying me in the desert? Yeah. Why *are* you doing this to me?"

Russo explained that he wanted to repackage my character. If I was buried in the desert, I could go away for a few months, then come back fresh. "Okay," I said. "Am I gonna get paid while I'm sitting at home?"

"Definitely you're getting paid."

"Let's see—I've already had a heart attack. I've been in the nuthouse. Now you're going to bury me alive. Well, I'm going to deal with this as a professional, and assume that you'll figure out a way to bring me back. But it has to be in at least three months. After getting buried alive, it makes no sense for me to come back tomorrow." Russo assured me that we were on the same page, and we shot the segment.

When I returned home to Charlotte and told Beth what had happened, she was confused. "They really *buried* you?" she asked, to which I replied, "Yeah, except this time, instead of just doing it in storylines, they did it to my face. *And* on TV."

I began my little vacation, but knew—like every time before—I'd be getting that phone call to return. In this case, it happened about three weeks after my burial.

Bill Banks was the one Russo had appointed to contact me. "Okay, the fans think these guys left me buried in the desert," I questioned him. "And now I'm supposed to walk out on TV? Just like nothing happened? First of all, how did I get out of the desert?"

"Well, we're not going to worry about that," he said.

"Listen, pal, I'm sixty miles outside of Vegas. Nobody's found me yet. I'm in the desert. You gave me the time off, and I'm taking the time off. I'm not coming back yet."

Even when I did appear on television again, a link was never made in the storyline between the incident outside of Vegas and my return. That was typical Russo—he could come up with an idea, but without a Vince McMahon around to edit and shape it, he couldn't figure out the next step. Yet to hear him speak, you'd imagine that he was solely responsible for the World Wrestling Federation's recent success.

Russo was no Vince McMahon, and he was no Paul Heyman, either. Heyman is another crazy wrestling fan who grew up in the New York area and ended up becoming a significant character in the business. When Heyman ran Extreme Championship Wrestling (ECW), he had a vision and acted on it. Did I like all that hardcore stuff he did? No. But Heyman paid his dues through the ups and downs of his company, and had an influence on other promotions. In his own way, he is a genius.

Initially, Russo told everyone that he didn't want to be on TV. Pretty soon, however, he had himself on camera playing a bad guy, interfering in matches, and giving long speeches about his brilliant wrestling mind. The guy wasn't brilliant; he was obsessed with making himself a star. And he fell in love with two guys who couldn't draw a dime—Jeff Jarrett and Scott Steiner.

I'd helped Scott Steiner get a job with WCW in 1989, when his brother Rick came to me and said that Scott was starving in the Memphis territory. I was impressed with Scott's amateur background, and thought that he had huge potential.

The Steiner brothers became a successful tag team in WCW, the World Wrestling Federation, and Japan—where they toured regularly, but never reached the level of popular foreigners like Stan Hansen, Bruiser Brody, and Steve "Dr. Death" Williams. They were also the only two stars with amateur credentials I knew who felt the need to disrespect bottom-card talent. It was completely uncalled for; I could never imagine Danny Hodge, Jack Brisco, Kurt Angle, or Brock Lesnar abusing people that way. It was among the most unprofessional things I'd ever witnessed, but WCW management apparently didn't want to address the issue. I can't count the number of times I heard agents say, "We don't want to get Scotty mad."

So Scotty did pretty much whatever he pleased. I remember the Steiners amusing themselves by taping up "Hacksaw" Butch Reed's hands and feet. Reed was such a fun-loving guy that he didn't care. Then I asked Reed's tag-team partner at the time, Ron Simmons, "When are they gonna do that to you?"

Simmons looked me dead in the eye: "Never."

"Well, what would happen if they did try to fuck around with you?"

"Flair, I'm *unfuckable.*"

Like Simmons, Dick Murdoch and Dick Slater were legitimately tough. But the Steiners considered these guys, like myself, too old to be teaming together in WCW. When the four wrestled in Gainesville one night, I called Arn over to the curtain. "Watch this," I said, as we looked through the curtain. The Steiners delivered no German suplexes, no Frankensteiners from the top rope, no belly-to-backs. They went along and did *exactly* as Murdoch and Slater dictated.

From what I've been told, the Steiners had a falling-out after Scott decided to leave Rick behind and become a singles star. As a singles performer, Scott had a tendency to get on the microphone and start ripping into people in a personal way. He did it to Diamond Dallas Page and his wife, Kimberly, Torrie Wilson, and Terry Taylor. But he always seemed to avoid insulting Kevin Nash, Scott Hall, Haku, Scott Norton, and other guys who might have had a rebuttal.

On February 7, 2000, Scott went on TV and greeted the end of my sabbatical with an idiotic diatribe, mentioning how WCW would have been better off hiring the late Buddy Rogers than "Nature Boy Number 2, Ric Flair," then addressing me directly. "When you walked down the aisle last week . . . the people at home, all they did was grab their remote and change their channel to the World Wrestling Federation and watch Stone Cold, a person who you and your friends got fired from here, 'cause you're a jealous old bastard. So Ric Flair, remember this . . . there's never been a bigger ass-kissing bastard in this business, but also in life. . . . You belong where you're at—in WCW, 'cause WCW *sucks*."

I don't know what possessed Steiner to do that so-called "shoot interview." Yeah, WCW sucked, but it wasn't smart to *advertise* that on your own show. And whose ass *did* I kiss? Jim Herd's? Bischoff's? What the hell was this guy talking about? The most upsetting thing about his comments was that Steiner said I played a role in having Austin fired from WCW. Hell, I knew—and I hoped Austin did, too—that I was one of his biggest advocates.

At the time of the speech, Steiner didn't have any kids. I *did*. And after hearing Scott's interview they asked me, "What's *that* all about?" The answer is that I'm not sure even Steiner understood what he was saying. He was irrational. Lex Luger told me that when the topic came up, Scott told him, "Yeah, Flair really screwed you around." Screwed Luger around? This guy didn't have the facts. If I did anything for Luger, it was make his career.

Today, Scott Steiner has a family. And the sad thing is that they're now going to have to read what I'm saying about him, the same way my kids had to listen to what he said about me. At one time, Scott was a decent athlete. After a number of injuries, though, he's a shadow of his former self. He took a cheap shot that I'll never understand and certainly didn't deserve. He's a guy who meant nothing as an attraction, drew no money, and has no legacy. People will forget him the minute he retires. Most wrestling fans have already forgotten him. He's mid-card talent now.

AS WCW'S RATINGS continued to slump, Bill Busch and Brad Siegel—who had now replaced Dr. Harvey Schiller as WCW's corporate overseer—demanded to know why Russo hadn't turned things around. Russo insisted that every time he came up with something good, the people above him would tinker with his writing. During one exchange, Busch suggested getting away from the risqué type of sports entertainment Russo had helped devise in the World Wrestling Federation, and returning to traditional wrestling. Busch also wanted Russo to be part of a booking committee. Russo rebelled, demanding total control of the wrestling product.

While both sides battled, Kevin Sullivan was placed in charge of the booking committee, sparking a backlash from some wrestlers who didn't want to work for him. One day after winning the WCW Championship in a very good match against Sid Vicious, Chris Benoit handed his championship belt to a referee and walked out of the company with Dean Malenko, Eddie Guerrero, and Perry Saturn. When they arrived at the World Wrestling Federation, Benoit was publicly quoted as comparing the value of the WCW title to a piece of tin.

The company was at a loss to solve the crisis, so on April 10, 2000, WCW did the unthinkable: bringing Eric Bischoff back to work side by side with Russo. Within two weeks, Bill Busch—the accountant who had tracked Eric's various financial blunders—had resigned.

On the same night that Eric returned to *Nitro,* I was booked in a match against Shane Douglas, a guy I remembered for his long, moronic monologues in ECW, calling me "*Dick* Flair" and claiming that I'd held him back in WCW during the Jim Herd era. Douglas had also gone on the Internet, psychoanalyzing me as an aging, insecure hack who couldn't handle working in the same company as a guy with his youth and looks. But when we finally met again at WCW, he told me, "All the stuff I was saying was just work. I was really hoping that we'd get to wrestle each other one day."

The less said about our match that night, the better. Douglas was disqualified when Russo ran into the ring and hit me with a bat. As for Douglas, this is a man who failed on every level. Remember Dean Douglas, his character in the World Wrestling Federation? You probably don't, because he was absolutely forgettable. According to him, though, that was Vince McMahon's fault. In his mind, someone was always holding him back.

Well, let me tell you something: if you're good in this business, you'll figure out a way to show it to people. If you're great, it will eventually come out. Douglas was neither good nor great. He was never a star of any significance. I've made more people than Shane Douglas ever entertained in his life.

JUST WHEN WE thought it couldn't get any worse, Bischoff and Russo outdid themselves by having actor David Arquette—the star of the WCW movie *Ready to Rumble*—win the championship. The title switch took place on April 25, 2000, in a tag-team match pitting Arquette and Diamond Dallas Page against Jeff Jarrett and Bischoff. The rules stipulated that whoever scored the pin would leave with the title. Arquette pinned Bischoff, and we had a new WCW champion.

BOBBY "THE BRAIN" HEENAN: When I found out that they were putting the championship belt on David Arquette, I replied, "Is Zsa Zsa Gabor sick this week?" That's the way it was in WCW. This is a company that had Buff Bagwell tag-team with *his mother.* It was like *Hee Haw* down there; they might as well have had Buck Owens picking at his guitar while wrestlers jumped out of the corn.

The strategy behind the Arquette victory was to promote *Ready to Rumble* and get WCW a burst of mainstream publicity—a goal that the company actually achieved. But the people who read about the win in *USA Today* still had no incentive to suddenly begin watching our show. Wrestling fans were mortified, but not as much as you'd think. The title was so dead at this point, who gave a damn? I think even Arquette was embarrassed by the situation.

"David," I told him after he'd won, "do something right with that championship belt. Wear it down to the bar, and buy everyone drinks."

That's what he did. He also, very quietly, donated his entire paycheck to the families of Owen Hart, Brian Pillman, and Bobby Duncum Jr.—wrestlers who'd recently passed away—and Darren "Droz" Drozdov, who'd been paralyzed during a World Wrestling Federation match. So how did I feel about David Arquette as a champion? Well, he had a hell of a lot more character than some other guys who'd worn the championship belt.

NO ONE EXPECTED David Arquette to take a leave of absence from Hollywood and actually go on the road to defend his title. So on May 7, 2000, he dropped the title to Jeff Jarrett in a three-man cage match that also involved Diamond Dallas Page—the first of *five* WCW championship changes that month.

On May 15, I beat Jarrett in Biloxi, Mississippi, in a match I enjoyed. Despite my opinions regarding his drawing power, I consider Jeff a wonderful wrestler and a wonderful guy. I was supposed to lose the title back to him, but at the next *Thunder* taping, my old inner ear problem returned, and I collapsed in the ring. As soon as it happened, I knew what it was and didn't even bother trying to get up. Russo came up with the term *braineurysm* to describe my condition, and announced that I was forfeiting the title. This was stupid, since the technology now existed to reattach the dislodged chip quickly; if everyone had been patient and waited an extra week, I could have given Jarrett another good match and lost to him clean in the center of the ring.

Instead, Jarrett got the title on May 22. On May 23, Kevin Nash won the title in a three-way match with Jarrett and Scott Steiner. On May 29, Kevin "awarded" me the championship in Salt Lake City because, he said, I'd never lost it. Immediately, Jarrett came out to challenge me. I resisted the challenge until my son David—who'd now become my enemy again—emerged from the curtain with Reid and Beth squirming under each arm. He was holding them hostage, fans were told, until I granted Jarrett his title shot.

BETH FLIEHR: It was pretty hokey. David had us each in a headlock. We went out onto the entrance ramp—just so Ric could see what was happening and agree to the match—then immediately returned backstage. What were fans supposed to think—that David was walking around with us backstage like that while everyone else just stood around and watched? What was he going to do to us, anyway?

My final WCW title reign ended later that night with David, as the referee, handing Jarrett a guitar so he could hit me over the head. At that point, I couldn't wait for the company to go out of business; I just didn't feel like walking out and getting sued again.

At least David had a contract and was making a good living. He'd also begun going out with Stacy Keibler, who was playing the role of "Miss Hancock," a sexy secretary. Stacy's a nice girl—and very hot—so everyone thought David was a lucky guy. As a father, though, I had a few concerns. He moved in with Stacy without talking to me first. I'm not saying I would have objected; I just wanted to have a discussion with my son about a decision like that. They found a condo in Baltimore, close to her family. That was another thing that I had questions about—was he putting his own needs first?

On camera, Russo had David and Stacy play up their real-life romance. He wanted to have them marry, only to discover that Stacy was *my* love child. He also considered doing a storyline in which David would find out that he was actually Russo's son. It seemed like whenever Russo had a hole in the show, he tried to plug it with something involving my family.

You know how other guys go to fantasy camps with ex-players from their favorite baseball teams? Well, Russo outdid them all on June 5, 2000, when he had a cage match with one of his favorite wrestlers, Ric Flair. Of course, Beth and Reid were with me; I'm surprised Russo didn't also try incorporating Ashley and Megan somehow. The bell rang, Russo started chopping me, and I had to make it look convincing. Then I removed Russo's shirt and chopped his chest red. With a guy that limited, that was about all that I could do.

Naturally, David was soon in the middle of things, coming up from under the ring to assault me. As I fought back, Russo got hold of a ladder and tried scurrying to safety through a trap door at the top of the cage. I followed him up there and chopped him some more, then Russo fell back through the door and into the ring.

I put Russo in the figure-four. I held him there . . . and kept holding him there as fans waited for something more to happen. Sensing their agitation, I looked upward about one hundred fifty feet to the catwalk, where stunt coordinator Ellis Edwards was sitting with a pressurized drum filled with seventy-five gallons of "blood." He couldn't press the release mechanism to drop it on us, though, until Russo was directly over most of the WCW logo on the mat. Otherwise, we'd have to roll into the "blood." Somehow we repositioned our bodies, and the blood came streaming down.

What was the point of all this? I can't tell you. All I know is that a similar situation had taken place while Russo was in the World Wrestling Federation, and he tended to rely on ideas that had previously worked there. Once I was drenched, my son David placed me in his own figure-four, setting me up to be pinned by Russo.

With everything that I had accomplished throughout my career, this is what it had come to at fifty-one years of age. Do you know how it felt, lying there on the canvas with fake blood splattered all over me after losing to a *magazine writer?* You figure it out.

GEORGE SOUTH: Wrestling had become so different than the wrestling I grew up watching and loving. Every time I saw Flair in the ring, I'd tell myself, "When he retires, the link will be over."

One of the last times WCW came to Charlotte, I was sitting with some wrestlers when Wahoo McDaniel tried walking in the back with his son, and the security guard stopped him. Wahoo had a ball cap on, hadn't worked in years, and the guy didn't know who he was. Can you imagine the embarrassment? Wahoo *built* Charlotte. He thought the guard was joking and tried to walk around him. And the guard grabbed Wahoo by the shoulder–in front of his son–and told him, "Sir, you can't go in."

Now, you know Wahoo–he'd fight you in a minute. And the guard said he was going to call more security. Well, Ric Flair–it was like it was meant to be–just happened to be walking by that second. It was like a scene from a movie of the week. Flair didn't holler. He explained to the security guard just who this man was, and how much respect this man deserved. And the security guard apologized. In fact, he even offered to get Wahoo's boy some T-shirts and stuff. Ric put his arm on Wahoo's shoulder, and I just stood there, watching the two of them walk off together.

I never got to go to Wahoo's funeral. When he died in 2002 from diabetes and kidney disease, the ceremony was held in this little place in Texas. I talked to his mom and his daughters, and they knew how sorry I felt. But I just won't forgive myself for missing the ceremony. Yes, I had a prior commitment, just like I did when "Mr. Perfect" Curt Hennig and Road Warrior Hawk—Mike Hegstrand—and Andre the Giant died. It's no excuse. Wahoo brought me to the Carolinas, taught me about wrestling, and rushed to the hospital to be with me after my plane crash. I drove Andre around when he was billed as "Jean Ferre" and still couldn't speak English. Mike used to carry toys back to Minnesota for my kids, and stood by my side during dozens of tense situations. No matter what kind of mood I was in, Curt could make me laugh. I should have been there for all of them.

I've told Dave and Earl Hebner, Arn Anderson, the General, Triple H, Piper, Vince McMahon, my real-estate partners Scott Storick and Pete Wirth, and other close friends that I want them to have a good time at my funeral. I want Shawn Michaels to come as well, and even though he doesn't drink, I want him to have one for me that day. I want them to remember that they lost a friend, but a friend who had a tremendous life—and who overstayed his welcome by at least twenty-five years. I want them to make it the biggest party that any of us have ever been to. If they die first, I'll do the same for them, and I promise that I'll be there. I'm not missing any more funerals.

But for the sake of entertainment, I hope I go first. My wife has told everybody that she's going to buy the yacht that she never let me have with the insurance money and call it *Natch's Dream.* She'll put the casket on the diving platform, then lower me into the ocean as everybody gives the Nature Boy his final toast.

I'VE BEEN MORE fortunate with injuries than other guys. I've had a cracked C5 vertebra in my neck, which hurt like hell but healed itself. There's been a little bit of atrophy in my arm and lat. There was a period when a group of wrestlers insured their bodies with Lloyd's of London and collected on fake injuries. I paid $140,000 in premiums and had legitimate claims, but my policy was canceled because of others' "career-ending" ailments.

Toward the end of my WCW career, I felt like I was starting to become injury-prone. I'd torn my other rotator cuff again in 1999 when Randy Savage came off the ropes on me, doing a run-in while I wrestled Diamond Dallas Page. I knew that I'd need an operation, and eventually I scheduled surgery with Dr. James Andrews in Birmingham, Alabama, on July 7, 2000. But Russo wanted me to do one more thing before I checked into the hospital: I was going to team up with Reid against Russo and David. Reid and I would lose, and we'd have our heads shaved.

My hair had been such a big part of my persona that it killed me to go through with it. But at that stage, I was so beaten down that I just rolled up into a ball. I was willing to do anything that would get me time off and away from all that bullshit in the dressing room.

Russo and I were talking over the finish when Bischoff ambled by. Everything was under control, but he couldn't resist chiming in, "Now, we mean *really* shave your head."

After it was over, I didn't feel as bad as I thought. I said, "Hey, I had both of my boys in the ring with me, and I'll have it on tape for the rest of my life. Who gives a shit?" The three of us went back to the hotel and had a really nice night.

My son Reid comes to the aid of his dad at the *Great American Bash 2000*.

I'D BEEN TOLD that I would be paid while I recovered from my surgery, but the company stiffed me. I could only put up with so much, so I called Russo. "Hey," I reminded him, "I had my head shaved. I did not do that for *me*. We had a deal."

"Yeah, Ric, we did," he answered. "You should have told me before. I honestly didn't know that they were doing this to you."

I've been double-talked and lied to a lot in wrestling, but Russo *was* telling me the truth. Despite our differences, when he gave his word to me, he wanted it to mean something. He got on the phone with management and leaned on Brad Siegel until I got some of my money back.

That's the strange thing about this business: people aren't always one way or another. If I made a list of positives and negatives, I could go back and forth with Vince Russo. The only one who will *never* come off the "asshole" side of the page is Eric Bischoff.

After fourteen years of wrestling each other, there was no one at WCW I respected and admired more than Sting.

After so many spectacular years in the business, I didn't know where I ranked anymore. Fans too young to have witnessed my matches with Harley and Steamboat would now live the rest of their lives with memories of me in a mental hospital, being buried in the desert, and having my head shaved by Vince Russo. It seemed to me like my legacy had been destroyed.

I was so removed from wanting to be in the business anymore. My emotions were out of control. Once I came back from rotator cuff surgery, I quit working out after an entire life of being in the gym. I just didn't care. The fans could tell that I was out of shape, and they heckled me about it.

CHAPTER **22**

WE KNOW YOU CAN HANDLE IT

Dave Meltzer wrote about my condition in the *Wrestling Observer* newsletter, and he didn't pull any punches. I'd met Meltzer a few years earlier, and I actually respected him. When he called me the greatest, my ring work lived up to it. And when he wrote—during the period I was both wrestling and on the booking committee—that I looked as tired as Jimmy Carter in the latter part of his presidency, it forced me to look in the mirror. Meltzer was implying that I didn't belong in the ring anymore. And he was right.

DAVE MELTZER: People were pointing at Flair's physique and forgetting that, as far as match quality went, he was still one of the top guys. Fans were used to paying attention to bodies because of all the muscular guys they'd seen in the eighties. They didn't notice that Ric's ability to make his opponents look good was the same as it had always been. It was sad to see the guy's legend get tarnished, and for people to not perceive him as special. There were times when I thought that Ric should retire.

There was nothing that WCW could do to prevent the inevitable, and their stories became more ridiculous—and more desperate. They made Goldberg a heel, put the championship belt on Russo, and staged a bogus funeral for Kevin Nash the day after Dale Earnhardt died. (That one went over *real* well in NASCAR country.) Company losses were projected to be as high as $80 million.

And now the people in WCW no longer just answered to Ted Turner, who had always had a soft spot for wrestling. Turner Broadcasting had become part of Time Warner, and a merger with AOL was on the horizon. Before that could happen, though, executives wanted to dump as many money-losing divisions as possible.

In January 2001, a tentative agreement between Turner Broadcasting and Fusient Media Ventures was announced. Fusient was going to buy WCW, with Turner retaining a minority interest. And guess who was going to be in charge of the new operation? Eric Bischoff. I was fairly close to certain that my wrestling career was over.

Before the deal was consummated, however, Jamie Kellner became the new CEO of Turner Broadcasting. In his first official act, Kellner declared that he was booting wrestling off TBS and TNT—not "upscale" enough for the audience he wanted to reach, I guess. With no television to promote the product, Fusient lost interest. And Vince

McMahon stepped in, buying WCW the way you would an old grill at a yard sale.

Even with all of the company's problems, I thought that WCW would sell for about $25 million. Instead, Vince picked it up for considerably less. If I'd known the price was going to be *that* low, I could have gotten investors and bought the company myself.

Like Vince, I would have purchased the WCW tape library—which included invaluable footage dating back to the Georgia Championship Wrestling and Jim Crockett Promotions days—but not bothered acquiring the wrestlers' contracts. If I had really wanted somebody, we'd negotiate one-on-one. I'm sure the investors would have wanted at least one big name to make the deal work, and I know that I could have counted on Sting to work for me once all the parasites who sank WCW were gone.

That said, I was glad that Vince was taking over. To me, the American wrestling business already consisted of one company; WCW might as well have been out of existence for two years. And I knew how much Vince loved this industry. The saddest part of the sale was thinking about all those people—wrestlers, announcers, office workers, backstage guys—who had to put up with working for idiots and were now losing their jobs.

THE FINAL EDITION of *Nitro* took place March 26, 2001, at an outdoor show in Panama City, Florida. WWE executive Gerald Brisco was backstage, and he made a point of bringing me over to Shane McMahon. Shane was friendly and respectful, and told me that Vince wanted to pay tribute to Sting and myself by having us wrestle on the program that night.

"Shane," I replied, "I'm so embarrassed. I've had surgery, and have barely wrestled this past year." But Shane was insistent. Sting and I had wrestled on the first *Nitro,* and this was a way of closing the circle.

Before the match, I was scheduled to do an interview, basically portraying Vince as the enemy who stole away our special company. Nothing could have been further from the truth, but I wanted to show Vince what I could contribute. Despite every other way that my confidence had eroded, I knew that I could still talk.

"We have run neck-and-neck with you, Vince McMahon, for years," I claimed in the ring, attempting to get the fans to feel remorseful about the passing of an era. "And just for trivia, Vince McMahon, do you know that in 1981, when you were trying to become an announcer, your dad was on the board of directors and voted for *me* as World Champion? *Woooo!* How about that?" To a lot of people who knew what I was talking about, it seemed like I was breaking wrestling's secret code, revealing how the NWA board voted on its champions. But those rules didn't exist anymore.

"And ever since that day," I continued, removing my jacket, "I have been a limousine-riding, jet-flying, kiss-stealing, wheeling, dealing son-of-a-gun that—along with the whole WCW, dammit all—have kissed the girls worldwide and made 'em cry!"

I was accomplishing my goal—some fans were chanting, "Vince sucks!" while one guy held up a sign proclaiming VINCE IS SATAN. So I started hyping my match for later that night: "In all my years in this sport, my greatest opponent with this company has been Sting. So tonight, if we're going out, we're going out on a high note. Stinger, the Nature Boy wants you right here, because it's your last chance to be—the man. You've gotta beat—the man. And Sting—*I'm! the! man! Woooo!*"

Unfortunately, our match didn't live up to my interview. It was terrible; I wrestled in a T-shirt because I was so ashamed of my physique. Sting had a bad shoulder, and some limitations because of it. Here were two guys who had sold out arenas all over the world. We'd been opponents for fourteen years and could tear it down every night. But it wasn't our finest moment. I wasn't ready, physically or mentally. When Sting threw me into the corner for my flip, I couldn't even make it over the turnbuckles. He set me up on the top rope and delivered a superplex, then turned me over and put me in his Scorpion Death Lock. I shook my head from side to side, unwilling to submit, then suddenly began nodding, and the bell rang. Sting definitely carried his end of the match. I couldn't carry mine.

Nitro ended just like it started—with me losing to my friend Steve Borden. He helped me to my feet and embraced me. Pretending to be injured by his finisher, I fell back down, but reached up to him. He took my hand, and we hugged again—and *that* was sincere.

JUST AFTER THE sale went down, I got a call from Jim Ross. In addition to his announcing chores, Ross had become the executive vice president of talent relations for World Wrestling Entertainment—the

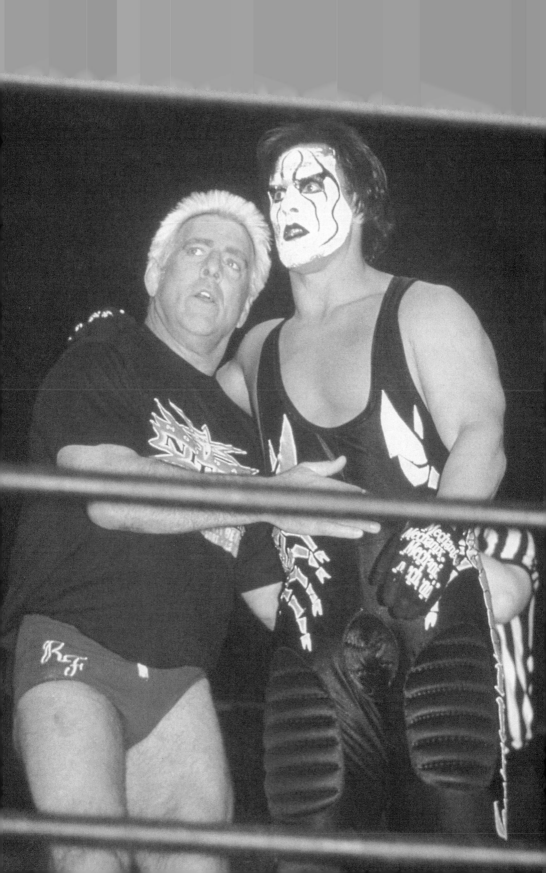

name the company adopted in 2002. "Are you ready to come to work?" he asked.

"Yeah."

"Are you still a wrestler?"

"I haven't been for a while, but I think I could be again."

"Well, we're looking forward to working with you."

I didn't hear from him again for more than six months, but I had other plans, anyway. My real-estate partners, Pete Wirth and Scott Storick, and I were busy looking for new opportunities. For years, Beth had tried to rein in my spending and persuade me to plan for the future, but I wouldn't listen. Well, when Wirth and Storick came into my life, they joined her cause. After a lifetime of denial, it took the three of them to convince me that the future wasn't tomorrow. The future was *now*. With Pete (who we call "Tony Soprano" because he's a New Yorker and looks like James Gandolfini) and Scott's encouragement, I was going to get my real-estate license, and hopefully use my name to develop our business.

Every week, I must have received a phone call from someone offering me between $5,000 and $10,000 to wrestle on an independent show. I wasn't interested. If there was any chance of getting my reputation back, it had to be done on the largest stage possible—in WWE.

In early November I received a call from my lawyer, John Taylor. WWE wanted to do a storyline later in the month, on the *Raw* following *Survivor Series*. I would be brought into the company in a non-wrestling role, as the new co-owner of the promotion. We didn't have much time to negotiate a deal, and there were a lot of things to work out. WCW still owed me a lot of money, and that arrangement would be nullified if I signed with a different wrestling company. But that wasn't what concerned me the most.

It's a terrible feeling to be nervous about walking across the dressing room, about being among your own peers. After being driven into the ground by Bischoff and Scott Steiner doing that terrible interview about me, my self-confidence was at an all-time low.

"Are you sure that the guys want me?" I asked Vince when we spoke on the phone.

"Of course, Ric. Everyone wants you."

I didn't know if he was speaking the truth, or just selling me. But I had to take him at his word. After all the negative shit that I'd been through, I really needed to try again.

JIM ROSS: I wanted Ric Flair in my locker room. We had a roster with younger guys who hadn't perfected the art of performing, or the art of telling a story. They needed role models that could teach them, and I'd be hiring the guy the vast majority looked up to as kids.

WWE was a much different place than the one I left in 1993. At one time, you were only as good as the last house you drew; now, it's your last quarter-hour TV rating. There were writers for the shows—not all of them wrestling people—who even scripted the interviews. I struggled with that, and we had to come to an understanding: they'd give me bullet points, and I'd take it from there. Even so, just being handed a set of instructions on paper added to my insecurity.

In some ways, though, I had matured. Part of this resulted from taking care of my mom as her condition deteriorated. I also wanted to be a role model for my two youngest kids. I took advice from people like T. J. Jaworski, a former NCAA champion who organized the wrestling camps at the University of North Carolina that Reid attended. T. J.'s everything I'd want my kids to be—someone who's accomplished his goals through hard work and mental discipline. I'll probably get some flack for that comment because, like me, T. J. has a wild side. He just always knows when enough is enough.

Reid's first wrestling coach, Tom Fiacco, helped teach me about priorities. After Reid lost to one kid on three consecutive occasions, I tried preparing my son for their next meet at the state championship finals. "We really need this one today," I said.

"No," Tom corrected me. "*Reid* really needs this one today."

The point was that your children don't forge their way in the world just to satisfy you. They need to achieve success on their own. Through Fiacco, I also learned that a father's job doesn't end when he drops his children off at school or at practice. You have to be an extension of everything they do, and live like a family all the time.

I've really cut back on drinking inside the house. I don't think it sets a good example for my children. God only knows, they've seen me in bad shape a few times and thought it was cool. It wasn't. And now, when I preach about living a certain type of lifestyle, they use my drinking against me. My one reservation about writing this book is that my children, especially Ashley and Reid, might suffer some embarrassment because of it.

Through my many years of partying, I also developed something called "alcoholic cardiomyopathy," a weakening of the heart muscles. I first detected that there was something wrong when my heart began skipping beats. I went to a cardiologist friend who told me that when your heart pumps, it expands like a rubber band. But mine was doing it too much. Initially, I thought that steroids might be responsible, but the doctor dismissed this theory. My heart was fluttering from thirty-five years of hitting it hard.

It's part of the price I've paid for being Ric Flair. In exchange for the glory and the good times, I acquired a heart condition, self-esteem issues, and cataracts from tanning beds—and very nearly wrecked my marriage to a great woman. But incredibly, I remained ageless in other ways. And in 2002, at nearly fifty-three years old, I was about to see if I could show a new generation of fans what they missed in the 1970s and '80s.

SHORTLY AFTER I arrived in WWE, Shane McMahon told me that his father believed I was worthy of more than a nonwrestling role.

At the *Royal Rumble 2002,* Vince wanted to wrestle me—ostensibly for the ownership of the company. I was horrified, and didn't know how to express it. Finally, I gathered Shane, his sister Stephanie—who oversees all the writing on WWE programs—and Vince in a room. Then, I melted down.

"Guys, I'm having a tough time," I confessed. "I'm struggling." It was the first time that I'd ever spoken out about losing my confidence.

The three of them looked at me in amazement as I wiped tears from my eyes. Then Vince walked over to my side of the room and embraced me. "We all have our things we have to work through," he told me. "I've been there."

I knew what they were thinking: This is Ric Flair, the invincible character who never has a bad day. I went into some detail about the last several years and admitted, "You're putting me in a marquee position, and I don't know if I can handle it."

Almost all three of them spoke at once: "*We* know you can handle it."

I TOOK IT as a challenge, and began working out hard. I still wasn't in shape on the day of the *Rumble,* but I had no choice but to go through with it. Vince had clearly thought about our conversation, though, and it seemed important to him that I regain my self-assurance. Before we went through the curtain, we had another discussion, and Vince actually became misty-eyed. "I want to make this night for you as big as I can," he told me.

I couldn't believe that I was hearing those words in *Atlanta*—the hometown of WCW. This is where the company, through Eric, had undermined me for so long.

Exactly ten years after I won the World Wrestling Federation Championship at the same event, Vince and I had a "street fight." Vince smashed me in the head with a metal KEEP OFF sign and a trash can. I started to bleed, and he dragged me around at ringside—to the spot where Reid was sitting with Megan. Vince reached forward, pulled Megan's camera away from her, held it in front of us, and took a photo of himself—beating me up.

BETH FLIEHR: Ashley and I were at a volleyball tournament in Baltimore, Maryland, and we were unable to be with Ric that night. Ric must have called me ten times during the day and into the early

evening, asking me to reinforce the fact that he could go out and perform that night. This was my first indication of how much he was really struggling with getting back into the ring. It was almost as if I was not speaking with the same man I've been married to for over twenty years. His self-confidence was really at an all-time low.

I was still embarrassed by my physique, and didn't feel like I was having a great match, but it was passable. Vince put me in the figure-four leglock and I reversed it. He crawled back to the arena floor, grabbed a lead pipe and went after me with it. Before he could make contact, I nailed him with a low blow, then snatched a TV monitor from the Spanish-language announcers' table and used it to bash McMahon's head. Before I put it down, though, I demanded to see a replay. Vince was bloody now, and I hit him in front of my kids while Megan snapped pictures. We got back in the ring, where I battered him with the lead pipe and won the match with the figure-four.

IT WAS NICE to hear that kind of applause again, but just a handful of people knew the true story. I had always prided myself on being a V-12 engine, and I was only working on three-and-a-half cylinders.

At least I was getting encouragement now. Michael Hayes—a former member of the Freebirds tag team, who now worked backstage for WWE—spent hours reinforcing my belief in myself. After my matches, road agents Pat Patterson and Blackjack Lanza would give me reviews of what they'd seen and offer advice. I had looked up to both of these guys when I broke into the business, and here it was, nearly thirty years later, and they were helping me regain my form.

Mark Callaway—Undertaker—has always been one of my favorite wrestlers. He can work, wrestle, and draw money. He also has one of the most enduring personas in the business, and the fact that he's a phenomenal athlete, who can walk across the top rope while holding an opponent in a wristlock, makes it even better. In my opinion, he's the most respected guy in the WWE dressing room. And in early 2002, when he didn't have an opponent for *WrestleMania X8,* Undertaker decided that he wanted me.

We made a lot of good television going into our match. Obviously, we didn't have the same notoriety as the most prominent match on the show—The Rock against the returning Hulk Hogan—but our storyline

Michael Hayes, a good buddy of mine, here in his early days as one of the Fabulous Freebirds.

was very intense. As the bad guy, Undertaker was doing things to mess with my emotions. He bloodied Arn Anderson, then invaded Ohio Valley Wrestling (OVW), the small, Kentucky-based promotion WWE uses as a developmental territory for new talent. My son David was training there at the time, and Undertaker dragged him out of the ring, pulled him into a bathroom, and beat the shit out of him. David even bled to make it look more realistic.

Here's the difference between Undertaker and Hogan—after shooting

the segment, Mark called me up and said, "I roughed up your kid a little bit. He did a great job." And David loved the guy. He was professional, and worked *with* my son instead of against him.

When I finally collided with Undertaker in Toronto's SkyDome on March 17, 2002, all 68,237 fans seemed ready to watch us rip each other apart. I sprinted down the ramp, jumped in the ring, went right after Undertaker, and started pummeling him. Later on, he sat me down in a folding chair and hammered me in the face. In the ring, he threw me into the corner, and I missed my flip over the turnbuckles. Before I could panic, he grabbed me and asked, "You ready to try it again, kid?"

It didn't matter that I was seventeen years older than him. He was leading the match, and if he wanted to call me "kid," that was fine with me. "Fuck," I answered, "I'm ready to go."

He hurled me toward the buckles, and this time I made it over the top—staggering down the ring apron into a big foot from Undertaker.

We never let up. I took a superplex from the top rope. When I locked Undertaker in my figure-four, he escaped by snatching me by the throat and delivering a chokeslam. Undertaker went outside the ring to grab a pipe, but Arn Anderson came racing down the aisle and gave my opponent a spinebuster. The fans were going nuts as Undertaker bloodied Arn, threw him in the ring, and applied a dragon sleeper. I broke it up with a chair shot to Undertaker's back. Dramatically, he turned around, kicked me in the face, and won the match with a tombstone piledriver.

As soon as I got to the dressing room, Blackjack Lanza was waiting there with a big smile on his face. "You old son of a bitch," he said, wrapping his arms around me, "you still got it in you!" I felt like a million bucks. With the exception of Arn, very few people had treated me like that at WCW in years.

The next night, before a broadcast of *Raw* in Montreal, Shane patted me on the back and gave me a hug. "I guess your performance last night cured you of any self-doubt," he smiled.

Sadly, he was wrong. Even after *WrestleMania X8,* I wasn't completely there. Yeah, I was carrying my weight—it just wasn't *Ric Flair's* weight. I beat Chris Jericho with a figure-four at *SummerSlam,* then submitted to his Walls of Jericho the following month at *Unforgiven,* but I later told Chris that I didn't feel I was good enough to be in the ring with him for either match. I felt the same way when I was pitted against Rob VanDam on a number of cards.

It seemed like I couldn't shake off the specter of Eric Bischoff.

There was actually a pretty good reason for this: on July 15, 2002, Vince brought Bischoff into WWE, playing off their long-standing business rivalry. Eric was strictly a character in the storylines, with *no* backstage stroke whatsoever. It didn't matter to me, though. I was just starting to get a grip on my own talent, and when I saw Bischoff walk through the dressing room at the Continental Airlines Arena in New Jersey, my heart sank.

I was scheduled to team up with Rob Van Dam that night against Undertaker and Brock Lesnar. There was so much on my mind, however, I didn't know if I was ready to walk through that curtain. Backstage, I told Brock about how I was feeling. He was a twenty-five-year-old kid who'd only been in WWE for four months, and I urged him to make sure that nothing disastrous happened. It was a lot to impose on a rookie. But when that bell rang, he was all man.

"Game time," he said. "Show's on. Let's go."

BROCK LESNAR: I already had some history with Ric's family. When David Flair and I were training in OVW, we were roommates and did everything together, so I got to know Ric and his family quite well. I knew nothing about what went on at WCW, but I could see that Ric wasn't himself. His head wasn't in the right place, and he asked if I could be in the driver's seat and lead him through the match. He was probably a bit nervous, since you can never be sure what a rookie will do, so I just let him know that I would take care of him. Just having a legend put that trust in me gave me the rub I needed with the boys. It also gave me another level of confidence. Ric said I helped him that day, but I think it was more of a godsend for me. Ric helped me mature as a wrestler.

I had a thousand reasons for never punching out Eric Bischoff in WCW. He was an executive. I had dragged my family through one lawsuit, and didn't want to get caught up in another—particularly one I would lose. But when I was alone, I'd think, Why didn't you just beat the shit out of him? And I blamed myself for never doing it.

Now that he was in WWE as a performer—no different than me or anyone else—I finally had my chance.

My "Flair for the Gold" carried over to WWE with
Evolution—Intercontinental Champion Randy Orton,
World Heavyweight Champion Triple H, and me and
Batista as World Tag-Team Champs.

Eric Bischoff had already tried to clear the air between us. The day after the World Trade Center bombing, he called me at home. "After what happened yesterday," he began, "I've been sitting here, thinking about all my friends, and just thought I'd call to see how you're doing."

I didn't know what to say. I was polite and made small talk, then went downstairs and told Beth, "Can you believe that Eric just called me and said he was thinking of his *friends? Now* I'm his *friend?*"

I assume that Bischoff was trying to cleanse his soul, but even if he felt better after our talk, I didn't. When he arrived in WWE,

CHAPTER **23**

DON'T YOU KNOW WHO I AM?

I was forced to act cordial to him, and it killed me. Finally I told myself, I've let him get away for too long. If I want to raise my boys to be men, it's about time I acted like one.

On March 17, 2003, before a broadcast of *Raw,* I saw Eric in the dressing room on his cell phone, talking about some *Girls Gone Wild* Pay-Per-View that he'd gotten involved with and how it was going to "revolutionize" television. I heard him use his classic cliché, "It's taking on a life of its own."

I went into the catering area and asked Arn Anderson if I could speak with him. He followed me into the hallway, and I said, "Please, just watch the door." He had no idea what I was talking about.

I returned to the dressing room and approached Bischoff. "I need to talk to you," I said.

He held up one finger so I would wait, but I had already waited too long. I slapped him hard across the face, knocking the cell phone out of his hand. He began backing up. I swung at him three times, but couldn't connect because he was moving so fast. When Bischoff got to the wall, I pushed him onto a couch, climbed on top of him, pressed my finger against his eye, and said, "I could take your fuckin' eye out right now." (I could have also used my fist to bust open his face while he was cowering underneath me, but that wasn't what I wanted to do. I wanted him to get up and fight.)

I backed away so he could rise from the couch. "Let's go! Right now!" I yelled. I swung my leg around and kicked the back of his leg, hoping it would jar him out of his seat.

"I'm not going to fight you," he said, but I wasn't going to give him a choice. Suddenly, Sergeant Slaughter—who's now a WWE road agent—was standing between us. "Ric, what are you doing?" he asked.

"Just paying a debt," I told him. Personally, I'm sure that Slaughter would have just as soon pulled me off a bloody Bischoff than separated us. But Vince doesn't want his agents to lose control of the dressing room, so I let Slaughter lead me away.

Vince was mad as hell when I was brought into his office in the arena. "What prompted this?" he demanded.

I explained, "This weekend, I was home with Reid, and I was thinking about the way I was raising him, the example I was setting for him. And you know, there's a fine line between getting along with people and taking shit."

Vince already knew my history with Bischoff, and didn't need elaboration. "Ric, this is unprofessional." He hesitated, then asked, "Was this planned? Was anybody else involved?" He suspected that Arn and I had conspired to set up Bischoff.

"No," I answered honestly. "I asked Arn to watch the door. That was it."

Vince shook his head. "This cannot happen again. When you're in the arena, you're on company property as far as I'm concerned." I nodded.

"One more thing, Ric. Is there anybody else you're planning to do this to?"

"Yeah. Hogan." I said this half joking, although I was still mad about him whipping David back in WCW.

Vince's eyes practically bugged out. "My God. *Please* don't do that."

As for Bischoff, he's tried to make peace with me on several occasions, saying things like "Life is too short." But he knows I'll never forgive him. Fuck, no.

IN THE WEEKS after the encounter, a number of guys came up to me and told me that they wished that they had done the same thing to Eric back at WCW. I felt relieved about finally standing up for myself. Then, two months later, I walked into the arena in Greenville, South Carolina. And everything changed for me.

Greenville has always been a special town to me—like so many other places from the old Charlotte territory. After WCW sued me in 1998 and I had to sit on the sidelines, I made my return in Greenville, and the people embraced me. No matter what names I'd called those fans over the years, they knew how much I truly loved them. And I knew that I could do no wrong in their eyes.

We had a *Raw* broadcast scheduled in Greenville on May 19, 2003. In the afternoon, I arrived backstage and inquired about what I'd be doing that night. I was told that I'd be in six of the program's eleven segments. "*Six* segments?" I thought. "They're dedicating the show to me. Why?"

Generally, Hunter Hearst Helmsley—Triple H—and I were partners, but for one night only, we were parting company so I could wrestle him for his world title. My self-doubt was still there. Could I really pull it off? I had to. This was my chance to be me again.

Since I'd returned to the company, Triple H had become one of my closest friends. When I was down, both he and Shawn Michaels would go out of their way to say an encouraging word to me. If Hunter saw me sitting by myself in the arena, he'd come over and talk to me.

In one televised match, Triple H and I were partners against Vince McMahon and Kurt Angle. When the battle ended and the cameras had shut off, Triple H called me back to the ring, grabbed the microphone, and said, in front of the live crowd, "*You're* the reason I'm in this business." I'll never forget that. I'd been Hunter's ringside adviser for a while, but now we were part of Evolution, a four-man gang that swaggered to the ring together like the original Horsemen. As the world champion, Triple H was the Ric Flair of the group. I was the wizened veteran, Randy Orton the future, and David Batista the enforcer.

Triple H first started talking about the concept of Evolution at the beginning of 2002 and I wanted to be part of it. From being in the Horsemen, to being in Evolution now, in some ways it feels like I've come full circle. Now, as then, we have four performers that are greater than the sum of the parts.

There's one major reason why Triple H truly is "The Game" in this industry: if he's in the ring with a guy who isn't up to par, Hunter takes it as *his responsibility* to make the guy look good. As I've said repeatedly, if you want to be the best—whether your philosophy is old school, new school, whatever—you go out and make your opponent look as good as humanly possible. That's the way I was my entire career, and that's the way Hunter is now.

> **TRIPLE H:** Ric was emotional all day long in Greenville. He did a vignette with Shawn where Shawn told Ric how much he admired him, and they both started to cry. I started to feel like we had something huge here.
>
> As our friendship had developed in WWE, Ric gave me one of his old championship belts with a note that said, "I wish I could have dropped this to you in 1985." I remembered that now and told Ric, "Let's go back to 1985, and fuckin' tear it up."

The story behind our match was that this was my one final shot at winning the gold, and I was getting it in a place where I'd experienced some of my greatest triumphs. Hunter and I had a rough draft of what we were going to do in our minds, but we mostly worked on the fly— the way it should be done.

At the beginning of the confrontation, I pulled out one of my favorite tricks from the early 1970s, extending my hand toward my adversary. Hunter paused, then moved forward to accept the handshake. I yanked my hand back, swept it through my hair, strutted across the ring, and shouted, *"Woooo!"*

I could hear the people *woooo*-ing as far away as Spartanburg.

MIKE MOONEYHAM: For the fans who couldn't be there, Jim Ross conveyed the significance and impact of the match. It's doubtful that there was a fan watching who didn't expect the Nature Boy to pull off the upset and remind everyone why he is the greatest of all time.

Hunter advanced toward me, and I poked him in the eye, hit him with three hard chops in the corner, and slung him toward the buckles. Then Hunter did the Harley Race reverse turnbuckle flip—all the way to the arena floor.

BUBBA-RAY DUDLEY: Everyone in the back couldn't take their eyes off the monitor. This was a classic Ric Flair match, except the roles were reversed. It's not the local babyface who nearly wins the title. It's fifty-four-year-old Ric Flair, and he may actually pull it off. Few people believed that Hunter was really going to drop the title, but he always made you think that Flair had a shot.

Triple H sent me into the corner. I did my flip over the turnbuckles, came running down the apron, climbed the ropes on the opposite side of the ring, and dove down on Hunter with my fists clenched. I placed him in the figure-four, and he rocked and thrashed back and forth, escaping the maneuver by grabbing the bottom rope. The fans let out a collective moan, like it was Flair and Harley in 1983. I was going out of my mind with excitement as we stood up. I held onto the top rope, chopping at Hunter again and again—the same way I saw Terry Funk do it when I first broke into the business.

TRIPLE H: The people were going crazy whenever he hit me. He'd hit me again, and it would blow the roof off even more. I kept goading him to hit me harder–"Come on, Ric! Hit me!"–and got him so fired up that he eventually blew himself up.

The entire *Raw* roster made me feel like a champion that night in Greenville.

Triple H put me in a sleeper, so I backed him into the referee. When the ref dropped to the canvas, Hunter went to ringside, picked up his championship belt, came back through the ropes, and tried to smash me with it. I ducked under the weapon, came up, stuck Hunter in the eyes, kicked him in the balls, and smacked *him* with the championship belt. I pulled the referee over to where he needed to be and covered Hunter for a two-count. The people were roaring, and I put on a little performance for them, strutting and discharging another "*Woooo!*"

Hunter carried me that night, bringing out what I still had inside. He later tried to claim that it was easy because he'd been watching me his entire life, but watching something, learning it, and applying it are three separate things. This was *not* a Ric Flair match; this was a Triple H match.

He attempted a Pedigree, but I turned it into a backdrop. Then I tried a Pedigree, and Hunter backdropped me. When I fell to the mat, he swept me up, turned my head toward the canvas, hooked his arms under my shoulders, and used the Pedigree to retain the championship.

SHAWN MICHAELS: A lot of people think that I'm the one who organized the post-match celebration for Flair that night, and I'd love to take credit for it. But it was really Tommy Dreamer who came over to me and asked, "Do you think you could get some guys together to go out to the ring, after the match, and kind of show Ric how we feel about him?" It was a great idea. To some of us, Greenville's another town, but in Ric's mind, we were in his backyard. It was the right place and the right time to let this guy know the impact he's had on the business, and on all of our lives.

Raw had just gone off the air, and I was still standing in the ring. I looked over at Earl Hebner and asked, "How was the match? Was it okay?"

"It was great," Earl said.

I shifted my eyes to the entrance ramp, and there was Shawn, leading Spike Dudley, Rico, Tommy Dreamer, and Stevie Richards out of the dressing room. And the guys kept coming and coming. The fans were giving me a standing ovation, and I was overwhelmed. Just thinking about it still makes me emotional. Suddenly, Shawn fell to his knees in the middle of the ramp and bowed to me.

SHAWN MICHAELS: In my life, I only bow down to one person, and that's Jesus Christ. But in my professional life, I wanted Ric to know, he *is* the man.

I burst into tears. For so long, it felt like I'd been in a vacuum-sealed chamber with my gloom. I could see the rest of the world on the other side of the glass, but I couldn't feel what the fans and my brothers in the wrestling fraternity wanted me to. Now the glass was shattered, and I could feel everything. And it wasn't bad anymore. It was great.

The boys were piling into the ring—Hurricane, Christian, Lance Storm, the Dudleyz, Chris Jericho—and more and more people kept coming out of the dressing room. J.R. and Jerry "The King" Lawler stood up at the announcers' table and joined in the applause. Over the PA, I heard the familiar sound of glass breaking—Stone Cold Steve Austin's entrance music. And here he came, not walking but trotting. When he got to the ring, I was handed a beer, and we toasted.

A flash flickered in my eyes, and the moment was recorded for posterity. And when I saw that white light, my mind drifted back in time—to Jim Herd saying that I was too old, and Eric Bischoff promising to bankrupt my family, and Scott Steiner screaming that I'd run Steve Austin out of WCW. Later, Stone Cold would ask me for a favor: he was having a photo of our toast blown up and framed, and would I mind autographing the picture before he hung it up in his house?

STONE COLD STEVE AUSTIN: Late in my career, before I walked out with some injuries and work problems, my last few matches were in a cage with Ric Flair. I've called 98, 99 percent of my matches since the beginning of my career because I don't hear so well. But I remember going out there for those cage matches and looking at him, and he'd smile; we knew where we were going. I just said, "I'm gonna listen to you, kid," and he said, "All right."

Those were some of the most fun matches I've had in my life. To go out there with a guy that I put on such a pedestal was an honor for me. Watching him is one thing. Working with him is an entirely different experience, and it's one of the most fun experiences you'll ever have. Go out there, put things on cruise control, and let Ric Flair guide the match. You can't go wrong.

Stephanie and Shane joined the mob in the ring, whispering kind words and toasting me as well. Then Vince's music filled the arena, and he strode toward me the way only Vince can. He was still playing Mr. McMahon with the angry face, but when we got close to one another, his eyes twinkled and he hugged me, raised my arm and made me feel like I belonged.

Finally, Triple H returned to the ring. We'd just had a match, so he tried to stage a face-off. I couldn't accommodate him, though—I was crying too hard. He contemplated me for another few seconds, then planted the championship belt on my left shoulder. The strains of *Also Sprach Zarathustra,* the theme song that Jimmy Crockett chose for me all those years ago, enveloped the ring while the fans pumped their arms in the air and Hunter and Bubba Dudley lifted me on their shoulders.

BUBBA-RAY DUDLEY: I told Vince afterward that this was everything that is good and right about our business. I was proud and honored to lift Ric on my shoulders, and let the world look at the greatest wrestler of all time.

Soon, the other wrestlers left the ring so I could stand alone and speak directly to the fans. "I've had some emotional moments in Greenville, haven't I?" I observed, wiping away my tears as the crowd clapped and shouted.

"I think the fans know that I've always thanked them. Even though we get paid sometimes to treat you guys bad, and you guys *like* to be treated bad because it's pro wrestling, we all know that each and every wrestler that gets in the ring every night is putting everything he has into making you guys happy, and is glad you bought a ticket to come here.

"I went through a period of time when the Nature Boy wasn't the Nature Boy. I lost a little confidence in myself. And . . . you wouldn't know, you would *not* know the quality of life I have right now. It is *so* good." The tears were back, streaming down my cheeks. "To be involved in something you love with so many positive people, with so many positive personalities, and to be with a company that has so much respect for the business, and so much respect for you, it's a great honor. At fifty-four, I'm as honored to walk down that aisle and get in the ring as I was at twenty-four. Thank you very much."

I looked over at the boys, standing on the entrance ramp and applauding me with the fans, then turned back to the crowd. "There's nothing, nothing, *nothing* in the world like the respect of your peers. I'll never forget this."

SHANE HELMS, AKA THE HURRICANE: Ric later thanked me for a match I had with him the week before he wrestled Triple H, and said that it helped set the mood that led into Greenville. Considering the impact that Flair had on me as a young kid, this was one of the biggest compliments I think I have ever received in any aspect of my life. And when Ric reads this, I want him to know that the honor was *all mine*.

The next day, David and I drove to the *SmackDown!* taping in Greensboro. I must have seen Hogan five times backstage, and he never said a word. But Roddy Piper was looking all over the arena for me, and when we finally saw each other, he gave me a hug. "I heard about last night," he said. "You deserve it."

After more than twenty years—and all the twists our lives had taken—Roddy was still my friend. I was worried about him, though, because he didn't seem to be fitting in as well as he should.

"Roddy, we all walk around with a defense mechanism," I told him. "It's the nature of the business. But these guys backstage love you. They grew up watching you on television. You're 'Hot Rod,' man. You can't be intimidated here, Roddy. Walk up to the guys, shake their hands, and let them know you're one of them."

Unfortunately, Piper left the company a short time later—still struggling to realize certain truths that I'd only just discovered myself.

WHEN I FIRST started in wrestling, Ray Stevens told me, "The day you walk through that curtain, Ric, and you don't have goose bumps, that's the day you never need to walk through it again." Well, I didn't have goose bumps at the end of WCW, and I'm ashamed to admit that I didn't have them when I first started in WWE. But I have goose bumps now, man. I can't wait to get out there.

I'm over my crisis of confidence. Like anybody, I still have days when I struggle with my self-esteem, but I've learned to deal with it. Any bitterness I may have had is long gone, washed away by the people I'm working with. And I can't say enough about Triple H. When I came to WWE after WCW folded, I would usually just sit by myself in the arenas during the time before the shows. I wasn't comfortable, I didn't know anybody, and I was down on myself. He befriended me and got me out of my shell.

I have a great support system professionally: Triple H, Shawn Michaels, Arn, Michael Hayes—Pat Patterson, Blackjack Lanza, and Paul Heyman a little bit, too. The McMahons have obviously been incredible—Stephanie, Shane, Linda, and Vince. Especially Vince. He'll tear me up if I do something wrong—he doesn't sugar-coat anything—but he treats me with all the respect in the world, too.

Vince and I are almost the same age. I once asked him how he keeps his game face on all the time. "Because I have to," he said. When I asked if he'd ever been insecure, Vince replied, "Of course. I just don't let anybody know it."

These are the people at WWE who have helped Ric Flair *be* Ric Flair again. They won't let me be anybody but who I am.

BETH FLIEHR: There are times when Ric has to be reminded who he is. Sometimes when we argue, he yells, "Don't you know who I am?" And I say, "Yeah. You're Richard Fliehr. Don't even *try* to pull a Ric Flair interview on me." But it is great to see Ric back with all his confidence being Ric Flair in the WWE. I guess I really didn't understand how bad Herd and Bischoff had hurt Ric's self-confidence. What Herd and Bischoff did to Ric is unforgivable. Ric is back with Vince, who has always treated him with respect. That was the past and this is the future. Of course I worry about him wrestling now, but it is in his blood. If it makes him happy then it makes us happy. I know he will always give a hundred percent of himself and the fans will always get their money's worth. Triple H has also been a great help to Ric, and I know that Ric truly values their friendship. Ric really enjoys working again and being with the guys. He has his self-confidence back.

In 2003, I celebrated my twentieth wedding anniversary. I think I spent about $1,000 for Beth's first diamond; this time, I paid about $100,000. She never asked for it. I just wanted to give it to her. She deserves even more for being so strong.

Sometimes Beth doesn't understand why I still wrestle. She thinks I work harder than I have to, and she's right. But she knows that wrestling is good for me mentally, and she understands why I beat myself up. It's so I can be Ric Flair again. I don't have anything to prove, but I love doing it. I absolutely still love doing it.

And WWE wants me to wrestle. I'm fifty-five, and they've made me a big part of the show. They rely on me, and that makes me feel better than you could ever imagine. Vince McMahon doesn't believe in charity when it comes to giving out TV time. He won't accept less than my best effort. That's what I've given him, and it's earned me my spot.

When I'm not working, I have no hobbies—only my children. When I was younger, I never went to my dad for advice. I was so stubborn that, even if he offered, I probably would have ignored him. That's not the way parents and kids should communicate. I look at Arn Anderson, who never even knew his father, yet he's been a strong role model for his kids. For so long, I wanted my children to look at me not as Ric Flair, the wrestler, but as *Richard Fliehr,* their *father,* a man who cares about them, can understand their problems, and will support them through anything. And I feel like I've finally broken through.

Over the years, my children–Ashley, Reid, Megan, and David
(not pictured)–have become the center of my world.

I talk to my younger kids several times a day, Megan about three times a week, and David at least once a week. As busy as I am, it's important for me to know what's going on every single day in their lives.

At home, my wife works on academics. I work on sports. I'm a firm believer that athletics lead to mental toughness, an essential quality for a teenager dealing with peer pressure. I want my children to be aggressive in life—not to take advantage of other people, but to strive for the best. If that's your goal, no matter what the endeavor, it's going to pay off.

BETH FLIEHR: I can see Reid in the wrestling business, but going to college is most important. I have to get on him sometimes about doing his homework. He's a smart kid, so he can pass tests without studying. That's not enough for me. He'll say, "Why does it matter? I'm either going to be a wrestler or a football player." That's plan A, but you need a plan B. What if that knee is blown out? What is your neck is hurt? What are you going to do if you can't wrestle or play football? That's why I've told him that he needs that degree. If he wants to wrestle after that, good luck.

Ashley's been in gymnastics and ballet since age four, and was cheerleading with a national traveling team, many of them high-school seniors, at twelve years old. Then she devoted herself completely to volleyball and made Charlotte Elite, an AAU team consisting of the area's top teenage players. I think that she's a better athlete than I ever was, and fortunately she can also focus on other things, like schoolwork.

Class Assignment: The Person Who Has Influenced My Life

My dad to some people is "Nature Boy" or "Ric Flair," the wrestler, but to me, he is a hard-working parent. Ever since he was old enough to move away from home, he has been on the road traveling to different cities every night. When I was younger, he would be away from home for two weeks at a time. When he is home he is either working out, doing promotions or always doing something for his kids. My dad's hard work at everything he has done has inspired me through the years.

My dad is also the most devoted father to his kids I know. When he is on the road he could be in Germany one night and a little town in Mississippi the next. Even if he has been driving all night to come home for just one day, he will be up at six o'clock to make us breakfast, although he only had two and a half hours sleep. Not a day of school has gone by in the last two years of school that if he was home, my little brother and I would have lunch brought to us although he might have a meeting that day. There has not been a volleyball or football game that my dad has missed when he is home. My dad enjoys devoting time to his children.

My dad is my biggest supporter and fan. No matter what sport I choose to play he will make sure by the next day that he will know everything he can about it. This winter I received seventeen letters from different colleges looking at me for volleyball and every single one my dad filled out the information and called the coaches. Even though he is hard on me when it come to getting sleep, making sure I do not miss a practice or workout, I would not be the athlete and person I am if it wasn't for him. His hard work through the years has been passed down to me making me the person I am today.

My dad will always be someone I look up to. If I could have half his dedication to what he has to his family, job and four kids, I could probably do anything I put my mind to. His efforts have given him a respectable name to viewers and the love from his family.

Ashley Fliehr
Providence High School

BETH FLIEHR: I'm the strict parent. All Ashley has to say is "Jump," and Ric asks, "How high, honey?" He's very loving and giving, but he goes overboard. One night, before he went on the road, I told him that I'd be busy the next day, and he said, "But who's going to take their lunch to them tomorrow?" I had to explain that most kids don't have their parents deliver their lunch at school. They can eat in the lunchroom with the rest of the kids.

MEGAN FLIEHR KETZNER: Today, all four of the kids in the family are in Charlotte. I moved there with my husband after graduating from college, and became a respiratory therapist. I wanted to be close to Ashley and Reid. In 2003, I told my father that I was pregnant with my first child. We were at Reid's football game, and he started to tease me. "You know," he said, "they're going to call me the grandfather of wrestling." I asked him what he wants the baby to call him, and he said Papa.

"You're really looking forward to being a grandfather?" I asked him, and he nodded.

He'll be a good one.

I was disappointed when David was released by OVW. I felt that there were other guys who weren't as good as David, but were already

Megan and Ashley.

locked into contracts with WWE, and the company had to trim money wherever it could. David didn't want to stay on just because he was Ric Flair's son. He wanted WWE to see something in him. Since then, he's wrestled in Puerto Rico, and picked up a lot of experience trying to improve as a wrestler—just as I did.

I believe that I'm better than I was a month ago. And next month, I'll be better than I am now. On December 14, 2003, at the *Armageddon* Pay-Per-View, Batista and I became world Tag Team Champions. That same night, Randy Orton won the Intercontinental, and Triple H recaptured the World Championship from Bill Goldberg. Like the original Horsemen, all four members of Evolution could now walk the aisle with titles around our waist. And I see a lot of opportunity ahead of me.

For all the negative experiences I've had, I feel like everything is leading toward a happy ending. When I step through the ropes today, no one's heckling me or calling me old. People are cheering my legacy. People are booing when they're supposed to. I'm working main events. I'm back in the limelight.

The fans are finally getting the Ric Flair they've paid for—not an imitation of Ric Flair, not a Ric Flair who doesn't want to be there, and not a Ric Flair who no one knows how to utilize.

In my life, I've been a movie star, a rock star, and a sports star, all wrapped up into one—and worked harder at it than anybody else. I've done things to embarrass myself, and to embarrass my family. Yet at the end of the day, it has nothing to do with how well my match goes tonight. In our business, you're only as good as your last match—unless you have a legacy. WWE has given me my legacy back. WWE made me realize that I have the respect of my peers. Hulk Hogan could never buy what I have.

The bottom line is this: Space Mountain may be the oldest ride in the park. But it still has the longest line.

One more time: *Woooooo!*

For more than thirty years, my fans have given me the opportunity to do something I've loved with an unbridled passion. Without them, my life would surely have fallen short of its mark. There would have been no "Nature Boy" Ric Flair. There would have been no book. Like I said in Greenville, South Carolina, on September 14, 1998, "It's real." You've given me the ride of a lifetime, and just remember: It's not over yet. Not by a long shot.

I've been truly blessed to have lived such a life and been able to meet so many wonderful and colorful characters who have helped shape who I am. Folks like "General" Bruce McArthur, who joined me as a teenager in exploring all of life's possibilities, and with whom I'm still close today. I'll forever be indebted to my buddy

ACKNOWLEDGMENTS

Mark Madden; without his editing talents this book wouldn't have taken the shape that it did. Dave Meltzer, whose astute observations of the business over the past two decades has provided a measuring stick for all those in the sport.

Someone once said there couldn't have been a Muhammad Ali without a Howard Cossell. Well, there couldn't have been a Ric Flair without a Mike Mooneyham. Besides being my close friend and sounding board, he's an outstanding journalist who has put my career into words over all these years. Verne Gagne gave me my start and refused to let quitting be an option. George Scott took a kid who was rough around the edges and molded him into a champion.

Those who have bled, sweat, and shed tears with me in the ring are too numerous to mention, but you all know who you are. My brother-in-arms, Arn Anderson, who is my friend for life. Guys like Ricky Steamboat, Wahoo McDaniel, and Harley Race, who made me a legend every time I climbed into the ring with them. Golden voices like Bob Caudle, Gordon Solie, and Jim Ross, who helped provide the soundtrack of my life. I've loved every day working with performers like Triple H and Shawn Michaels, who feel so passionately about our business. I can never give Vince and Linda McMahon enough thanks for giving me the chance to prove that "Nature Boy" Ric Flair still had what it takes.

I'd also like to thank the talented folks at Simon & Schuster who have guided me throughout the book-writing process, as well as WWE's Stacey Pascarella. They all deserve special kudos for their patience.

Most of all, I'd like to thank my family, who have supported me through the good times and the bad times. My beautiful wife, Beth, has endured more than a woman should ever have to. She's been the rock of the family, and I plan to spend the rest of my life proving to her that diamonds are forever. I've been blessed with four wonderful children, Megan, David, Ashley, and Reid, who have touched my life in ways I can't even begin to describe. And although they're not around to read this book, I know my mom and dad are looking down and smiling. It was their special love that took a baby boy that no one else wanted and taught him "To Be The Man."